PRAISE ... FFECT

"An insightful, instructive guide and user-friendly roadmap that helps steer us Type A's away from burnout and onto the path of sustainable productivity."

~ **Trudi Roth, Writer & Founder, It's The TruStory**

"In a busy world of distractions, finding focus is difficult. Mich Bondesio perfectly articulates how these external factors impact our lives, and shares practical and meaningful ways to establish better rhythm and purpose in what we do."

~ **Catarina King, Co-Founder, Society1**

"You can't force yourself to be productive. After reading this book, I am feeling more in tune with my mind and body. Terrific thoughts and ideas on ways to be far more productive with less time!"

~ **Kelly Berry, Founder, Learn Start Grow**

ABOUT THE AUTHOR

Michelle Bondesio is a writer, speaker, coach and entrepreneur.

Mich *(pronounced Mish with an 'ish')* is the founder of Creating Cadence, the host of the Creating Cadence Podcast, and the author of The Cadence Effect.

The focus of her work is on transforming our habits and practices to activate more of our potential, both at work and in life. Mich's aim is to change the global conversation around traditional views of productivity, so that we can create better cadence in our days, more momentum in our work, and more joy in our lives.

Originally from South Africa, Mich currently lives between the UK and France, and works with clients around the world. Through her podcast, talks, workshops, courses and coaching programmes, she helps high-achieving strivers step off the treadmill of overwork, so they can thrive in mid-life and beyond.

Website: CreatingCadence.co

Book Site: TheCadenceEffect.com

Newsletter: CreatingCadence.co/subscribe

Instagram: instagram.com/michbondesio

Twitter: twitter.com/michbondesio

YouTube: youtube.com/@MichBondesio

LinkTree: https://linktr.ee/michbondesio

Full author bio at the end of the book

THE CADENCE EFFECT

TRANSFORM YOUR LIFE WITH INTENTIONALLY PRODUCTIVE HABITS

MICHELLE BONDESIO

There's always another way!
Mich

Bondesio
Media

The Cadence Effect: Transform Your Life With Intentionally Productive Habits

Copyright © 2023 Michelle Bondesio

All rights reserved. No part of this publication may be reproduced, stored in a retrieval system, or transmitted in any form or by any electronic, or mechanical means, or by any other means, without the prior written permission of the author, excepting for the use of brief quotations in a book review.

No part of this publication may be used, reproduced, or sub-licensed for the purposes of training artificial intelligence technologies to generate text, including without limitation, technologies that are capable of generating works in the same style or genre as this publication, unless the author's specific and express permission has been obtained to do so.

PAPERBACK ISBN: 978-1-7393788-0-6

EBOOK ISBN: 978-1-7393788-1-3

WORKBOOK ISBN: 978-1-7393788-3-7

AUDIOBOOK ISBN: 978-1-7393788-2-0

Published by Bondesio Media (Bondesio C&C)

For media enquiries, or requests to publish excerpts from this book, contact books@bondesio.com.

Interior book design by Michelle Bondesio.

Book cover design, framework and interior illustrations by Rachel Simpson, We Are Bird.

Back cover photo by Rachel Ovenden Photography.

Doodle illustrations © Michelle Bondesio.

❦ Created with Vellum

For my past self, who would have benefitted from this guidance during a difficult time. And for my family, whose love and support created the foundation for me to find my way.

"THERE IS ALWAYS ANOTHER WAY, AND WE HAVE THE POWER WITHIN US TO FIND IT."

~ MICH BONDESIO

THE CADENCE EFFECT

TRANSFORM YOUR LIFE WITH INTENTIONALLY
PRODUCTIVE HABITS

BUILD MOMENTUM

WORK WITH PURPOSE

CRAFT A MEANINGFUL LIFE

CONTENTS

An End & A Beginning   1

PART ONE
CADENCE & INTENTIONAL PRODUCTIVITY

1. Introduction   15
2. Cadence vs Balance   21
3. Intentional Productivity   35
4. Life in the Digital Age   44
5. Reflection Exercises No.1   53

PART TWO
THE REAL CHALLENGES

6. Stress & Stressors   61
7. Procrastination   75
8. Burnout Part 1 - Work   87
9. Burnout Part 2 - Life   102
10. Reflection Exercises No.2   118

PART THREE
HOW WE WORK

11. Seeking Flexibility   127
12. Work Styles   132
13. Work Environments   146
14. Our Work Tools   157
15. Workflows   170
16. Reflection Exercises No.3   174

PART FOUR
LEVERAGING OPPORTUNITIES

17. Habits & Behaviour Change   183
18. Mindsets for Intentional Productivity   192
19. Building Strong Foundations   205
20. Cycles of Productivity   220
21. Reflection Exercises No.4   239

PART FIVE
MANAGING OUR FOCUS & FLOW

22. Rewiring Our Brain for Focus — 251
23. Managing Our Flow — 267
24. Building Rituals into Our Workflow — 277

PART SIX
NEXT STEPS

25. Making a Cadence Canvas — 293
26. Crafting Your Canvas — 297
27. Implementing Your Canvas — 303
28. Moving Forwards — 306

Acknowledgements — 317
Full Author Biography — 321
Bibliography — 323

AN END & A BEGINNING

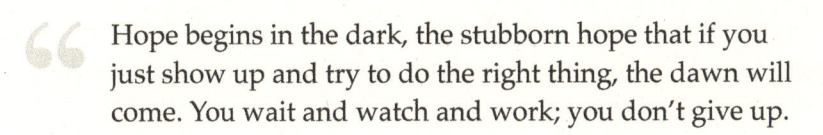

> Hope begins in the dark, the stubborn hope that if you just show up and try to do the right thing, the dawn will come. You wait and watch and work; you don't give up.
>
> ~ ANN LAMOTT

A DARK & MESSY START

A roller coaster ride of major life events and radical changes turned my brain and body upside down and twisted my perspective all around.

With a background in project management and communications, I've found myself in high-pressure situations and deadline-driven environments for most of my work life.

The work culture often felt like burning the candle at both ends, which meant burnout was a common occurrence in these environments. When I ran out of steam, often all it required was a few days off or a change of project to help me bounce back and crack on.

That all changed in 2015, when I suffered from an epic bout of burnout. Caused by a culmination of chronic, ongoing stress over a two-year period on both the work and the home front, this burnout forced me to check out of life.

In the lead up to my health crisis, I was working very long hours in a toxic workplace, alongside a lengthy rush-hour commute. My personal life was also crumbling, and I was dealing with difficult, sad, and traumatic things, some of which were beyond my control.

These compounding experiences were disorienting, and I felt like I was losing my sense of self and identity.

After feeling stuck and stressed for a long time, I made three major life decisions, all at the same time - moving countries (again), leaving my marriage, and leaving my career. I hoped these decisions would help me ease the stress so that I could once again find myself.

Within three months of making these decisions, and after ten years away, I was on a plane back to the UK with only a bag and a bicycle.

IT WAS MEANT TO BE A FRESH START.

My plan was to hit the ground running, and I then found myself in a situation where I had to just keep going. I didn't have the time (or the tools) to properly process and deal with the ramifications of these major decisions and changes.

Something eventually gave out, and that something was me. The fallout was that my body called time out.

In 2015, I succumbed to illness and was incapable of working for more than a year. 18 Months, to be exact.

Burnout can manifest in several ways, so it can be different for everyone. I experienced both physical and mental fatigue and a host of physiological, emotional, and cognitive health issues. This meant there was more than one thing to fix.

AN END & A BEGINNING

Trying to understand how to fix everything was like trying to unravel a knotted ball of string while blindfolded.

My choices ended up taking me far from my family, to a place where I didn't know anyone. I became depressed, whilst also juggling panic attacks. The extreme anxiety put me into hyper-alert survival mode, and I was also battling chronic insomnia. When I wasn't feeling like an agitated energiser bunny, I was crying my eyes out for the littlest thing, with little energy to face my challenges.

There was a period of about six months at the start of this saga, where I can't actually tell you what I was doing. I have little recollection of how these days unfolded, perhaps because every day felt like the same trudge through treacle.

What I do remember is being in the H&M store trying to make a simple decision about which set of socks to buy. The pressure of making that choice felt so hard that I started hyperventilating. The walls closed in and I had to run out of the mall before I had a meltdown.

I would also have days where I just felt numb, with no joy despite the cheerful things happening around me. The depressive feeling would come at me in palpable waves. I likened it to a grey roller shutter coming down over life as all the colours would leach from my view.

During this time, I had to get ID pictures taken, and I didn't recognise myself. In those photos I'd aged 20 years, my face drawn and sallow, my eyes so sad and lost. I still find it painful to look at those pics.

BUT THERE WAS MORE.

I developed skin allergies to the toiletries I was using, and sensitivities to several random foods. I had to throw out so many soaps and shampoos, and it's only recently that I've been able to eat bananas again. My adult acne went into overdrive because of hormonal imbalances caused by the stress. To make matters worse, I developed a stomach ulcer and IBS.

Everything in my body was so out of whack and my skin looked so bad that I didn't want to be seen in public.

Burnout also shot my attention span to shit. I couldn't focus on something for over two minutes. My memory faltered as my mind became a sieve, and I couldn't remember what I was doing tomorrow. I went from being an avid book lover to being unable to read more than two pages at a time.

Although spending time on social media was an opportunity to connect with the outside world and reduce my sense of isolation, it also became an anxiety-inducing stress magnet, which aggravated my symptoms.

I became addicted to the dopamine hit of seeking engagement and interactions, whilst also experiencing comparison fatigue from seeing all these beautiful people with supposedly perfect lives, while mine was rapidly imploding.

These things compounded to the point where I became physically incapable of doing anything work-related.

I had prided myself on being the capable, reliable, responsible, 'multi-tasking spreadsheet queen' that everyone else came to for help with their thing. But I turned into the person who struggled to tie her shoelaces without falling apart.

At one point, I recall dejectedly sitting in the local Job Centre. I was trying to explain to the stern DWP Officer why I couldn't rely on my 20 years of skills and experience to get me a job. He looked at my work history and said I should apply for Project Manager roles.

I could barely speak. My throat was so tight. In a whisper, with tears running down my face, I said I didn't trust myself to do that work anymore.

Trying to apply for basic roles didn't help either, as potential employers deemed me too experienced. And how to explain a massive chunk of missing time on my CV without coming across as unreliable?

AN END & A BEGINNING

So, for a long time, I couldn't earn an income, and alongside meagre state support, I burned through my savings trying to keep my head above water. As I later discovered, for a time, I became what the government technically classes as "destitute". I just thought I was going through an incredibly difficult time, and that I needed to do what I could to endure it.

But things felt hopeless, and I once again felt trapped, with no control over what was happening in my life. My confidence took a major dive and my self-esteem was in the toilet. I became nervous, socially awkward and reclusive, unable to trust my own decisions. The self-doubt, shame, and loneliness were crippling.

It was an extremely tough place to be, and in that murky time, I really wasn't sure if I was ever going to make it back.

But I eventually found all the help I needed, and I could slowly heal and rebuild myself.

© Michelle Bondesio

I mentioned that there was more than one thing to fix. Turns out there was also more than one way to fix everything, too. I was lucky to meet an inspiring career coach, Peter Jones, who would motivate me by saying, **"There's always another way, let's find it."**

So, I set about finding the best way to move forward in all parts of my life, despite the limitations of my situation.

I had no money to throw at the problem, so I started with what I did have - the resolve to keep trying, even if I kept failing.

To create a supportive mindset, I adopted two mottos that I would say out loud whenever I encountered a hurdle or felt like I was failing.

1. "What if I can?"

This question helped me change my perspective and find new ways of dealing with my situation. When things felt impossible, I would ponder this question. It would open up new possibilities and confirm that the answer to the question "What if I can?" is always: "I can!"

2. "Tomorrow is another day."

This motivation gave me the impetus to keep working on getting better day by day, even if I accomplished little in a day. Tomorrow became another chance to try again, to show up, and to make change, with each day's progress building the foundation for the next.

Alongside these words of wisdom, I put my hands and feet to work.

I began walking the hills and dales of my local area, in the sunshine, rain, sleet and snow. At first, it would take a good hour of hard walking before my busy brain would slow down and I'd feel more connected to myself and my surroundings.

Being in nature was a soothing salve. I started challenging myself to find one beautiful thing (no matter how small) on each of these walks. Then I'd share photos of those things on Instagram as a kind of personal diary.

I also started keeping a daily gratitude journal, writing my thoughts both in the morning and in the evening.

Next, I tried my hand at art therapy, drawing what would become a series of 50 simple doodles, some of which are in this book. A few of these rudimentary illustrations unexpectedly led to me winning a competition.

The prize was a ticket to the Do Lectures, something that had been on my wish list to attend before I'd crashed and burned.

My regular yoga practice, that I'd developed in my 20s, had fallen by the wayside during my burnout. Restarting this also helped to ground me and reconnect my mind to my body.

I found these practices powerful, and they helped me rebuild my health and rewire my brain. But I also had to resort to clinical support.

My doctor put me on a host of medications to sort out my hormones and gut issues, and I had to change my diet considerably. However, my body was too sensitive for antidepressants. Instead, I was prescribed conscious breathing and meditation practices to deal with the anxiety and Cognitive Behavioural Therapy (CBT) to help with the depression.

I had to relearn how to live and work, how to do and be... only better and differently.

With a lot of hope, the right support, and by taking one small step at a time, I found my way out of this dark mire, this place of difficulty and despair. I found a better place where the light gets in. In doing so, I found a new dawn, a new career, and a new way of being.

As my racing mind calmed down to a reasonable pace and my hormones balanced out, my sleep, memory, and concentration slowly improved. I eventually came off most of the medication. What also brought joy was that I could start reading again. At first just a few pages at a time, until I could build up to a full chapter and then a full book.

With my natural curiosity re-engaged, I set out to learn more about how my brain and body worked, so I could better understand what had happened to me and why. That's when I realised something important.

Things didn't stop at the point where I "got better".

I needed to develop a blueprint that would help me to "stay better" over the long run too, so I'd never be in danger of succumbing to these threats again.

My realisation led to the voracious consumption of books on habits, neuroscience, psychology, performance, and behaviour change. I also started trying out lots of different activities and systems reputed to support health and productivity.

This holistic endeavour had me experimenting with a variety of modalities, practices and functional medicine approaches. My aim became figuring out how best to support my wellbeing, restore my capabilities, and rebuild my life.

My transformation required learning and behaviour change on lots of different fronts. It meant I had to become more self-aware and more disciplined. I had to learn to overcome my fears and develop a more open mind about trying new things.

From these experiments and experiences, I developed a toolkit of valuable skills which many of us never get the chance to be taught as part of 'growing up'. Often these are skills we're forced to adopt only once we're thrown into a crisis. And being in crisis mode is not always the best time for new learning to stick!

So, the topics and skills we cover in this book are the accumulated knowledge I've gleaned so far. Some the hard way as part of my recovery, and some from my subsequent learning and doing.

AN ONGOING JOURNEY

> In this life or the next, what goes down will come up. It's a matter of how we see the challenge in front of us and

> how we engage with it. Persist, pivot, or concede. It's up to us, our choice every time.
>
> ~ MATTHEW MCCONAUGHEY

Fast forward to today, and I've transitioned from my previous career in communications and project management. I've become a more purpose-driven entrepreneur who puts wellbeing at the centre of her business.

Why did I choose to take this path?

In preparing to return to work, I reached a crossroads where I had to make another big decision.

I knew I couldn't go back to the way I had previously worked. My stamina could no longer endure that style of working, nor did I have the desire to work that way. Despite being the norm, I knew it would also be extremely toxic for me in the long run. If I was to maintain my slowly improving good health, I had to pivot with my work. Both the type of work I was doing and how I was going about doing it.

So my decision was to buck the norms of the time and become more intentional about my approach to work. But that's not the only reason I headed in this direction. I also discovered something exciting through both my experience and subsequent research.

When we put purpose and wellbeing at the centre of how we work, this approach leads to benefits and outcomes that compound positively over time.

- It supports our creativity, productivity, and wellbeing better.
- It helps us manage our time, attention and stress better.
- It helps us create momentum, build resilience, and craft a more meaningful life.

The positive effects of putting purpose and wellbeing at the centre of how you work are exponential. It cascades out into the rest of your life.

When I could eventually go back to work in late 2017, I became a freelance technical copywriter working from home. This way, I could have more control over my working environment and work style.

I also wanted to share what I'd learned, to raise awareness of the dangers of burnout and to educate people on ways to work differently. So, in 2018, I founded a side project called Growth Sessions.

My mission was to help people transform their working practices, activate more of their potential, and build more supportive work cultures. Growth Sessions became an umbrella brand for talks, workshops, training, coaching and mentoring programmes, both online and in person.

Later that year, I also started a newsletter called **'Cadence - Life & Work in Motion'** so I could share more about these topics.

I chose the word *cadence* as it connects to rhythm or flow. For me, it was apt as life is always moving, and we need to develop the skills and resilience to keep pace with these changes.

I'll dive deeper into the meaning and importance of cadence in future chapters.

Then in 2020, I launched the **Creating Cadence Podcast**. Each season centres around the impact that habits, mindfulness, and emerging technology can have on our wellbeing, creativity and productivity, as well as the future of how we work.

The topics proved popular as the idea of *creating cadence,* and the concept of *intentional productivity* connected to it, resonated with listeners. This path has led me to help busy, high-achieving strivers to find better ways to thrive, and Growth Sessions has since become assimilated into the Creating Cadence brand, with a more refined focus.

In 2022, the University of Central Lancashire invited me to become one of their **Entrepreneurs in Residence** at the Lancashire School of Business & Enterprise. It's an immense honour to be recognised in this way for what I've been slowly building since 2018.

I would never have imagined back when I first started on this alternative path that I would end up here.

I'm not telling you these things to brag, or to sell you something!

These achievements have all been possible because of my experiments in intentional productivity. They are outcomes from seeking ways to create more cadence in my days and to build more momentum in my life and work.

Each of these business developments and results is an example of the cadence effect in action. They show what is possible when we focus on building more mindful and sustainable work practices that support our wellbeing, our productivity, and our creativity.

These accomplishments are stepping stones on my path to seeking fulfilment and crafting a more meaningful life.

NEXT STEPS

My journey of discovery continues, and this is my invitation for you to join me. This book is the next step on that path, and I'm thankful that you're here with me.

I wrote this book for three reasons:

- To help you build supportive skills <u>before</u> you might need them.
- To help you navigate what might otherwise be a hard path, if you're already experiencing these types of challenges.
- To spread the word that there is another way for us to be living and working. One which supports our wellbeing and productivity far better than our ingrained, traditional norms and current working cultures dictate.

In the next few chapters, I'm going to share what you can expect from this book. I'm also going to introduce the concept of *cadence* more fully and explain why I think it's a more helpful term than the notion of *balance*.

THE CADENCE EFFECT

I'll reveal the connections between creating cadence and developing intentionally productive habits, and why this approach is so transformative that it leads to what I call *the cadence effect*.

You'll also find out about the blueprint I created that helped me to get better and stay better. This framework has subsequently become what I call the Cadence Canvas™. This canvas will provide the structure which helps you to develop more intentionally productive habits that are going to transform your approach to work and help you live the life you've dreamed of!

If you're struggling with your current situation, or wanting to make change and not sure where to start, take heart! There is always another way, and I'm here to show you the path.

So, if you're ready, let's get started.

© Michelle Bondesio

PART ONE
CADENCE & INTENTIONAL PRODUCTIVITY

1. INTRODUCTION
2. Challenges
3. How We Work
4. Opportunities
5. Focus & Flow
6. Next Steps

ONE
INTRODUCTION

> Building habits is a lifelong practice.
>
> JAMES CLEAR

Now that I've shared where this book has come from, in this chapter, I'll be clarifying the aims and purpose of this book. This includes who I wrote it for, and what to expect from your experience of engaging with this content.

FOUNDATION VS DESTINATION

Learning and behaviour change is an ongoing journey and we can't put a time limit on when we will reach our destination.

In this book, our focus isn't on the destination or on quick, unsustainable fixes.

It's on the steady journey, the lessons you gather along the way, and the skills you build on the path to your destination.

The focus is on creating consistent, foundational practices that can support you in the various parts of your life and work, both now and in the future.

In the modern digital age, our health spans are increasing, our work lives are extending, and we are choosing <u>not</u> to retire (out of choice or necessity). Alongside extended lives and work hours, there is also a rise in burnout. This means that while we need to be prolific in our output for longer, we also need to do it in a way that supports us better.

So, the aim of this book is to help you build stronger foundations so that you don't have to experience the burnout (and fallout) that I did.

It explores ways for you to lead a more productive life, not just for the sake of being productive. But also so that you can improve your focus and get more meaningful work done without sacrificing your health along the way.

- This book is a call for us to transform how we work.
- To throw down the mantle of overwork.
- To redesign traditional work systems that no longer support us.

We do this by becoming more intentional about HOW we work.

It's as simple as that.

However, simple is not always easy. If it was, this book would end at this page.

To make change, we first need to understand the baseline. So getting to where we want to go means we need to truly comprehend where we currently find ourselves.

We will look at what causes your stress, the effects of burnout and procrastination on your performance, and how to develop more supportive digital, work, and life habits.

So you can activate more of your creativity, improve your productivity, and look after your wellbeing better too.

WHO IS THIS BOOK FOR?

If you're a high achiever who needs help stepping off the treadmill of overwork, then this is for you.

This book is beneficial for business owners, consultants, entrepreneurs, freelancers, graduates, teams, and leaders of teams.

It's for people like you and me, who are striving for better business outcomes and seeking to integrate more meaning into your life and work. Although the primary focus is on work-related activities and activities that support working better, you'll find that the skills we cover will aid you in other parts of your life, too.

This book is about considering the bigger picture and then taking smaller, manageable steps to achieve that broader outcome. It's my hope that it will inspire you to develop your skills and activate more of your potential. So that you can become even better at what you do, and how you do it, in a way that is more meaningful for you.

WHAT TO EXPECT FROM THIS BOOK

Let's set the foundation for what you can expect from this learning experience.

Most of us spend a vast amount of time using digital tools as part of our workday. The exercises in this book will assist you in identifying exactly how your current use is helping or hindering your wellbeing and performance, and enable you to make positive change.

We'll look at how you can develop better digital habits and behaviours, and what you can do to build stronger work foundations and a healthier culture around work.

This includes reviewing **the current context of our modern working environments**, with digital tools and emerging technologies, and the impact they all have on our ability to do good work.

At some points, things get a little scientific to help you understand **the physiological roles** that things like habits, procrastination, stress and burnout play in affecting our performance. There are other factors at play too, which may surprise you, including... wait for it... the moon!

We'll look at **cycles of productivity** and how we can build practical habits and routines that help us become healthier, more creative, and more productive.

Our mindset also has a major influence on our wellbeing, focus abilities, behaviours, performance, and perception of the world. So we'll dig into the different mindsets we can cultivate to support us better, too.

To round things off, I share some **handy tips, tricks, and hacks**. These include simple ways that you can prepare yourself for digital work and intentional productivity, and practical actions you can take to improve your working environment, work style, and workflow.

In **the final chapter of the book - Moving Forwards -** I recap what we've covered and conclude by sharing my perspective on where I see the future of work going and the important things we need to prepare for.

Alongside prompts within each chapter, you'll also find **detailed, practical reflection exercises** at the end of each section, to help you examine your current situation and explore ways to improve it. Your responses will guide you in creating your own Cadence Canvas™ for intentional productivity, which is the final exercise in the book.

Note: These reflection exercises are excluded from the eBook version, and are instead available to purchase as a separate Workbook from TheCadenceEffect.com.

Get a special bonus - a free downloadable Canvas Cheat Sheet - by signing up to the Cadence newsletter. The cheat sheet has quick actions and activity suggestions to help you create your own canvas.

Subscribe here: CreatingCadence.co/subscribe

The Bibliography lists references and resources for further reading and learning on the various topics covered in each chapter.

INTRODUCTION

If you listen to the audio version of this book, I include the bibliography list as a PDF download with your purchase.

NOW, AN IMPORTANT POINT.

You <u>don't</u> have to do everything that is recommended in this book to feel and experience the benefits of *the cadence effect*.

Start small and simple, pick a few manageable changes you can implement, and build slowly from there.

Although you will feel the effects of your consistent improvements almost immediately, this approach isn't a quick fix.

It's about developing a lifelong love affair with the process of activating your potential.

Fill this journey with learning, curiosity and fun. Be open to getting to know yourself better.

A quick note on grammar, spelling and style…

- I'm South African by birth, and at the time of writing this book, I'm living in the UK. I write in a relaxed way and the language, structure, format, and spelling I use here may differ from what you're accustomed to in your country.

- I deliberately spell *'wellbeing'* and *'burnout'* <u>without</u> the hyphen, primarily because my brain doesn't like unnecessary hyphens. *For the record, we can spell them either way.*

- Also, usually when I'm referring to wellbeing, it's in a collective sense. To me, well-being implies the wellness of only one being, but in my work, I'm considering wellbeing from the standpoint of both individuals and communities.

Please don't let these differences distract you from the message and learning you can gain from this book.

So, if you're ready, let's begin by considering the concept of *cadence* and what I mean by *the cadence effect*.

We'll look at how cadence connects with productivity, and why creating work-life cadence is far more helpful for our wellbeing than attempting to achieve work/life balance.

TWO
CADENCE VS BALANCE

> Life is like riding a bicycle. To keep your balance, you must keep moving.
>
> ~ ALBERT EINSTEIN

A KEY LEARNING FROM MY BURNOUT EXPERIENCE WAS THAT MY LIFE WAS UNBALANCED.

It had become skewed towards stress-inducing experiences, which caused a lot of bumps in the road.

What had pushed me over the edge into an epically long bout of burnout was chronic, ongoing stress, both on the work and home front. After attempting to endure it for over two years, things fell apart, and so did I.

During my recovery, as I set about figuring out how to create more balance, I realised that needing to achieve that 'balanced life' we all strive for was an impossible challenge. That's because, in this context, the term 'balance' is flawed and unhelpful, for a few different reasons.

THE CADENCE EFFECT

The idea of work/life balance is misleading, as it is difficult to both attain and maintain what is a static construct. It is unsustainable for longer than a moment.

THE SEESAW

Imagine a seesaw in a playground, like the one in this diagram.

If this is unfamiliar, a seesaw looks a bit like a big, old-fashioned scale, with a long metal or wooden beam attached to a central plinth. The beam has seats with handrails on either end, and it moves by pivoting up and down from that central point. Kids (and adults) use their feet to create momentum, pushing off from the ground to make the seesaw tilt up and down for fun.

Just like a scale, keeping the seesaw balanced means keeping it level. And that's where the static element comes in, because to stay level in the midrange, it can't move. However, that is very difficult to achieve with a seesaw, especially if one passenger might be heavier than the other, or pushing harder than the other.

On the flip side, an imbalance occurs when things aren't level. The motion of pushing off the ground propels the seesaw in the other direction, so as one side of our seesaw goes up, the other goes down. If we apply this to our life scenarios, this implies that to win at one thing, we have to potentially lose at another.

CADENCE VS BALANCE

This led to a big realisation for me.

When we strive for work/life balance, we're setting ourselves up to fail by using a limiting term like *balance*, as life is always moving and we need to move with it.

Attempting to keep everything 'just so' and in balance doesn't allow for movement. It doesn't enable us to adapt to our changing environment without throwing things out of balance.

THE BICYCLE WHEEL

If, like me, you're a fan of riding a bicycle, push bike, or vélo, (depending on what you call it in your part of the world), you'll know that a good wheel makes all the difference in getting you where you want to go.

If your wheel has a broken spoke or two, or you've hit one too many large rocks or potholes, then your rim will bend or buckle, making for a bumpy ride that can take you off course.

If your wheels run true, it makes for a smooth ride, helping you to stay on track. And a smooth ride also means you are better able to build momentum and then maintain a good pace.

It's time to get off the seesaw and onto the bicycle!

THE CADENCE EFFECT

As part of my journey to building a framework that would help me live and work better, I realised that balance is bullshit. It's unsustainable as it is impossible to maintain.

I decided that instead of aiming for balance, there was another way to approach this. What I needed was a way to create cadence. But what exactly is cadence?

THE CADENCE EFFECT

Cadence equates to the concepts of rhythm and pace, movement and flow.

It's linked to mathematical, musical and artistic pursuits, but is also increasingly common in arenas like sports and marketing.

For example, in cycling, cadence denotes the speed and fluidity of your pedal stroke. More recently, I note that content marketers and digital creators are now referring to their publishing cadence to explain the cycles in which they post content.

For me, cadence connects with this idea of our life and work being constantly in motion. If we can create cadence, then we don't get stuck on attempting to create a perfect, but static moment of balance, one that is unsustainable over the long term.

Creating work-life cadence facilitates forward motion.

It enables us to build momentum in all parts of our life, even when one part is demanding more than the rest.

There will be times when we need to move more or less, or at a faster or slower pace. Cadence is about keeping the rhythm of our actions fluid. So we can easily adjust to the ups and downs of our environment without needing to stop.

As I mentioned in the Prologue, I built a framework based on my learning to help me get better and stay better. It's the same framework I now use with clients to help them on their journey of changing how they work, so they can create more space and meaning in their lives, too.

Creating cadence is about creating space, creating place, and creating momentum.

When we experience these things in our life and work, then we benefit from *the cadence effect*. Before we consider these three elements in more detail, we need to understand how our environments affect our ability to create space, place, and momentum.

OUR ENVIRONMENTS

One of the core themes in my work as a performance coach and business consultant is that of our environments and how they affect our ability to live and work with cadence.

First, there's our internal environment - the things that happen in our bodies and brains.

Then there's our external environment, such as our homes and workplaces.

What happens outside of us influences our internal system, and vice versa.

If we have a strong internal foundation, we're better equipped to handle what happens around us. Likewise, if our physical environments support us well, then our minds and bodies have more opportunities to thrive.

But there's a third environment too, which affects us both inside and out. It's the virtual world, created by our relationship with digital technology.

With the rise of the 4th Industrial Revolution, technology has become a ubiquitous and essential part of how we live and work. But tech overuse and misuse is also making us unwell. This affects us both as individuals and as communities. There are implications for our productivity and performance. These things impact on our health, and that of our business bottom lines.

The impact that tech and digital have on us is even more relevant now, after being forced to spend more time online because of the Covid-19 pandemic.

These environments are the context in which we're trying to create space, place, and momentum to build cadence into our days. We can't avoid the tech, but we can leverage it to our benefit, in many cases, better than we currently do.

CREATING SPACE

In 2017, I first experimented with minimalism and digital minimalism after being influenced by Cal Newport and the Minimalists. The practice of minimalism involves becoming more purposeful about the stuff (including digital tools) that you choose to use and have around you.

Since then, we've become more aware of the benefits of minimalism, as psychologists, neuroscientists, and advocates have shone huge spotlights on how clutter of any kind affects our health and wellness.

Due to the ever-increasing need to be online, there is a danger that the way we use our digital tools can become more of a hindrance than a help. And it takes practice to create space away from the blue lights and the deluge of information constantly coming at us.

Room to Think

Many of our job roles have turned us into knowledge workers, where we partake in using both mandatory and optional technologies as part of creating value. In this situation, our brains are our primary form of capital. Cal Newport calls this *value attention capital*.

Social media, unless it's your profession, is actually an optional technology.

A big issue with optional tech-use is the distraction it can cause.

So consider this… if it's not your profession, how often do you use social media like a professional? By that I mean using a structured dashboard on your computer to schedule your messaging, rather than tweeting on the fly or on the couch.

Often we <u>don't</u> engage with this tech in a structured way, especially if we're a busy solopreneur or a micro-business owner trying to do all the things and fit everything in.

The problem is this …. our brains get hijacked by social tools and apps, as companies have purposefully designed them to trick our dopamine response. This raises our cortisol levels and plays havoc with our hormones. *(I talk about this more in the Challenges chapter).*

This bombardment and manipulation means our focus and attention are all over the place.

- We lose time down rabbit holes.
- We develop conditioned behaviours.
- We feel compelled to do things on autopilot, even though we know they aren't good for us.
- Our perceived lack of control makes us feel worse about ourselves.

When we're in this state, we compromise our performance and our health. It's no wonder our productivity levels suck!

When we're perpetually distracted, we can't do the deep, meaningful, creative, clever and innovative work that generates our attention capital and helps move us and our businesses forward.

So, to create cadence and benefit from the cadence effect, the first area of focus is to CREATE SPACE away from the distractions. Then we have the room to consider how our sense of place affects creating cadence.

CREATING PLACE

As the future of how we work evolves, we need to upgrade our understanding of how we can use technology and design to support our wellbeing in our homes, workplaces and communities.

Let's consider our modern workplace and world.

Our work spaces extend beyond the physical office. Our office hours extend across time zones. Before the 2020 lockdown started, we were already working in a fragmented way, which became amplified during and after this enforced sheltering in place.

At the time of writing, we've emerged from a global pandemic, but we're also experiencing a global economic downturn and destabilising conflict across the world. There's some serious triage needed to support our economies, communities and businesses, but we can't be as productive as we need to be to do this, if our health and wellbeing are suffering too.

Wellbeing First, Productivity Second

Pre-pandemic, that might have sounded controversial, but just a few months of lockdown helped many of us to realise what matters most.

Even now that we are well out of the pandemic zone, many people have elected to continue working from home, or adopted a hybrid work approach, instead of returning to a physical workplace permanently. Others have left unfulfilling work to explore something new.

There's plenty of research (some of which I cite in later chapters) which proves that **"better selves" are better for our business bottom lines**. So it's also in our financial interest to focus on wellbeing first and productivity second.

When we consider the idea of place making in relation to wellbeing and productivity, how can our organisations (big and small) be more human-centred workplaces which cater to a diverse range of needs and requirements? If we can support our individual wellbeing, that enables both businesses and communities to flourish, despite the adversity of whatever our current situation is.

Based on our life-changing pandemic experiences, we have learned to interact with our urban infrastructure in different ways. Aside from new opportunities to make alternative places in the virtual world, place making also needs to take different forms to enable connection in the physical world.

So, CREATING PLACE is the second important focus point for creating cadence. This brings us to how motion, movement, and momentum play a role in activating the cadence effect.

CREATING MOMENTUM

There's a difference between creating movement by taking action versus succumbing to an indoctrinated culture of perpetual hustle and grind.

I explore the concept of the "hustle culture" in more depth in the Challenges section, but in brief, it promotes autopilot behaviours because it focuses on time scarcity. So much to do, and so little time to do it, yet we put more time into doing more.

> In the past, the brilliant Elon Musk has not so brilliantly boasted about his 100-hour work weeks, saying that "nobody ever changed the world on 40 hours a week".

I disagree vehemently with Mr Musk!

Having crashed and burned due to overwork, I now rail against the hustle culture. I devote a sizeable chunk of attention to the notion of overwork in the next section.

My experience of burnout helped me find a much healthier, better way of working. I discovered that there are ways to disrupt and innovate without killing yourself. It starts with being more intentional.

> To quote Dan Pink, "what's even scarcer today than attention is intention".

Living and working with intention requires us to pay more attention to the things we've become accustomed to doing on autopilot.

It means changing our approach, our way of thinking, our behaviours and actions. Making change of any kind is challenging, especially when we try to do it in big steps. Being intentional is no different.

But based on my experience, I'm happy to say that there is a way to make this more doable.

The way to develop and sustain the habit of being more intentional is through small, simple, incremental steps and repeated practice.

Small steps help us build momentum by moving forward at a slow and steady pace. A pace that works for us.

We create meaning through movement. This movement doesn't have to be at breakneck speed. It may sound counterintuitive, but we achieve a lot more when we slow things down.

Maintaining perpetual motion is about building momentum, one step at a time.

How we do one thing is how we do everything. We can decide how we show up in this new world we're facing. As we transition into a post-pandemic life, which could take years, give some thought to how you want to move forward.

- What are your goals for this next part of work and life?
- Are these goals aligned with your values and your identity?

When we align our thoughts with our actions, it becomes easier to activate the potential we need to achieve our goals.

What we cover in this book will help you develop a foundational approach for moving through life in a way which helps you to incorporate your core values into how you work.

It's helpful to have a framework that we can use to guide us and to implement what we learn on this journey.

INTRODUCING THE CADENCE CANVAS FRAMEWORK™

We'll be using my framework to help you build your new productivity practices.

The Cadence Canvas Framework™ addresses four aspects of HOW we approach work and life, and the impact they have on our experience and our outputs.

They are Foundation, Process, Culture and Performance.

1. FOUNDATION

Building strong physical, mental, emotional, and environmental foundations helps us thrive over the long term.

2. PROCESS

Developing a personal workflow of systems, practices and processes supports our focus, wellbeing, creativity and productivity.

3. CULTURE

Placing purpose, wellbeing, and meaning at the centre of how we work creates connection and aligns our values with our goals.

4. PERFORMANCE

Improving our self-leadership abilities and being more intentional about our productivity activates more of our potential.

Let's see how these four elements interact with each other as shown in this visual of my Cadence Canvas Framework™.

THE CADENCE EFFECT

THE CADENCE CANVAS FRAMEWORK™

PROCESS

Developing a personal workflow of systems and processes supports our focus, wellbeing, creativity and productivity.

PERFORMANCE

Improving our self-leadership abilities and being more intentional about our productivity activates more of our potential.

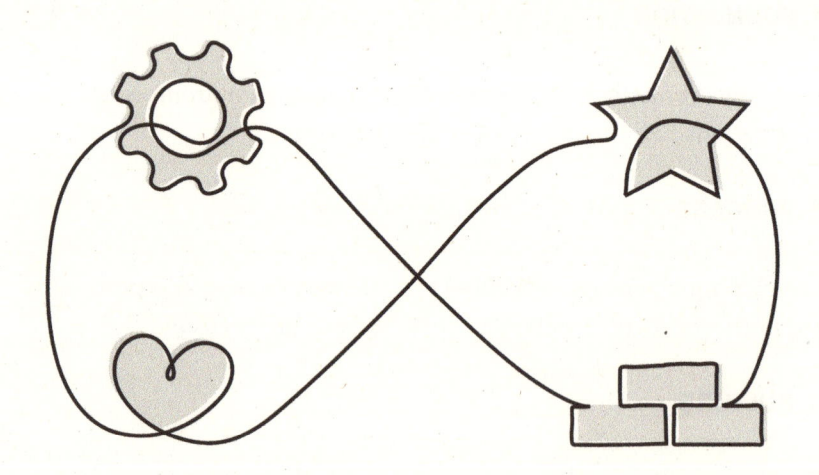

CULTURE

Placing purpose, wellbeing and meaning at the centre of how we work creates connection and aligns our values with our goals.

FOUNDATION

Building strong physical, mental, emotional, and environmental foundations helps us thrive over the long term.

THE CADENCE EFFECT IN ACTION

By reviewing and working on our foundations, processes, and culture, we improve our performance.

By activating our potential through the building of sustainable habits and behaviours, we have the power to transform our lives.

These actions enable us to create momentum, work with purpose and live with more intention, which all contribute to a more meaningful life.

All the topics covered in this book come together to help you build firm foundations, and develop better processes, to enhance your performance and cultivate a healthier, happier culture.

They apply whether you work alone or in a team.

CREATING CADENCE IS A CONTINUOUS CYCLE

I set up my framework as **an infinity symbol**, because the journey of creating cadence never stops. It's like a dance, with endless opportunities to keep moving.

It's in our human nature to problem solve, and as part of this process, we are continually experimenting, testing, and improving.

So, the cadence cycle is continually moving through the four aspects of how we approach our life and work.

Something to note, I have not visibly structured the chapters of this book according to the Cadence Canvas Framework™.

Instead, I've woven these principles and the guidance relating to these elements into the topics covered in each section.

You will see how it all comes together when it's time for you to create your own Cadence Canvas at the end of the book.

Before we continue, consider these two questions about your current state of productivity.

    1. Are you feeling stressed and/or overwhelmed by your work?
    2. Are you struggling with focus and completing your work?

If you answered yes to either, don't worry, you are not alone! In this book, you'll learn about tips, tricks and methods that can help you feel less stressed and more focused, so you can get back on track with your work (and your life).

Now let's discover more about the concept of Intentional Productivity, and the practices which make it easier to benefit from *the cadence effect*.

We'll be looking at what productivity means, the influences on productivity, and how we need to rethink our approach to it.

THREE
INTENTIONAL PRODUCTIVITY

> It is only by becoming a minimalist that we can become a maximalist.
>
> ~ BRAD STULBERG & STEVE MAGNESS

'Intentional Productivity' is about focusing on the things that matter.

This is a concept I've used in my coaching and writing work ever since I first launched Growth Sessions in 2018, when not many people were really referring to it as "a thing".

The idea of Intentional Productivity has since become more widely known, but it's still not mainstream. Yet. For me, the concept grew out of the things I learned and implemented during my lengthy burnout experience and subsequent recovery. Rooting my work in this concept has had transformative results for both me and my clients.

> I've found that when we develop practices that enable us to be more intentional about how we work, it improves our focus, elevates our creativity, supports our wellbeing and has a positive effect in other parts of our lives, too.

There are many research examples out there to back this up. But traditional notions of productivity don't make room for these good things to happen. They are more of a trap than a benefit. *I elaborate on these traditional traps later in the book.*

IT'S MORE THAN JUST A PHRASE

Intentional Productivity isn't productivity for productivity's sake.

It requires that we define productivity from a place of personal value. So, our output is also based on what is meaningful for us to put in.

> Intentional Productivity is about building sustainable, mindful, and focused working practices that help us create momentum, work with purpose, and craft a more meaningful life.
>
> ~ MICH BONDESIO

When we become more mindful about how we engage with our tools and our environments, that's the first step towards helping us perform better at work and in life.

The research shows that better selves are better for business outcomes.

A 2019 meta-analysis of 339 studies, conducted by Gallup and the London School of Economics, confirmed that "higher employee wellbeing is associated with higher productivity and firm performance".

When we become more intentional about how we work, we can activate more of our business potential, too. This applies whether you work as in a company, or whether you work for yourself as an entrepreneur, consultant, or freelancer.

As knowledge workers, we spend most of our days doing work that requires focus, so it makes sense that we're able to do that work in a way that helps us to work at our best.

Focused, intentional productivity is even more crucial if you work in a team.

> Effective, aligned teams require strong, supportive foundations to function cohesively, so that they can perform consistently and collaboratively at a high level.

Our world has now become increasingly virtual because of the pandemic and the fast adoption of rapidly progressing emerging technologies.

Spending so much time in virtual spaces has implications for our health and performance - both positive and negative.

So, prioritising our digital health and wellness is something <u>none</u> of us can afford to ignore. However, putting wellbeing first also clashes with the traditional view of productivity.

THE STANDARD PRODUCTIVITY METRIC

The typical technical (boring) definition of productivity is based on the factory model of work that harks back to the Industrial Revolution.

This definition by the US Bureau of Labor Statistics is about as dry as it gets.

> Productivity is represented by the volume of outputs we're able to produce, based on how efficiently we use our input resources, such as labor and capital.
>
> ~ US BUREAU OF LABOR STATISTICS

Using this format of productivity linked to deliverables, we and our outputs typically appear as data points on a business balance sheet or management tracking system. And that's fine, if we were all just a number. But that's not the case.

It's important to remember:

> Traditional notions of productivity are flawed, as we are humans first and resources second.

We are <u>not</u> commodities! Even though advertisers, industry bodies, policymakers, and business analysts label us that way.

THE CONTEXT FOR INTENTIONAL PRODUCTIVITY

Our outputs and ability to deliver can fluctuate based on several factors and influences.

- **Physical Factors:** For example, a poor night's sleep or having to work in a very noisy environment.
- **Emotional Factors:** We could experience conflict caused by office politics, or poor communication with a client or a team member. The state of our relationships, both at work and at home, matters.
- **Physiological Factors:** We carry how we feel with us, and chronic stress, anxiety, and / or depression cause physical, mental, and emotional fallout.
- **Control Factors:** Whether we have agency over how we do our work and what we produce is important, as a lack of autonomy increases stress.
- **External Factors:** Things beyond our control can also cause overwhelm, pressure and stress. A lengthy pandemic is a case in point.

We need to understand the landscape, which gives rise to the need for a change in the way we perceive productivity.

The need to spend too many hours on Zoom calls, and stretch ourselves too thin, taking on too many roles, has worn thin.

We've been through the ringer, adjusting to a world plagued by Covid. It forced many of us to reconsider what is important in life, and several interesting changes occurred that affected organisational culture.

'The Great Resignation' aka *'The Big Quit'* or *'Great Reshuffle'* was about people leaving their jobs with companies, largely because of distrust or dissatisfaction with their working conditions. They activated their dream of starting something on their own, or finding a better role elsewhere. And according to the Microsoft Work Trend Index 2022, the movement has gained momentum, particularly with Gen Z and Millennials.

Quiet Quitting was another outcome of the pandemic and hustle culture. When people could not leave their work or workplace, but were dissatisfied with their situation, they downgraded their investment in their work and sought meaning elsewhere instead.

This led to **employee disengagement** and a **reduction in productivity**. Although this trend has stopped being discussed in the press, most likely because of the cost-of-living crisis, I surmise it is still happening.

Although we are now well into the phase of "new normal", people are fed up juggling massive workloads with burning out. Especially when others around us fall ill, budgets get cut, and job constraints tightened, all adding more pressure to our days.

Productivity-related issues can also be due to whether we **find meaning in the work we do**. Does our work give us a sense of purpose? That purpose doesn't have to be world-shaking or life-changing, but it needs to be meaningful within our specific context.

DEFINED BY OUR WORK

We often identify so closely with what we do that when we take the work away, we can feel lost. It's common for us to lose our sense of meaning and identity outside of what we do for a living.

When work is the 'be-all-and-end-all', when the focus is solely on being productive to get the most out of yourself and out of others, this has a negative impact on both productivity and wellbeing. And it can lead to burnout. One example of this is when people who stop working to retire suddenly find their health declining, as they have no meaning or purpose left in their lives.

There are other dangers that come with attaching our "self worth to our net worth". In her book *Dare to Lead*, Brené Brown talks about how both armoured leadership and society's expectations reward exhaustion and cause us to attach our self-worth to our productivity.

> When worthiness is a function of productivity, we lose the ability to pump the brakes. The idea of doing something that doesn't add to the bottom line provokes stress and anxiety. It feels completely contrary to what we believe we want to achieve in life.
>
> ~ BRENÉ BROWN

Let me be clear.

I'm not saying work is not important. It is.

But life is about more than just work. Without the other parts of our life to influence and support us and also provide us with meaning, our work is just work.

Part of what spearheaded me making those major life decisions prior to experiencing my epic burnout was that I had lost the meaning in my work. It no longer brought me joy, it just brought me down. That loss of meaning was the start of a downward spiral that spread across my life and took me to a tough place.

Thankfully, I found meaning again with the work I now do, primarily because I've become much clearer about what matters to me, both in my work and in my life. I've been able to align my work and life goals with my values and beliefs.

Creating this type of alignment contributes to our ability to experience the cadence effect.

RETHINKING PRODUCTIVITY

Now more than ever, how we view productivity needs to change.

When we engage in Intentional Productivity practices, we're not just focusing on the work, we're also being more mindful of how our work fits into the bigger picture of our lives.

Intentional productivity connects our personal values and a more purpose-driven way of doing business, with the other usual requirements essential for our businesses to sustain and thrive.

It helps us to create more cadence in our workday and build more momentum in our work projects. And it supports our wellbeing and creativity, too.

I really like James Clear's definition of productivity.

> We often assume that productivity means getting more things done each day. Wrong. Productivity is getting important things done consistently.
>
> ~ JAMES CLEAR

However, with my definition of productivity, I take it a step further as Intentional Productivity is an even more nuanced way of thinking about being productive.

It still includes a focus on working efficiently, effectively and consistently. But it also considers our desire to produce meaningful work in a way that doesn't place ALL of our meaning on our work.

So distilling my definition to its essence:

> Intentional productivity is about getting important things done consistently and meaningfully, in a way that activates and encourages our potential, and supports our wellbeing and creativity.
>
> ~ MICH BONDESIO

WHY IS INTENTIONAL PRODUCTIVITY IMPORTANT?

We're in an increasingly fragile economic landscape and we're experiencing unprecedented amounts of stress and burnout due to a variety of factors both in and outside of our work.

It can feel like there's always more that needs to be done, with less time, less money, and fewer people or resources. These are threats which put an incredible strain on our wellbeing and ability to perform well.

As humans, we're the weakest link in the business production process, but we're also the most important link, and our most valuable asset.

> To thrive in business, both in the current world situation, and in the long run, we need to put ourselves, our people, and our purpose at the heart of how we do business.

High-performing employees, successful entrepreneurs and cohesive teams strive and thrive over the long-term, because they build firm foundations. They work according to a supportive framework that focuses not just on productivity, process and performance, but also on creativity, connection, health and wellbeing.

Choosing to work in this way also becomes a 'positioning' choice. It differentiates their business offering in a busy marketplace, enhances their business longevity, and improves their potential for growth.

We all have the means to build these firm foundations.

Studies have proven that when we create healthy work cultures that support our wellbeing, it also improves productivity, creativity and communication, as well as our business bottom line. This applies whether you work on your own, as part of a small team, or as part of a big organisation.

Intentional Productivity is about treating ourselves like the valuable assets we are.

So, how do we improve ourselves and our outputs? We start by mastering Intentional Productivity. And you're in luck, as that's what this entire book is about!

I'm a convert to this approach to work, having experimented with a host of different working styles and productivity habits which place wellbeing at the centre of how I work.

To me, it's clear that this is one of the most effective ways to overcome the challenges we face.

Before we go deep into specific challenges that threaten our wellbeing and productivity, let's understand the lay of the land.

The next chapter explores Life in the Digital Age.

We'll consider the digital context we find ourselves in to get clarity on how that influences our performance.

FOUR
LIFE IN THE DIGITAL AGE

> Sometimes speed doesn't get us to our destination faster.
>
> ~ AMY BLANKSON

After checking out of life from burnout, I started the slow journey of recovery, figuring out how to get better and to stay better. As I set off down this path to the other side, I encountered a lot of resistance, both from myself and from others, based on the social and cultural norms around me.

It really hit home how the typical ways in which we work (and live) can be harmful to our existence. Yet this is how many of us have learned to do and be. It's just the way we do things in our digital society.

Now, there are a lot of pros to living and working in virtual worlds. Our tech tools have a tremendous capacity to support us in working more efficiently and effectively. However, be aware that in this book, I'm going to be sharing a lot of the cons of our digital world. This is not because I particularly like being a harbinger of doom. Rather, because you can't make change if you're not aware of the true effect these influences can have on your wellbeing and productivity.

Remember, there is always another way.

Knowledge arms us with the power to make better-informed decisions so we can take more appropriate action.

THE DOWNSIDE OF DIGITAL

Our fast-paced and fast-developing online lifestyles, and the gadgets and tools we use in our day-to-day, trigger autopilot behaviours which slay our focus, fracture our attention, and dumb us down.

- A deluge of content stops us from focusing on the important stuff.
- We're tweaking out on social media, and screened up to our eyeballs.
- Shiny triggers distract us everywhere.

Technology occupies every minute of our days (and often nights). It's accessed via our phones, screens, gaming consoles, ear pods, microphones, cameras, you name it.

Mostly, these tools support us, yet increasingly some of them do not, and we're becoming too distracted to realise what's happening.

You may think you know exactly what's going on, and that you are in total control of your usage and behaviour, but some of the knock-on effects of our daily digital use may surprise you.

As Dr Anna Lembke points out in her book *Dopamine Nation*, compulsive overuse combined with access to the products of transformational technology are leading to a rise in addictions of all kinds.

THE AGE OF DISTRACTION

Research quoted by Johann Hari in his book *Stolen Focus* confirms that we are experiencing a rapid decline in our attention resources.

In his book *Hyperfocus*, Chris Bailey shares studies that show that most people can only focus on what's in front of them for 53% of the time.

The content available for us to consume is contributing to that. The deluge of data we face, and often need to deal with as part of our work, is **forcing us to stay shallow** in all facets of our lives.

We no longer have the space to create depth in our work and relationships.

The fallout? It's making us unhappy and unwell, less connected to ourselves and others, and less productive. So, where do some of these actual issues lie?

THE SMOKING GUN

The biggest culprit in our digital addiction is the ubiquitous extension of our hands. It's that modern day "box of cigarettes" - the smartphone - that tethers us. It's not just the box, it's also the contents that can be harmful to our health.

How we engage with our smartphones also leads to habits that fracture our attention. Our phone is typically by our side *all the time!* It has become an extension of our physical selves as we carry, hold, touch, and use it continuously throughout the day.

It has also become a key component in creating our identity, as we use it to communicate with the world and to signal how we want others to see us.

With social media, gaming and AR/VR experiences becoming an even bigger part of our lives, this enabling tech now includes headsets, glasses and goggles. Their use can contribute to excessive time spent in unsupportive spaces.

LIFE IN THE DIGITAL AGE

However, it's important to note that these other types of equipment may also be our saviour, as their evolution and increasing adoption will free our hands from the shackles of our phones.

Overall, these tech tools were designed to make our lives easier, and they do, but they also take up space in our lives and contribute to the clutter in our minds.

The autopilot behaviours that often stem from using digital tools can lead to an existence where there is little room for our brains to engage in quiet deep thought, creative problem solving, and meaningful internal discussion.

I'm not suggesting we turn our backs on them, as these tools are here to stay and they can play a valuable role in how we work and in achieving the outcomes we're seeking.

Instead, we need to create space in our lives — both whilst using these tools and away from them — so that we can make room for things that matter.

And what do I consider as something that matters?

Birthing new ideas, for one thing. There are heaps of small, big, and momentous challenges out there that require lovely, bold, imaginative, innovative and game-changing creative ideas. Ideas that could make someone's day, make life easier, or literally save the world *(and I'm not kidding when I say that)*.

This is where Intentional Productivity comes in.

> Intentional Productivity is an essential practice, framework and guide to help us carve out space and time for creating more meaning in our lives and for doing more of the work that matters.

UNDER PRESSURE

To develop our Intentional Productivity, we first need to exercise our awareness skills. It's important to understand the true impact of our broader cultural context.

What pressure does our digitally-focused world place on our ability to be productive and focused over time?

Many of us now work in the knowledge economy.

For this kind of work, our brains are our most important asset. But they are also the weakest link, as they don't have the same stamina as a computer or the latest AI Language Learning Model application.

For our brains to operate at their best, they need regular down time for rest and recovery. They also need environments which support their ability to work in a focused and productive way. Unfortunately, our environments don't always provide what our brain needs to function at a high level.

What else is affecting our productivity in this world?

To start, the lines between our home lives and work lives have become blurred. There's no more traditional 9-5. Now we're always contactable and always on.

The good side of this is that we now have opportunities to work more flexibly in ways that fit around the other responsibilities in our lives.

The downside is that it's easy to get into cycles of behaviour where we don't switch off when our workday is done. We continue to answer emails and message colleagues during what should be down time.

Our workday extends beyond what is feasible for ongoing, sustainable productivity.

Even post-pandemic, many of us are now in positions where we are juggling both personal and work responsibilities simultaneously, with no distinction between where they start and stop, and that puts an additional strain on our cognitive load and attention span.

Being connected and online means we have content and information coming at us from all sides, all the time. It's a lot for our brain to process, so we end up trying to multitask in autopilot mode.

This deluge of stimuli puts our bodies into an anxious, reactionary, fire-fighting state of perpetual alertness. It can trigger our brain to go into survival mode and spike our cortisol levels, so we feel more stressed than is optimal.

A CULTURE OF CORTISOL

Cortisol is called the stress hormone. It performs certain much-needed natural functions in the body. However, an overproduction of cortisol can be toxic for brain function.

A degree of stress is beneficial for us. When it energises us, it can motivate us to make change. When the stress we experience has a positive effect, this is called being in a state of "eustress".

But when cortisol triggers too often for the wrong reasons, that puts a strain on our body and mind. Too much cortisol and stress for too long puts our body into a state of "distress".

Operating in a culture of cortisol, where our overactive stress responses are perpetually being activated, eventually causes burnout, that umbrella term for physical and mental fatigue.

I dive deeper into stress, stressors and burnout in the next section on Challenges, but before we get there, let's consider what is perpetuating this culture of cortisol.

THE DOPAMINE ECONOMY

Dopamine is our pleasure hormone. Our need for dopamine causes our attachment to our devices. The dopamine economy leverages and manipulates this response **for financial gain**.

The creators of most social media and gaming platforms have purposefully designed these systems to hijack our brain's dopamine response.

The aim is to get us to spend more time on these platforms, seeking hits of pleasure. We are the product, targeted by advertisers who are the clients of these platforms. For the user, they help us escape the pain and discomfort that stressful work and life can bring, but over-usage can give rise to autopilot, addictive and anti-social behaviours.

In *The Chaos Machine*, author Max Fisher explores how the design of social media and its algorithms has rewired our minds. Through research, whistleblower revelations and interviews with the creators of this technology, he shows how they "deliberately shape our experiences" and cause "a powerful pull on our psychology and our identity which changes how we think, behave and relate to one another".

The examples Max Fisher cites are chilling reminders of how these spaces can manipulate our behaviour and alter our identity, both online and offline, even when we're not using them.

> Now, this might be ok if the outcomes of their influence were positive in every respect, but the findings are that these social media systems and algorithms amplify negative moral sentiment more than positive. Antagonistic content drives more views and likes, which perniciously perpetuates over-reactive behaviour such as hate and outrage.

Things become too personal and we feel the need to take sides. It's also much easier to ridicule, demean or defame someone online in the form of your avatar, than doing so in person where you can see first hand the hurt or pain your response truly brings.

As Max Fisher indicates, these systems and platforms "play on the frailties of our human nature and our most basic social impulses and needs. They bring out instincts and behaviours we try to suppress in modernity."

There are further ramifications from the over-production of dopamine.

As Dr Anna Lembke explains in *Dopamine Nation*, homeostasis works to keep our body's physiology in balance. So the more pleasure (and dopamine) we seek, the more pain it creates in the body to balance things out. And the body is always seeking more dopamine, so it never stays balanced for long.

Our overuse of whatever releases more of this pleasure hormone becomes part of a cycle of addiction, as we continue to combat the pain, but with an ever-diminishing pleasure return.

Remember that seesaw analogy from the chapter about Cadence vs Balance? Same thing applies here.

OUR DIGITAL HEALTH

Research shows that our attachment to our phones and the way we engage with their contents can cause mental health issues, such as body dysmorphia, poor self-esteem, anxiety and depression, as well as addiction responses and withdrawal symptoms.

For example, 'Nomophobia' is a classified anxiety disorder, which relates to the fear of being without, or being unable to see or touch, our phone.

The way we've become conditioned to use our smartphones and digital devices damages our focus and concentration, and this is incredibly disruptive for our productivity.

Aside from causing us to "lose time", digital behaviours such as perpetual scrolling also result in repetitive autopilot behavioural responses.

> The idea of these learned behaviours really hit home for me one day when I was travelling on the train. I used to check out Instagram on my commute, using my right thumb to scroll up the screen. On this day, my phone battery had died, but I had my Kindle with me, so I was reading an eBook. To flip pages on my Kindle, I tap left or right with my index finger. About 10 minutes into reading, I became aware that my right thumb was moving up and down of its own accord. My zombie thumb bemused me trying to scroll on its own, because my brain was having Insta withdrawal!

We crave spending time with these tools in these spaces because of their design, and we're likely to spend more of our time in them as technology advances even further. But we can leverage these tools and technologies to support us better. As I always say, there is another way!

To start, if we want our brains to operate at their best when we're doing attention-focused work, we can work on two things:

1. Supporting our ability to concentrate better when we use our tools.
2. Managing our dependence and attachment to our tools by taking extended time away from them.

How do cadence and intentional productivity tie in?

Building intentionally productive habits helps us to work at an adjustable pace with adaptable practices that support our creativity, wellbeing and productivity in both the online and physical world.

It incorporates a flexible toolkit of techniques and behaviours that we can leverage as needed to suit our ever-changing situation.

Now let's reflect on your current situation.

Answer the preliminary questions in the Reflection chapter for this section, which will help to highlight your current situation and how it might be affecting you.

As we progress, we'll go into more detailed reflection exercises in each of the sections in this book. And we will save our responses as we go along, to add to our Cadence Canvas at the end.

FIVE
REFLECTION EXERCISES NO.1

> Awareness is the greatest agent for change.
>
> ~ ECKHART TOLLE

"WHERE" ARE YOU NOW?

Making change first requires understanding where you are now and what got you here.

Consider your current situation and respond to the following questions:

1. Do you ever feel stressed and distracted in your work and life?
2. Can you identify some autopilot behaviours you regularly engage in at work and at home? *(E.g. reaching for your phone when you're bored or stressed; opening the fridge to snack when you are not hungry to avoid doing challenging work or having a tough conversation.)*
3. How much time do you spend playing games or watching TV?
4. How much time do you spend using your phone every day?
5. How much time do you spend on social media daily?

THE CADENCE EFFECT

6. What are you doing on your phone, other than making phone calls?
7. What impact does your gaming, TV watching and/or phone usage have on your productivity?
8. What impact does your social media usage have on your productivity?
9. Are you able to give sufficient time, focus and attention to something that matters (in your work and/or personal life)? If not, what's stopping you?
10. Are you willing to make changes that will improve your productivity and your life?
11. In an ideal world, what's one minor change you might be willing and able to make to your current habits that will give you more time for what matters?

Make a note of your answers to these questions.

Writing things down helps to bring issues into focus so that you can address them and take action.

WHO ARE YOU, REALLY?

Making change also requires identifying your values, so that as part of doing this work, you can align your life and work goals to those values.

Consider these questions:

1. What type of person are you?
2. What is important to you?

A few examples of my own values to guide you in creating your answers:

- "I'm the type of person who follows through and finishes what I start".
- "I'm the type of person who shows up for those I care about."

REFLECTION EXERCISES NO.1

- "I'm the type of person who aims to be patient and calm."
- "I'm the type of person who doesn't give up."
- "I'm the type of person who approaches challenges with grit and determination."

Here are some longer examples:

"When I take action or engage in activities in a way that aligns with my values, I feel at peace in my mind and energised in my body. Things flow. There is less friction or resistance."

"Things that are important to me in the way I work: simplicity, professionalism, pragmatism, connection, empathy and loyalty."

"Things that are important to me in my life: my family, being kind, showing up with love, connecting with nature, and protecting the environment."

YOUR TURN...

Complete the guide sentence below as a starting point:

"I'm the type of person who...."

Your answers can be short phrases. They don't have to be long and involved. If you're not sure where to start, take another look at my examples above for guidance.

Consider your responses based on a first impression of yourself and what is meaningful to you. They should reflect the beliefs which affect how you respond in the world.

Other prompts:

- What are your most important values?
- What is it like "you" to do to keep your life moving forward?
- How will aligning your values and goals make you feel?
- What will this help you achieve?

Make a note of your answers and consider the small changes you can start making to how you view and engage with your world.

SMALL STEPS OVER TIME LEAD TO BIG CHANGE.

If you alter your thinking and become more aware of your approach to life, it will direct your attention and impact your productivity in a good way.

Before we continue, let's recap what we've covered in this first section.

- First, I shared my story of how an awful experience with epic burnout transformed my approach to life and work.
- I've introduced you to the concepts of cadence and intentional productivity, which sit at the heart of a fresh approach to productivity that we'll be exploring further in later sections.
- You got to see the Cadence Canvas™, my framework for activating potential, which you can use for developing your own productivity practices as we work through this book, to help you harness *the cadence effect*.
- We've briefly looked at the challenges and opportunities that come with living and working in a digital age.
- Finally, we reflected on where you find yourself at this moment, so that you have a baseline from which to work.

YOUR IDENTITY & YOUR CADENCE CANVAS

Your identity reflects your culture. Who it is like you to be is a key part of the culture you want to build around you, your behaviours, work practices, interactions, and life experiences?

So, consider the identity you want to emulate based on the answers you've given above. Keep a note of your answers so you can add them to the CULTURE section of the Cadence Canvas Framework™ once we've completed all the sections in the book.

REFLECTION EXERCISES NO.1

Part 2 is about The Real Challenges we face.

We're going much deeper into the key challenges that impact our emotional and physical health, and which have implications for how we build our intentional productivity practices.

Some of these challenges are so deeply embedded in our culture, they have also created ingrained behaviours.

The first chapter of this next section focuses on the origins of stress, the stressors which cause it, and ways we can manage it better.

NOTES

PART TWO
THE REAL CHALLENGES

1. Introduction
2. **CHALLENGES**
3. How We Work
4. Opportunities
5. Focus & Flow
6. Next Steps

SIX
STRESS & STRESSORS

> The greatest weapon against stress is our ability to choose one thought over another.
>
> ~ WILLIAM JAMES

The things which cause friction, overwhelm and pressure in our lives elevate the impact of stress on our bodies and minds.

As I mentioned in the previous section about cortisol, some stress is good and/or natural and can help us perform better. However, too much for too long causes a host of health and performance issues.

As part of developing more mindful approaches to work, we need to address stress. We need to accept its role and manage it, so it helps rather than hinders us.

And now for the science bit. Let's clarify how stress gets activated and what triggers it.

THE STRESS RESPONSE 101

Our bodies are absolutely amazing works of wonder. We have so many interlinking systems which affect and protect how this physiological place we call 'home' works.

The **stress response system** is just one of these sets of tools that provides the energy we need to perform and respond. When our stress levels elevate, it's a response designed to keep us safe.

Here's what happens when it's activated:

- The stress hormones cortisol and adrenaline (epinephrine and norepinephrine) signal to our body to prepare for action.
- Energy sources (glucose, fatty acids and amino acids) get activated and sent to critical muscles, priming our body for action and our brain for reaction.
- Our breathing and metabolic rate (heart rate, blood pressure) increase to help transport nutrients and oxygen to protect our body and brain.
- Our body's energy diverts from longer-term processes, such as digestion, so it's available for immediate use.
- Our muscles tense, preparing to provide speed and strength, our pupils dilate to sharpen vision, and we sweat more to prevent overheating.
- Our immune function gets a surge of energy in anticipation of injury or infection.

All of this is happening in micro-seconds, and when all is working in sync, this system runs like a well-oiled machine for keeping us safe. However, our brain can't tell the difference between real and perceived threats. When the stress response repeatedly activates, it can cause havoc with our body's homeostatic system, putting a strain on its ability to function correctly and appropriately.

Stressors activate the stress response in our body before we feel it in our minds (our thoughts).

STRESS & STRESSORS

Our brain and body perceive stressors as potential threats. They put us into **'fight, flight, freeze or please' mode**. This is a built-in response mechanism, which ensures our survival.

As described earlier, a certain amount of stress in our bodies is natural, and can be helpful in getting us to overcome fear and take action.

Most of us are also being exposed to a lot of stressors beyond our control, as we're in a time of major upheaval, conflict, and transformation in the world. The stress that comes from being in these sometimes overwhelming situations can cause our brains to default to survival mode.

Too much stress or oft-recurring stress puts excessive strain on our body and mind, as they have to overwork to deal with the stressors, often with insufficient time for recovery in between.

Repeating or ongoing stressors can cause **chronic stress**. Over the long term, chronic stress causes physical damage to our bodies and creates mental fatigue. And we know where that takes us… it's the road to burnout.

WHAT ARE YOUR STRESSORS?

To tackle excess stress, you first need to understand what is causing the stress. These triggers are called stressors. They can be physical or emotional stressors. They can be external or internal stressors.

1. EXTERNAL STRESSORS

Stressors can relate to things such as work, money, family, culture, and community.

Perhaps you have to deal with money worries. Maybe someone at work is repeatedly engaging in discriminatory behaviour against you. Perhaps you are dealing with long-standing familial conflicts; or trying to juggle an excess of caring responsibilities on top of a burgeoning career.

Consider this example of how an external stressor may cause increased stress on the body:

> If you (or your partner) are made redundant and suddenly there's only one (or no) income to cover all the bills, this is going to cause extra stress.
>
> The stress might manifest through increased anxiety as you worry more. You may find it difficult to concentrate on your tasks and responsibilities. Your heart rate might speed up, so you feel jittery. You may experience insomnia and a loss of appetite (or crave carbs and sugar).
>
> The lack of sleep affects your performance each day, and the anxiety makes it difficult to focus. You become irritable with your coworkers and clients, and short-tempered with your kids and partner.

We may not be able to control the stressor that causes these responses, but we can learn to control or manage our response to that stressor.

We'll look at ways to do this as we progress through the book.

2. INTERNAL STRESSORS

They can link to things like thoughts, emotions, and our mindset.

They can relate to psychosocial issues, such as self-criticism, poor body image, a crisis of identity, traumatic experiences, painful memories, and so forth.

For example, someone may have criticised our body shape or our abilities when we were young, which was then internalised and is now triggered every time a similar situation arises in adulthood. It can be a challenge to overcome the emotional pain caused by the original experience. We may still feel stress whenever we're put in a position that forces us to relive it, or to feel the same way we did in that original situation.

Research shows that what is lightly referred to as "emotional baggage" and more seriously as "unresolved trauma" gets stored in the mind and body. We can continue to feel the effects of this trauma, both mentally and physically, well past the original event.

These effects - also known as "post-traumatic stress" - can show also up physically in the body, triggered whenever recollections of a traumatic experience arise, even if the original stressor no longer exists.

In these situations, some form of talk therapy can be beneficial in helping us manage our response to internal stress.

The key is to build our self-awareness.

So that we become more aware of when these responses are being triggered; recognise the responses for what they are; and develop tools to help us respond more appropriately each time we recognise it coming up.

Physical pain or dysfunction can also be an internal stressor.

> For example, in my 20s, I slipped a disc in my lower back while picking up a TV remote of all things! I had to spend two weeks in bed, and several weeks being inactive, as part of the recovery. I've paid the price of intermittent back pain ever since. In the beginning, that intense physical pain and lack of mobility affected my mood and mindset considerably, and it led to a short period of depression.
>
> These health indicators are examples of stress that was placed on my body and mind, which came from an internal stressor. It took physiotherapy, meditation, yoga, pain killers and learning how to move my body differently, for me to manage my response to this stressor better. Now, when that back injury niggles or flares, usually because I've been sitting for too long, I know what to do.

As with external stressors, there are opportunities to develop skills, habits and behaviours that can help us manage our response to internal stressors.

We'll be delving into the science of habit creation and behaviour change, and considering some simple ways to manage our responses in the section on Leveraging Opportunities later in the book.

THE IMPACT OF STRESS ON PRODUCTIVITY

Stress can aid us in our work performance. The pressure of a tight deadline can be great for activating our best creativity. The right amount of stress, experienced at the right time, for a limited amount of time, can make us more productive.

> ... performance increases with physiological or mental arousal (stress), but only up to a point. When the level of stress becomes too high, performance decreases.
>
> ~ THE YERKES-DODSON LAW

Research has found that the optimal point varies based on the complexity and familiarity of the tasks causing the stress/arousal, and the degree of control you have over the stressors and stress response.

The science shows that when our stress levels are elevated, we are better at doing simple tasks. But, if we're trying to do complex tasks, an increase in stress <u>decreases</u> our focus and performance.

If pressure and stress only occur occasionally at work, then our brains and bodies can usually cope and bounce back.

However, our brain associates work that might be difficult with pain and discomfort. This is something our brain actively wants to avoid, because it's perceived as a threat, especially if we're already experiencing pressure and overwhelm.

When we're in survival mode - a constant state of heightened alertness - be it from work challenges or something outside of work - then we struggle to do deep, focused work, because our attention and wellbeing is affected.

In this situation, our brain doesn't identify work as a priority. Instead, it's constantly jumping around, checking for threats and making sure we're doing what we can to be safe.

So, concentrating on creating that overdue business presentation is the last thing on your mind! It just knows that the presentation is making you stressed, and for your mind, that is a threat to your very survival!

How often is your work not causing stress?

Chances are you feel stressed more of the time, than less.

In a work scenario, if we're feeling too stressed, we may become more distracted, feel more anxious, and procrastinate more, (which I talk about in the next chapter).

If the stress persists, we may succumb to burnout, or experience other health issues.

WORK CULTURE & STRESS

I talk about the hustle culture and the culture of overwork in more detail in the chapter on burnout and work, but I want to touch briefly on work culture here, as it can be a trigger for increased stress.

A pressured work culture forces us to do more with less. This is only sustainable in the short term. When it's ever present, it breeds the same effects as a culture of cortisol, where we are adrenalised to the max, working on borrowed time and seeking dopamine like there's no tomorrow. As a result, we become stressed to our eyeballs.

Your personal scenario might not be as hectic as what I've just described, but the culture within which you work can still put pressure on your health.

If we're working in a high-pressure culture, where everything is a tight deadline and we feel like all we do is fight fires reactively, then

we're working in a way that leads to chronic stress and eventually burnout.

We all know that ongoing, elevated stress is incredibly damaging for our physical and mental health. What you might not know is that this type of stress also affects things like our memory, our reasoning, judgement, decision making, and communication skills.

CHANGING OUR APPROACH TO STRESSORS

We might not always be able to control what's causing the surrounding stress, but we can change HOW we respond to these triggers. We can alter our perspective.

OUR LOCUS OF CONTROL

Wellbeing-focused practices sit at the heart of what's within our control.

Self-care is essential to help us build sound health foundations and manage our stress.

Strong foundations enable us to develop and maintain robust bodies and healthy immune systems. They also help to keep us grounded and centred, so that we can respond more calmly and effectively in times of stress. They provide the basis for building our resilience so that when we face challenges; we can bounce back more quickly.

I go in to a lot more detail about these foundational practices in the section on Leveraging Opportunities, but here's a taster of what I'm talking about.

It's within our control to engage in practices such as:

- Getting enough sleep and practising good sleep hygiene
- Daily exercise and regular movement
- Proper nutrition for your age and body type
- Mindfulness techniques such as yoga, meditation, journaling & conscious breathing

STRESS & STRESSORS

These types of supportive activities are becoming non-negotiable in our fight to stay well and resilient in turbulent times.

However, there are also a lot of stress triggers that are outside of our locus of control. So how do we handle those?

MANAGING STRESSORS BEYOND OUR LOCUS OF CONTROL

Often when we are feeling pressured or overwhelmed because of stress-activating situations beyond our control, we get so frustrated that it causes us to respond emotionally.

We freak out, start crying, get grumbly, or snap at others. Sound familiar?

- Think about times when you felt super-stressed.
- How did you respond at that moment?
- What would you have done instead, to handle it differently, if you could?

Self-regulation is an effective way to help us handle stress-activating situations. Here are two ways that you can develop your self-regulating skills.

1. MENTAL SELF-REGULATION

One way is to change our approach to these triggers, working to become more aware of the automatic behaviours we default to when things feel challenging.

Then we can practise better responses, learning to create a gap between the trigger and how we respond to that trigger.

- When exposed to a stressor, cortisol releases that triggers our fight/flight response.

- It stays in our system for about 90 seconds and during this time it also brings up emotions, which can be something real or imagined - our brain doesn't know the difference.

Often we let the cortisol-induced emotions (justified or not) continue to rule us once the 'threat' has passed, but <u>we have the choice</u> to alter our response to that perceived threat.

We can either perpetuate the cycle or we can shift our thinking.

If, during those first 90 seconds, we can realise there's a reaction about to kick off, and then pause, then we can choose <u>not</u> to react (or overreact) in full-on threat response mode.

Let's break the process down more simply…

Trigger >> Awareness >> Pause >> Respond

- The trigger is the thing causing you stress.
- Awareness is when you first note how the trigger is causing you to feel and respond.
- The pause is when you stop and take a moment to consider how you're responding and whether you can change your response to something more supportive. (It could be as simple as taking a few deep breaths to clear your mind and body).
- Then you continue with a considered (and potentially different) response, behaviour, approach, or outlook.
- This takes practice, and also the ability to accept and apologise when you don't get it right. Especially if your overreaction causes emotional pain to those around you.

Mental self-regulation is a learned behaviour that can help you manage your response, but there will always be triggers, and it's a given that you will still overreact at certain times.

However, once you build the habit of becoming more aware of when stressors are triggering you, then it becomes easier to adjust your response more quickly over time, to reduce the level and frequency of overreaction.

STRESS & STRESSORS

Letting go of what you can't control is accepting what you can't change.

We are natural problem solvers, but sometimes there are no solutions for a situation that just needs to be endured.

If you can't change the unwanted situation causing your stress response, can you reframe and accept it? By practising what is known as radical acceptance, you can shift your perception of a situation so that it no longer has such a powerful hold on you.

We exacerbate our level of stress when we spend copious amounts of time ruminating about events, situations and experiences we can't change. If we can instead acknowledge them for what they are, then we can loosen their hold on us and reduce our stress.

Accepting that this is just how things are at this moment, helps us to let go of living with past regrets or seeking impossible outcomes in the future, so that we can become more present in our lives.

As part of this reframing, you may even find some positives or benefits to the experience you are in. What can you learn from this challenge? What is the situation trying to teach you?

2. PHYSICAL SELF-REGULATION

Often during periods of high stress, we carry the after-effects of that stress in our bodies long after the stressor's direct influence subsides.

Wild animals have an inbuilt automatic system for releasing stress in their bodies. They literally shake it off and then move on with their lives.

Humans need to do it mindfully and manually. Otherwise, it builds up and causes chronic health issues.

"Shaking off" the stress in human terms means engaging in activities that help to change our physical state.

When we do this, our homeostatic system recalibrates itself and we feel better able to carry on with our day and our life.

Examples of ways to complete the stress cycle:

- Movement, such as dance, yoga or vigorous physical exercise *(including sex)*.
- Meditation and conscious breath work help you get grounded.
- You can change your visual focus and the stimuli you're able to see and hear.
- Release tension by having a good ugly cry or laughing until you pee in your pants.
- Hugging, kissing and physical touch with someone also releases endorphins to make you feel better.
- You can also create touch moments on your own, e.g. rubbing your hands, tickling your arm, hugging a pillow, or stroking with your cat can be just as effective.

Amidst my burnout, sometimes the loneliness was overwhelming.

I felt starved of touch long before the pandemic limited our ability to hug others, and my pet allergies meant I couldn't emulate that connection by cuddling a fur ball. Instead, in bed at night, I got into the habit of positioning pillows alongside me, so that it would mimic the feeling of a warm body next to me. That made me feel calmer and safer and helped me to fall asleep.

Later on, Friday night "Kitchen Disco" also became a thing. I'd put on some 80s tunes to boogie while cooking. My neighbours probably thought I was batty, but busting dirty dance moves always lifted my mood and put a smile on my face. :)

3. VIVA THE VAGUS

The vagus (aka the wandering nerve) connects the brain stem to various parts of the body. It's the longest nerve in the body and affects the regulation of sensory, motor and parasympathetic responses in our body, and our cardiovascular, respiratory and gastrointestinal functioning.

STRESS & STRESSORS

The vagus nerve also supports our endocrine and immune systems in managing the body's inflammatory response. The vagus can also help to counteract the fight/flight response we experience in our autonomic nervous system in times of high stress.

Stimulating our vagus nerve brings us into a calmer, clearer state. Maintaining a healthy vagal response (or vagal tone) ensures we're able to balance our parasympathetic system and makes it easier for us to regulate our emotions so we can also support our mental health better.

You can consciously stimulate the vagus nerve in a few different ways, including:

- Diaphragmatic breathing, such as conscious breathing or meditation, which I talk about in more detail later in the book.
- Gargling with water, as the nerve runs down the throat.
- Applying pressure in the ear, as this is where it lies closest to the skin.
- Cold water immersion, such as wild swimming, taking cold showers, or learning and doing the Wim Hof Method.

BEING PREPARED FOR STRESS

What do you currently do to help you manage your stress?

- What are your favourite ways of moving? Do you like running, walking or cycling?
- How do you usually let off steam when stressed? Hot yoga, HIIT, strength training, or deep breathing?
- If you like dancing, then dance more, guaranteed, it will elevate your mood and keep you limber in the process!
- Can you hug or hold hands with someone today? Pets and pillows are excellent substitutes if you live on your own.

Consider which of these you can try out, or do more of, to help you let go of the effects of stress.

In our online future of work, we're going to need to do more work with fewer resources. These circumstances are bound to cause more stress.

Our first line of defence against changeable circumstances is building stronger foundations, by increasing our self-awareness, building our resilience and engaging in proper self-care.

We also need to consider and implement ways to work better, that help us manage our stress and reduce the impact of stressors. To leverage the outputs that good stress can bring and limit the effects of bad stress. *We'll look at ways to change your working practices in later sections of this book.*

Recommended Further Reading:

- The Stress Prescription: 7 Days to More Joy & Ease - Dr Elissa Epel, PhD
- Burnout: The Secret to Solving the Stress Cycle - Emily & Emilia Nagoski

Before moving on, consider your existing stress situation.

- How do you typically respond, react, and feel when stressed?
- Which stress triggers are within / outside of your locus of control?
- How might you manage your stress better AND shake off your stress response?
- If you can't change the stressors, how can you change your perspective or reframe your outlook on the stress you face?

Up next is Procrastination and the havoc it can wreak on our productivity.

It can be the bane of our lives. But did you know it stems from a built-in protection response and our mind is just trying to keep us safe?

SEVEN
PROCRASTINATION

> Procrastination is the thief of time.
>
> ~ EDWARD YOUNG

I mentioned in my burnout story how there was a period of about six months where I felt like I'd lost time, where I couldn't remember what I was doing day to day. Everything I had to do in a day also seemed to take so long to do, because of the strong resistance I felt to doing anything that was outside of my comfort zone. At that point in time, I was in such a heightened state of anxiety that EVERYTHING felt like a threat. So I would often freeze and avoid doing things, as they seemed too scary or too difficult to do.

You don't need to be trapped in this kind of worst-case scenario to be crippled by procrastination.

As a species, we've lost the tolerance for discomfort, and we indulge in behaviours which compromise our attention. We've also become uncomfortable being bored or alone with our thoughts. The pressures most of us experience daily can be overwhelming, prompting us to avoid them in any way we can.

We procrastinate on doing the hard things, avoid dealing with the urgent things, and put off facing the important things in our life.

Procrastinating is a common occurrence due to the way our brain is built. But it can derail our good intentions for being productive, as it can affect how we manage our time.

As a concept, procrastination is not something new. It is not just a result of our modern way of living; it has been around for way longer than you may realise.

- The word is derived from *procrastinare* (Latin) which means 'to put off until tomorrow'
- It also has Greek roots in the word *acrasia*, which relates to "doing things against our better judgement".

We think we procrastinate because we're failing at controlling our willpower or managing our time, but there are deeper reasons why we do it.

WIRED TO PROCRASTINATE

Procrastination serves a bigger purpose, and from an evolutionary perspective, it is hard wired into our behaviour patterns.

Our brains are designed to:

- Favour short-term thinking and immediate reward.
- Seek pleasure, safety and comfort.
- Avoid danger, threats and discomfort.

These are the same actions we take when we procrastinate. Procrastinating isn't specifically a problem with our ability to manage time. It is a behaviour driven by emotion.

Procrastination is a system for protecting us and repairing our mood.

Research has identified it as being part of our emotional response to stress. It's a coping mechanism for dealing with challenging emotions. These are the emotions we may feel when our brain identifies a potentially stressful or uncomfortable situation as a threat.

A study in 2005 considered two types of procrastination: active and passive.

- **Active procrastination:** purposefully delaying an action, so you work better under pressure.
- **Passive procrastination:** you find yourself paralysed, unable to complete a task.

Active, intentional procrastination can have some benefits. And an avoidance response is natural in certain circumstances.

However, procrastination can become an automated habit when we experience continued periods of high stress over time (aka chronic stress).

When procrastinating becomes our default response to taking action in our life, this compulsive behaviour takes over our lives, and prevents us from doing the things we really want to do. It may even harm us.

WHAT REALLY CAUSES US TO PROCRASTINATE?

Situations, experiences, tasks, and actions, which can make us feel bored, anxious, insecure, fearful, negative, or uncertain, bring about the desire to procrastinate.

There are plenty of things in a work context that make us feel the need to avoid doing our work.

The uncomfortable emotions we feel in these situations cause feelings of stress in our body, as our brain battles against thoughts of doing something it finds uncomfortable or threatening, in favour of doing something that makes us feel better.

And, as previously mentioned, aside from work, our current world context has lots of scary, threatening things pushing us to avoid discomfort and seek safety and consolation in something else.

This need to avoid discomfort and seek pleasure is why:

- We end up doom scrolling Twitter when we're trying to do that very important piece of work.
- We reach for our phones to bury our heads in a rabbit hole of dancing babies on TikTok, when the news of the day is too depressing to contemplate.
- We settle for the deluxe chocolate bar instead of dealing with and resolving coworker or partner conflict.
- We end up rearranging our kitchen cupboards, binge watching Netflix, or raiding the fridge, when we should do our accounts.

Immediate rewards help us escape discomfort temporarily.

The irony is that we process pleasure and pain in exactly the same part of the brain. But there is a dopamine reward we experience when we gain pleasure and comfort. So we seek it out.

The short-term gain feels more important than the longer term outcome, but this avoidance tactic results in a loss of performance over time.

The efficacy of that dopamine release diminishes over time too, so we seek more of it to get the same pleasurable response, creating a negative, addictive cycle.

THE COST OF OVER-PROCRASTINATION

Several studies have found that when procrastination becomes a default habit over time, it negatively affects our moods, our stress levels, and our physiology. It puts our wellbeing and happiness at risk.

There are further ramifications.

CONFLICT

It affects our relationships. Procrastination impacts on our ability to communicate clearly. We become so focused on the distraction and we stop paying attention to other things happening around us. We may end up letting people down, causing arguments, or creating larger repercussions because of our inaction.

Revelling in the distraction takes us away from interacting with other people so it reduces our socialisation opportunities, something important for our overall health.

SHAME & GUILT

Actively avoiding doing something we know we should do also makes us feel guilty for not doing it. Again, this becomes a repetitive vicious cycle, as we procrastinate more to avoid feeling bad, only to have it make us feel worse.

Not only do we feel shame, but depending on what we are doing to procrastinate, it can also give rise to poor self-esteem or anger at oneself for having no control.

LOSS OF AUTONOMY

When we procrastinate too much, and it becomes our default, autopilot response, it feels beyond our control. We just do it. It just happens. When we finally notice what's going on, we discover we've wasted what could be hours doing something unhealthy or unproductive.

We can feel helpless to control it or make change. But feeling helpless is a learned response.

In his book *Learned Optimism*, the psychologist Martin Seligman talks about learned helplessness. The more we encounter situations which we feel we can't change, the less we try to change our situation.

So we stop trying and become resigned to letting the situation rule us. But it <u>doesn't</u> have to be this way!

ADDICTION & SELF-HARM

Researchers use dopamine levels to quantify the addictiveness of an experience. The dopamine hit we get from a procrastination behaviour means that the more we do it, the more we want to do it, which can lead to an addiction to that behaviour.

Procrastination can also be the reason some people continue to smoke or vape tobacco, take harmful drugs, gamble with their savings, watch too much porn, or self-harm in other ways, despite knowing it's an unhealthy activity.

They know the risks of what they are doing, but they can't stop themselves. The addictive activity can serve a purpose as a coping mechanism for dealing with or avoiding the stress they're feeling - be it from current circumstances or past trauma.

It can happen to all of us!

> During my burnout, I would lose chunks of time on social media. It was to avoid writing job applications when I was finding this so hard to do. I developed these repetitive behaviours where I would cycle through every social channel multiple times, pressing refresh again and again, seeking novelty and distraction to keep me occupied rather than facing the difficulties of my reality. It was like gambling on a one-armed bandit. I couldn't get enough. I hated the fact I did not seem able to stop myself from doing it.
>
> It was only after I read Cal Newport's *Deep Work* that I realised the limiting effect these distractions were having on my ability to move forward in my life. Nowadays, reducing distractions is a priority for helping to manage my procrastination tendencies.

I'm still susceptible to procrastination, as I'm still human. But I've become better at recognising exactly what is making me feel the need to procrastinate, so I can put it in to context, and crack on.

Putting a name to the perceived threat causing my need to procrastinate, and then being kind to myself in understanding why I was feeling threatened, helps to reduce procrastination's hold on me.

I've also discovered some great ways to help manage procrastination which I share in the next part of this chapter.

PROCRASTINATION & PRODUCTIVITY

We all procrastinate in some way or another. Typically, small bouts of procrastination don't do us any harm. But the amount of distractions and the levels of discomfort caused by uncertainty in our world means we are procrastinating now more than ever, and it is having a negative impact on our productivity.

Procrastination compromises our concentration and fractures our focus. This has massive implications for our ability to produce our best work out in the world.

According to research quoted by Chris Bailey, an author and expert in productivity, many of us self-distract every 30 to 40 seconds.

And it seems that most of us can only focus for 53% of the time when we're trying to do focused work. Our mind is wandering for the other 47%!

Let's get real ... it's impossible to be focused for 100% of our time, nor would we want to be.

But we can improve our focus ability by reducing our proclivity for procrastination. We also need to understand the difference between procrastinating and day dreaming. They are not the same thing! Day dreaming can be a helpful, creative problem solving activity. It is not work avoidance, it can supplement and support our work.

However, if we want to perform better for specific periods of time in our workday, then we need to get more intentional, so that we can manage some of that mind wandering and overcome our resistance in a better way.

As mentioned in the Stress & Stressors chapter, we can do this by working on our self-awareness, our self-regulation, and our habits.

RESETTING OUR ATTENTION

To support our productivity more intentionally, we need to build more supportive emotional habits. And we need to identify better emotional rewards that override our typical 'avoidance' behaviours.

As our brains are built to procrastinate, we can't stop ourselves from doing it from time to time. But we can get better at noticing when we're doing it, so we can change our behaviour.

Learning to reset our attention takes practice and there is no one 'right' way to do this.

It's important to experiment to find ways that work best for you, and it's a good idea to have a few methods in your toolkit to call on in different situations. Here are some activities that can help you reset your attention.

1. GET CURIOUS

Acknowledge when you're procrastinating and question what's causing you to do it? Bring attention to the sensations in your body and mind, so you can get to the root cause of what you're feeling and why. Building your self-awareness skills makes it easier to notice when you're doing it.

You can build your attention skills through practising meditation and other mindful activities, such as journaling.

I'll talk about these more in the section on Preparing For Focus & Flow.

When you become aware that you're procrastinating, ask yourself:

"Why am I really doing this?"

The reason you find yourself standing in front of the fridge for the third time in an hour probably isn't because you're hungry. Instead, it's probably because you're feeling afraid of what your brain perceives to be a difficult / challenging / boring / annoying / scary / *[insert your descriptor here]* task that you need to do.

Identify the real reason you're avoiding the task at hand. By addressing the procrastination and recognising it, you diminish its power, which allows you to move on and take action.

- Getting to the root of why you are avoiding a task, or have interrupted it, reduces procrastination's hold on you, helping you to take back control.

2. ZOOM IN

Break down overwhelming tasks into bite-sized actions to reduce the resistance you're feeling. "Bite-sized" might mean micro, teeny-tiny steps to get you over that first hurdle of starting.

Motivation, momentum and confidence happen <u>after</u> we take action, not before. So, we need to take a first step, to feel motivated to take more steps.

The simpler the starting point is, the easier it is to get into the task and continue. So, when you're feeling resistance to getting started, make a list of the first five things you need to do to take action on a task.

A micro list could look something like this:

1. Open browser
2. Type search term
3. Bookmark top three article links
4. Read top three articles
5. Make notes on each of these articles

By the time you've ticked off the first three on your list, you'll more than likely find that you're well on your way to accomplishing your task with more ease.

- Set out the very next actions you can take to progress on your work. When you keep your focus close and reduce things down to their simplest steps, it makes the task more manageable.

3. CREATE FRICTION

Put obstacles, barriers and boundaries in the path of your "go to" procrastination behaviours and temptations. You can also remove friction from the harder tasks at hand.

When we make it more challenging to do the easy "avoidance activity", the less likely we are going to do it. And if we make the arduous task easier to do, then through practice we can develop habits and behaviours that help us do these harder activities without, or with less, resistance.

- Make it more difficult to engage in avoidance tactics and easier to do what matters, even if it's hard.

Examples: Create obstacles to default procrastination behaviours:

- If you must buy and have treats in the house, hide them from yourself. Put them in a difficult to reach place.
- Put your phone out of line of sight behind you, out of arm's reach, and turn off your notifications.
- Delete addictive games and apps from your phone or lock yourself out of social media on your browser during times you need to get work done.
- Turn off notifications for things you don't need to know about while doing deep work.

Examples: Reduce friction on more supportive / strenuous activities:

- Put your healthy snacks at eye level in the cupboard, on the shelf, or in the fridge.

PROCRASTINATION

- Put your computer and phone on *"do not disturb"* or *"focus"* mode when doing deep work.
- Have your fitness clothes laid out the night before so they're the first thing you see in the morning (or sleep in them, if you need a tad more reinforcement to exercise!).

4. ADD DIFFICULTY

If you're stuck in a deep rut of perpetual procrastination, then try doing something that is MORE challenging than the thing you are procrastinating on doing.

It may seem counterintuitive, but by doing something that is more psychologically straining or painful than the actual thing we're trying to do, we leverage our dopamine to change our "pain / discomfort" threshold. It ends up making the perceived difficulty of the actual task less challenging, and therefore easier to get started on.

> According to Dr Andrew Huberman, of The Huberman Lab, "the discomfort associated with *[doing the more difficult thing]* will quickly rebound your dopamine to a higher baseline level that in turn, you can devote to the bigger task at hand."

The replacement activity has to be something that is well outside of your comfort zone, though, so if you enjoy folding laundry or doing your accounts, then find something more "painful" to do to reset your dopamine levels.

BECOME A PRO AT MANAGING PROCRASTINATION

Remember, procrastination isn't about our inability to manage our time or control our willpower, it's our coping response to stress and challenging emotions.

Our brain battles against thoughts of doing something it finds uncomfortable, in favour of doing something that makes us feel better. We can take back our control by becoming more intentional and practising more supportive behaviours. We need to be kind and understanding to ourselves, too.

When you procrastinate, first get curious about why.

- What are you feeling? Name the emotion. Is it fear, uncertainty, boredom, anxiety, or insecurity?
- Why are you feeling it? Get to grips with the real reason you're procrastinating.
- Break down the next steps into micro steps to get you back on track with your tasks.

Make it more difficult to default to avoidance tactics. And set yourself up to win by making the things you want to do as easy as possible to get started on.

In the next two chapters, we're going to look at Burnout and consider ways to get better at dealing with it.

First, we'll define what burnout is, and consider it specifically in a work context. Although our work environment is just one landscape in which burnout occurs, the hustle culture has a lot to answer for in causing it to become an epidemic.

EIGHT
BURNOUT PART 1 - WORK

> The land of burnout is not a place I ever want to go back to.
>
> ~ ARIANNA HUFFINGTON

In this chapter, we'll explore unhealthy productivity, define what burnout is and how it shows up, and consider some current statistics relating to burnout. I also elaborate on the origins of the term *hustle culture* and take a specific look at entrepreneurial burnout.

WORK & UNHEALTHY PRODUCTIVITY

When I shared my story at the start of this book, I mentioned that one precursor to my burnout was chronic stress because of working in a toxic environment.

> The company had brought me in on a fixed-term contract to work on a specific project. I found myself in a fractious situation, dealing with ridiculous deadlines, using clunky systems and complicated, outdated software.

THE CADENCE EFFECT

It was an open-plan office with about 60 people working in a noisy space. Everyone was overworked and overwhelmed, being called in on weekends, or having to work late into the evening to meet meagre and inaccurately calculated project timelines. In fact, I even remember having to do work to sort out a problem on Christmas Day!

Many of us were arriving early and staying late. Both to avoid being stuck in horrendous traffic for two hours, and because we couldn't do any focused work during the day due to all the distractions in the office.

I was working with people who were tiptoeing around a few domineering and disrespectful individuals whose behaviour instilled fear across the company. Gossip was rife, as each department would bad mouth the next around the water cooler or in the kitchen. Like everyone else, they also subjected me to criticism and ridicule behind my back.

Now, dealing with the occasional ridiculous deadline or "difficult" person was nothing new to me, because I cut my teeth in the film industry. However, having to work this way continually every day for several months was totally unsustainable.

There was no respite, and I was not in a position to leave until the end of the contract. It became a hardship as I dreaded dragging myself to work each day. I wasn't sleeping well and my jaw was so sore from clenching it all the time. The tension of being on tenterhooks around unpredictable people and working with unreliable software created so much uncertainty.

The knock-on effect was that I was struggling to focus, so everything felt like it was taking twice as long, which would then garner criticism from those difficult people. I felt like I couldn't speak out about the situation, as I was only on contract, but also because I felt intimidated. So, like many others in the company, I felt I just had to endure.

Unsustainable and unhealthy work practices can have dramatic consequences, one of which is burnout.

As mentioned in the prologue, I eventually became a burnout statistic.

I was one of the almost 50% of the global workforce affected by this phenomenon. But my epic burnout unfolded long before the pandemic came along to raise our risk factors for it, or our awareness of it.

Although the constraints of the pandemic are now subsiding, burnout is still on the rise.

It's happening across industries and across countries, whether you work from home, in a hospital, a restaurant, a manufacturing plant, or in an office.

It has become a prevalent health threat in our lives and workplaces, yet we still don't seem able to take it seriously or avoid it, as you'll see by what I uncover in this chapter.

The threat of burnout may seem scary and reading about it may trigger you. For that I apologise in advance, but awareness of the depth of the problem is the first step to resolving it.

A rise in the intensity of our workloads combined with skills gaps in a rapidly changing working landscape, topped off with increased pressure and expectations (initially caused by the pandemic, but still in place), are primary reasons for increasing burnout in our workplaces.

The consequences of burnout from a business perspective are multiple and loss of productivity is just one element of this.

It creates a breeding ground for distrust and apathy amongst the team. It can extend to decreased engagement, a drop in retention, increased sick days, and the additional pressure placed on other employees who have to pick up the slack. Along with the extra costs of rehiring or temporary replacement, these are just some of the knock-on effects which impact work culture and our business bottom lines.

But just how prevalent is Burnout? And is it really such a threat to our future health, wellbeing and productivity?

BURNOUT STATISTICS

UK research reported in 2022 shows that 46% of people working across industries are at risk of burnout from their job. This risk profile increases for those of us working from home.

Let's look more closely at the impact of burnout specifically on knowledge workers. As part of Yerbo's Burnout Index 2022, they interviewed over 30,000 tech workers for their "State of Burnout in Tech" report, with staggering results:

- 2 in 5 people working in tech are at high risk of burnout
- Burnout is more prevalent in women than men in these industries
- 62% of tech workers feel physically and emotionally drained
- 42% of tech professionals who feel they are at risk of burnout, are considering leaving their jobs (also contributing to The Great Resignation)

According to Converkit's State of the Creator Economy Report for 2022, 61% of over 2000 content entrepreneurs surveyed had experienced burnout in 2021.

So burnout is affecting a LOT of us, but what does it really mean when we burn out?

DEFINING BURNOUT

Burnout is an umbrella term which covers mental, emotional and physical fatigue. It occurs because of a prolonged exposure to stress.

The term has been around since 1976. It is attributed to the psychologist Herbert Freudenberger, who based it on his observations of the physiological symptoms experienced by volunteers at a free clinic in NY City.

In 2019, the World Health Organisation (WHO) recognised it as a workplace phenomenon, but it's not yet classified as a medical condition.

> The WHO defines burnout as "a syndrome conceptualised as resulting from chronic workplace stress that has not been successfully managed".

They characterise burnout across three dimensions:

1. Feelings of energy depletion or exhaustion
2. Increased mental distance from one's job, or feelings of negativity or cynicism relating that job, and
3. Reduced professional efficacy because of 1 and 2

Burnout is most commonly referenced in a work context, but it can span the breadth of both our work and our life.

A Université de Montréal's 2014 study, reported in Science Daily, revealed that the mental health factors which impact on burnout in the workplace don't exist in a vacuum. Burnout is "deeply affected by the rest of a person's day-to-day life. And vice versa."

As I mentioned in the first chapter, burnout can contribute to a host of physical, mental and emotional health issues, so often there's more than one thing that needs fixing.

Trying to earn money to support yourself and your family by working in a stressful job can become overwhelming, placing an additional burden on your coping skills.

If you're an entrepreneur like myself, there are particular challenges that we face, which can increase our stress and cause entrepreneurial burnout too.

As we've covered, certain levels of stress in the short term can be motivating. But ongoing, intense stress of any kind puts pressure on the body and mind, causing the physiological fatigue associated with burnout. But what does it actually look like?

BURNOUT SIGNS & SYMPTOMS

Some of these burnout indicators may already be familiar to you, but some may be surprising too.

The following signs, symptoms or behaviours are risk factors for burnout.

- Depression
- Anxiety
- Insomnia
- Adrenal fatigue
- Gut issues
- Hormonal imbalances
- Food sensitivities
- Low energy and being tired all the time
- Lack of motivation
- Listlessness and languishing
- Low morale with a strong negativity bias
- Over-reactive emotional behaviour: cynicism, hostility, anger or irritability
- Recurring dreams or nightmares
- Tearfulness
- Brain fog
- Feeling unproductive
- Continuous procrastination
- Indecision
- Relationship conflict and breakdowns
- Feeling less sociable
- Avoidant behaviour, such as not answering emails or responding to texts
- Living and working in a state of clutter and disrepair

It's important to note that these symptoms can also be standalone issues or attributable to other things on their own too. So it can be tricky to identify that you might be experiencing burnout.

Many of these symptoms may require professional help or clinical support alongside improving our self-care practices. However, even if your symptoms don't merit traditional medical treatment, they put a lot of pressure on the body and mind. And if they persist, that then causes the fatigue associated with burnout.

Studies also show that burnout can damage our brain.

It changes the structure and chemistry of our brain and influences our empathic responses. Sometimes, people suffering from burnout experience more fear and display more aggression.

Let's dive deeper into the work perspective, and the different layers of complexity our working lives add to the burnout issue.

THE HUSTLE CULTURE

Our traditional work culture normalises OVERWORK.

Whether you're an employee, a freelancer, or an entrepreneur, the culture we are trying to work within plays the biggest role in our perceptions of productivity and what we consider being productive.

It's more acceptable for us to "stay late" to get shit done, and do the same again tomorrow, than it is to leave early to spend time with family, rest more, so we can come in tomorrow feeling more refreshed, so we can be more productive!

BEWARE THE HUSTLE

> Always be hustlin' - get more done with less, working longer, harder, and smarter, not just two out of three.
>
> ~ TRAVIS KALANICK (FORMER UBER CEO)

THE CADENCE EFFECT

Across knowledge worker industries, the hustle culture is a root contributor to burnout.

The hustle culture relates to a mindset focused on the pursuit of more at any cost. It's a social pressure to produce constantly.

At its essence, the hustle culture in a work context involves doing whatever it takes to make a living and to make a success of your life. To get noticed, you need to keep doing, keep moving and shaking.

In theory, that sounds fine, until you realise that taking part in the hustle culture also involves doing those things at the cost of sleep, relationships, wellbeing, and your integrity, if that's what it takes to get ahead.

The hustle culture is a trade-off.

But where does this term actually come from?

- The concept of hustling became a thing back in the late 1800s, with a colourful and often discriminatory trajectory to our modern day.
- 'The hustle' then became a symbol of black empowerment through gangsta rap in the 1980s.
- It later gained popularity in Silicon Valley, where tech startups encouraged their employees to stay at work for as long as possible. They offered incentives such as meals and fun activities, bean bags and pool tables, sleep pods, and in-house laundry services, in exchange for staying at work. This translated to working late into the evening and on weekends, (and in some cases sleeping under their desks).
- Online services and larger corporations then appropriated the term, enticing potential workers with the promise of freedom and self-reliance. It was an unfair exchange though, as what they got was low pay, inconsistent work and minimal benefits (think Uber).

The hustle culture is pervasive across industries, but is not conducive to healthy productivity. It is unsustainable over the long term.

It can lead to burnout, as keeping up with the hustle takes a lot of energy, putting pressure on our cognitive load and depleting our resilience.

Yet, whilst people and organisations are cottoning on, this culture persists, with disastrous results.

This normalising of overwork, which has become accepted as part of traditional ways of working, sits at the heart of burnout in the workplace. It's affecting our confidence and sense of self-worth, too.

PRODUCTIVITY DYSMORPHIA

Dysmorphia is a term that is used to describe when our perception of something is flawed or out of alignment with what is accurate or appropriate. Our skewed view could be about our bodies, a situation, our skills, and yes, even our productivity.

A culture of overwork is turning us into insecure overachievers who feel the pressure to perform and then experience self-doubt over our abilities.

The concept of Productivity Dysmorphia was first shared online in 2020 by Ben Uyeda, a California-based designer.

Writer and author Anna Codrea-Rado later explored this further. After researching the phenomenon and talking to experts, she defined how it fits into our work landscape:

> Productivity dysmorphia sits at the intersection of burnout, imposter syndrome and anxiety. It is ambition's alter ago: the pursuit of productivity spurs us to do more while robbing us of the ability to savour any success we might encounter along the way.
>
> ~ ANNA CODREA-RADO

When we are experiencing productivity dysmorphia, we feel no sense of achievement for the fruits of our labours, so we try to work harder to gain that sense of achievement. Again, and again. So the vicious cycle of overwork continues.

WHEN WORK BECOMES TOO STRESSFUL

Every sector has its own brand of stress that typically comes from working in a high-pressure, deadline-driven environment with specific industry-related demands. As you've seen from my example from the beginning of this chapter, toxic work cultures also play a role in burnout.

These working situations, conditions and negative organisational cultures are primary fodder for increasing workplace stress:

1. An unsustainable workload
2. A lack of autonomy, control, or agency over how we work
3. Feelings of self-doubt and a loss of self-efficacy
4. A lack of connection with our work community
5. Insufficient recognition or reward for our perceived value
6. A sense of depersonalisation, where we feel unrecognised as an individual
7. Unfair discrimination or judgement against us
8. A disconnect between external circumstances and internal values

The depersonalisation, emotional exhaustion and decreased sense of accomplishment that accompany chronic work stress are damaging our ability to function effectively and to lead fulfilling lives.

- When there's a lack of congruency between our internal and external worlds, where the work we do doesn't align with our values, it causes stress.
- Where we are having to continually do things that hold no meaning, it causes dissonance, which leads to stress.
- When we don't feel seen, acknowledged, valued or appreciated in our roles, by our work community, our bosses or peers, it causes stress.

- When there's always so much work to do that we feel constantly overwhelmed, perpetually fighting fires in reactive mode, it causes stress.
- When we don't feel equipped with the required professional, practical, physical or emotional skills to complete our work, it causes stress.

When this stress doesn't abate because these situations don't change, we end up hitting a wall.

As we've discovered throughout the pandemic, continued uncertainty, chaos and ambiguity over a long period puts strain on our physical and mental ability to cope.

The volatility of the economy and the complexity of our online-focused work lives compounds matters too. As we mentioned, the hustle culture we find ourselves in also depletes our resilience.

But what happens if you're also your 'own boss'? What implications does burnout have for you if you work on your own as a solo entrepreneur or freelancer?

The short answer is that burnout is an even bigger threat to you!

ENTREPRENEURIAL BURNOUT

Whether we work in tech industries or elsewhere, it turns out that entrepreneurs of all kinds are particularly susceptible to burnout, for a few reasons.

A VUCA WORLD

The first reason is because of the VUCA challenges we face in typical entrepreneurial environments.

VUCA stands for Volatility + Uncertainty + Complexity + Ambiguity

An extra 'C' is sometimes added, representing Chaos (i.e. VUCCA).

This acronym first came into use in the late 1980s in the military, and later adopted in strategic leadership and organisational management practices.

We are all exposed to VUCA challenges and situations at some points in our lives, *(the pandemic is a case in point).*

However, VUCA elements are also typical factors that entrepreneurs face <u>daily</u> in their business endeavours, and these threat factors can be relentless.

So what other reasons might also cause burnout specifically for entrepreneurs?

ENTREPRENEURS & MENTAL HEALTH

It turns out that entrepreneurs are also more predisposed to mental health challenges.

Research quoted the National Institute for Mental Health has found that 72% of entrepreneurs are directly or indirectly affected by mental health issues, compared to just 48% of non-entrepreneurs.

Specific influences that impact on entrepreneurial mental health:

- Entrepreneurs have an intense and intimate connection with our businesses. So we often link our self worth to our business success.

- We are often working long hours that there are few opportunities to socialise. This contributes to a sense of isolation and loneliness, a primary cause of depression.

- We experience prolonged periods of high stress because of the risks we take when starting our own business. This interrupts our social engagement system and if we don't already have a strong social system in place, this may prevent us from reaching out for help.

- Even if we have strong social ties, not everyone gets the entrepreneurial experience and what's involved, as it's very different from working in a traditional business as an employee. So we may also feel like we have a lack of support from those we care about, as they don't understand what we do or what we need.

- Studies have found that there's also often a perceived need amongst entrepreneurs for impression management and social acceptance. They want to be seen and acknowledged on social media. And as we know, too much time playing in those arenas can cause attention fatigue.

- Then there's the issue of *entrepreneurial poverty*, where we don't spend time and money on our wellbeing, because we feel we need to invest all of our resources in the business to get it going and keep it going.

Overall, the entrepreneurial journey can be extremely challenging, and it's definitely not for everyone.

However, based on my experience, it can also be extremely rewarding to start your own thing and make a success of it, not just from a monetary perspective.

It requires a greater resilience.

So it helps if you have good practices in place to support your health, wellbeing and productivity, despite the uncertainty and unpredictability of your environments.

Whether you are an employee or an entrepreneur, the key thing is that you need to sustain and thrive over the long haul. This means addressing issues like overwork right from the start.

Remember, it's also about focusing on creating cadence. This helps us to adjust our pace and be more flexible, so we can continuously adapt to the fluctuations of our external environments more easily.

HOW TO PREVENT BURNOUT

> If we want to live a life of meaning and contribution, we have to become intentional about cultivating sleep and play. We have to let go of exhaustion, busyness and productivity as status symbols and measures of self-worth. We are impressing no-one.
>
> ~ BRENÉ BROWN

We can no longer embrace a culture where productivity comes at the cost of wellbeing.

Not only is burnout damaging our health, wellbeing and productivity, as well as our relationships with ourselves and others, it also has immense costs for businesses, healthcare systems and economies.

We have to build healthier work cultures, and given the statistics I quoted, this is becoming non-negotiable for both companies and the individuals who work within them.

The good news is….

It's not all doom and gloom. We don't have to become a number, or a victim. We do have a choice!

We can find ways to live and work which support our ability to thrive. We can earn an income to support ourselves and our loved ones in a way that doesn't strain us at the same time.

We can decide to either participate in unhealthy and unproductive work cultures.

Or we can stand up for ourselves and step out of this detrimental construct.

We need to get serious about changing our approach to our working practices, to get better at both handling stress and burnout, and combating them.

> As Brené Brown shares in her book *Dare to Lead*, "the daring leadership response to exhaustion is modelling and supporting rest, play and recovery", rather than tying up our self-worth with productivity and the hustle!

This is why the practice of Intentional Productivity is so important.

- Implementing foundational practices that can support your wellbeing and productivity can boost your resilience and help prevent burnout, or help you bounce back more quickly when it threatens.
- Engaging in mindful approaches to work can go a long way to helping us improve our wellbeing and creativity, as well as our focus and our performance.
- When we can do our job better, and are recognised for doing it, without feeling continually overwhelmed, this leads to increased productivity and employee retention.

Getting clear on what connects you, energises you, and makes it easier for you to be productive sets you up to win.

And when we embed intentional productivity practices into how we work, everybody wins! That's the cadence effect in action.

We'll look at several ways we can support ourselves better in the Opportunities section of this book, coming up soon. However, it's not just stress at work that influences our health and productivity.

There are other stressors outside of our work sphere that can influence our performance and increase our risk of burnout.

So, let's look more closely at what else is causing stress in our lives. The next chapter focuses on Other Burnout Influences.

Some of the contributing cultural and socio-economic factors which can lead to excess stress and burnout may surprise you.

NINE
BURNOUT PART 2 - LIFE

> In a culture fuelled by burnout, a culture that has run itself down, our national resilience becomes compromised. And when our collective immune system is weakened, we become more susceptible to viruses that are part of every culture, because they're part of human nature….
>
> ~ ARIANNA HUFFINGTON

Burnout is a dangerous threat not just to our productivity, performance and personal wellbeing, but also to our collective and social wellbeing, which is why it warrants two chapters.

As I mentioned in the previous chapter, while we often see burnout as a workplace-focused affliction, it can span the breadth of life, too. Let's look at some examples.

A GLOBAL PANDEMIC

The Covid-19 Pandemic is a perfect example of a VUCCA experience - a concept introduced in the last chapter.

BURNOUT PART 2 - LIFE

The pandemic ticked all the boxes for a complex, volatile situation filled with uncertainty, chaos and ambiguity. All amped up to eleven!

It also had extensive repercussions beyond the immediate threat of illness and death.

- It led to a massive rise in burnout, as we tried to carry on as normal in our working lives despite the ever-present threats around us.
- The relentless fear and uncertainty, and needing to spend so much time online for all aspects of communication and connection, wore us down.
- Many experienced a form of brain fog known as *pandemic brain*, affecting their ability to be productive.
- Those left with the legacy of "long Covid" were forced to recalibrate their lives dramatically, as they no longer had the stamina to live and work as they'd done previously.
- Being forced to shelter in place also caused an increase in loneliness and isolation, especially for people living on their own. Loneliness and social detachment can be killers in themselves without a pandemic along for the ride. As studies show, being isolated from community and connection can be severely detrimental to our physical and mental health.
- Money worries were exacerbated for many when businesses were forced to close, or jobs were made redundant.
- And those who lost loved ones to the pandemic were forced to navigate the heavy experience of grief, on top of these other intense stressors.

As the months and years progressed, many of us developed coping mechanisms for managing our responses to this experience. The long-term effects of the pandemic are still being felt across the world.

There are other stressors in our environments which create VUCA-type situations we may experience in our day-to-day.

SOCIETAL & CULTURAL STRESSORS

Aspects of our lifestyles, environments and societal structures can increase stress, reduce productivity and affect our wellbeing, leading to burnout.

- The time we spend online with **digital distractions and dopamine-inducing tools** - whether that's for work, play or procrastination - overloads our minds and fractures our attention.
- **A patriarchal society** which dictates what we wear, how we should behave, who has more power, who gets preferential treatment, and so forth, causes ongoing stress.
- **Unsupportive behaviours** such as people-pleasing syndrome, and **harmful practices** such as social shaming, cancel culture, discrimination and systemic racism.... these things create stress too.
- Juggling **increased family responsibilities** with our burgeoning workload and **economic uncertainties** puts an immense strain on our resilience.
- Less obvious contributors include **processed foods**, **pollution** and the **climate crisis.** *Wait, what?! you may say.*

Let's look at some of these in more detail.

THE PATRIARCHY

In their book *Burnout: The Secret to Solving the Stress Cycle*, Emily and Emilia Nagoski highlight how traditional patriarchal cultural systems have played an underlying role in incidences of burnout over our modern history.

> We're all susceptible to burnout. However, it's most common for women, Black, Asian and minority groups, people with disabilities, and LGBTQ+ communities to be subjected to the stressors which cause it.

The patriarchy supports the conditions for burnout and affects on our ability to be productive. It influences and holds sway over other factors and conditions which contribute to burnout too, such as racism and discrimination, conformity and social shame, people pleasing, perfectionism and more.

SYSTEMIC DISCRIMINATION*

Discrimination includes any form of bias — from sexism, racism and homophobia to misogyny and xenophobia. It includes any form of unfair judgement based on ability, disability, culture, gender, race, religion, sexual orientation, and more.

We have a long history of raising awareness about, and fighting, injustices against the marginalised and disenfranchised. Here are a few examples…

The Anti-slavery movement came into being in the UK in the 1770s and the Abolitionist movement in the US became formalised around 1830.

The Feminist Movement began in the 1840s with the first Women's Rights Convention in the US, and Emmeline Pankhurst's UK Suffragettes mobilised in 1903.

The Civil Rights Movement in the US gained momentum in the 1950s and the Women's Rights Movement in the 1960s and 70s.

More recently, the #MeToo and #BlackLivesMatter movements have put these types of issues in the spotlight in a way we can't ignore.

So, much progress has been made, and yet… we are still fighting against discrimination and inequality daily. Things like gender parity and cultural equity are still pipe dreams in many industries and countries.

Our patriarchal systems (which extend to our cultural mores, laws and religions) limit our freedoms and even put our lives at risk.

For example, these systems affect:

- Whether a woman has control over her body and the freedom to decide whether she wants to get or stay pregnant.
- Or whether she can show her hair, face or body without fear of being raped, beaten or murdered.
- They determine whether a non-binary person can use the ladies' loo.
- They affect whether someone with a disability can apply for certain jobs.
- They affect the salaries which women and people of colour can command.
- They impact on whether a black man can go for a jog through a neighbourhood without fear of getting stopped, searched, shot, or killed.
- In some countries, they dictate whether a gay person can marry or even publicly identify as being gay, without fear of arrest, punishment, or death.

It's a contentious topic and unfortunately there isn't sufficient space in this book to explore it in further depth.

What you need to know is that the pervasiveness of the patriarchy, its societal constructs and its behavioural offshoots, are major influences on chronic stress and burnout.

Being constantly judged or discriminated against causes underlying stress.

This makes it ten times more difficult to do your work and live your life. If you face these pressures daily, they force your body into a threatened state of hyper-awareness.

Navigating these frequent discriminations, whether it's at work, on the bus, in the park, in the supermarket, or in a job interview, compounds over time and becomes exhausting.

Most of us are oblivious to the daily micro aggressions we might mete out to people who we perceive as 'different to ourselves'.

Behaving this way has been so ingrained in our societal structures for far too long. These practices are baked into our cultural norms, and as a result, many of us don't realise we are hurting other people.

As both a society, and as individuals, we have to work harder on raising awareness and changing our behaviours. We need to keep working on developing our self-awareness about our hidden biases. We need to practise operating from a place of love and kindness, not judgement and ridicule.

THE BIKINI INDUSTRIAL COMPLEX & SOCIAL SHAME

This term *bikini industrial complex* was introduced by the Nagoski sisters in their Burnout book. It's a point of reference for what is a consumer-focused movement that starts influencing us from a young age.

When all the advertising we see tells us we need to look a specific way and wear a specific thing to fit in, we feel inadequate when we can't.

Competing with Artificial Constructs

Airbrushed, touched up "beautiful people" pouting perfectly at us from the pages of an online magazine, or an Instagram post, can be an impossible physical ideal for many of us to achieve.

It can be exhausting trying to keep up appearances when our bodies might not be shaped to carry off *that* type of clothing, or *that* kind of makeup, or to look lithe, skinny and sexy.

Our experiences of not matching up to a perceived norm lead to comparison fatigue and self-esteem issues.

What's worse? There's a marked rise in body dysmorphia, depression, eating disorders, self-harming and suicidal tendencies, particularly in pre-teens girls and young adults, because of their feelings of inadequacy.

Even for adults, invasive plastic surgery such as facelifts, bum lifts, Botox and boob jobs are on the rise.

We're falling for the spiel that we need to buy all those extra products to paint our eyebrows (and then waterproof them), or fill our lips, or cover our freckles. According to the advertising that bombards us, we are not enough without these things. So we are spending money on things we don't actually need, all for the sake of driving the greedy, capitalist, consumer machine.

We're fighting Ageing instead of Ageism

Fashion dictates we remove our natural hair (in places it's actually meant to be, to protect our bodies), for the simple sake of men's comfort. In other words, to appeal to the "male gaze", or to look more "appropriate" so that we fit these ridiculous societal standards that have been set.

The norms around ageism demand that we need to do things like colour our hair so that we forever look "under 40". People with visible greys start to experience invisibility issues, being discriminated against in the workplace and elsewhere.

A public example of this was the firing of Lisa LaFlamme, a prominent Canadian TV journalist and anchorwoman, in August 2022.

During the pandemic, Lisa stopped colouring her hair and shared her natural look with the world. She received much criticism from TV executives, who then abruptly ended her contract. There was a backlash from viewers who complained about the blatant sexism and ageism apparent in the decision.

> Like most people, I too have been influenced by the threat of ageing and ageism. I originally started going grey at 23 and I coloured my hair to hide it. I was concerned with what these chemicals were doing to the environment and to my brain. However, I felt I had to adhere to an unspoken rule about women needing to look "young" to be attractive!
>
> After over 20 years of succumbing to this messaging, during the pandemic, I decided it was time to terminate my relationship with a dye bottle. It wasn't a simple transition. It took two years to grow

out, and I felt vulnerable during that time. But now that it's done, I feel so much more at home and confident in myself.

However, now when people meet me for the first time, they think I'm older than I am. I can also attest to the invisibility issues that many women in mid-life speak about, as I've started experiencing this too. I've had to become a lot more assertive, both in how I carry myself in the world, and how I respond in these situations. *Basically, now I call bullshit on it!*

Many women in much later stages of life still colour their hair, and each to their own. It's a deeply personal decision to go against the flow, one that makes us feel unsafe.

You're too much! Or not enough!

All of us - but especially women - get shamed for being too fat, too old, too intense, too different, too outspoken. The list goes on.

We are told we're giving up on life when we choose to grow out our grey.

Yet pre-teens are objectified and sexualised when society robs them of their innocence by encouraging them to grow up, don make-up, and wear suggestive outfits that make them look 25, not 12!

And then we're blamed for being groped or raped, or worse, and told we were asking for it dressing like that!

We're informed we are too pushy when we stand up for ourselves in a meeting. We are told we are under-qualified when we ask for the same salary as our lesser-qualified male counterparts. We are asked to speak at events for free, and told it will be great exposure.

Perhaps you are reading this and nodding along, feeling annoyed at having experienced some form of this bullshit yourself!

Irrespective of your gender, what's even worse is that this thinking is so pervasive that when we aren't shamed by others, we have learnt to shame ourselves!

CANCELLED BY OUR CULTURE

Cancel Culture is another factor supported by this notion of the bikini industrial complex. Cancel culture correlates with the rise of social media shaming. It involves the boycotting, shunning or ostracisation of a (usually public) person for saying or acting in a manner which is deemed as unacceptable.

Often, these decisions to ridicule someone publicly seem to be made without considering all the facts. It's that pernicious knee jerk response I spoke about in the chapter on Our Digital World. Like a runaway wildfire, there's no going back once the tinder has caught.

This culture has become so ubiquitous that the fear of being outcast is apparent in the false lives people curate on social media. Yet we are all drawn in by these fake environments.

As mentioned in the last chapter, when our external environment and our internal values aren't aligned, it causes friction. This disconnect between our lived experience and our projected experience has implications for our mental health in the long term.

The pressure to either conform to, or even rebel against, a society dominated by these confines and constructs can cause burnout, precisely because of the relentless perceived pressures involved.

PEOPLE-PLEASING SYNDROME & PERFECTIONISM

> Research shows that perfectionism hampers success. In fact, it's often the path to depression, anxiety, addiction and life paralysis.
>
> ~ BRENÉ BROWN

I'm a fan of everything Brené Brown does, and she's not afraid to bring uncomfortable topics out into the open. When talking about armoured leadership in her book *Dare to Lead*, she refers to perfectionism as "a hustle" and "a defensive move to protect ourselves from being seen".

In *The Gifts of Imperfection*, Brené suggests that to overcome perfectionism and reclaim our lives, we need to understand the difference between healthy striving and perfectionism. You may wonder how these two things connect.

We are Dying to Belong

It's a basic human need to desire a sense of belonging.

We want to feel seen and to be acknowledged. We want to be accepted in, and feel part of, our community.

So we are conscious of what other people think. We also have an evolutionary need to be accepted as part of the group, as there is safety in numbers. So wanting to be accepted is something we strive for. Rejection feels like a failure to belong. And when we are in survival mode, rejection can feel like a death sentence.

Being our perfect selves at the expense of our best selves.

It's natural to want to be liked, but many of us find ourselves caught in this web of people-pleasing. It's because our need for belonging is not being met, so we overcompensate by doing more to gain what we need.

Remember those insecure overachievers I referenced in relation to productivity dysmorphia in the previous chapter? Same, same, just a little different.

We're constantly over-producing, overworking, over-helping, and doing more than we need to, just to feel recognised, to feel validated, to prove ourselves, and to keep others happy. We do this so we can feel like we belong as "part of the group".

Perfectionism correlates with People-Pleasing

There are a few reasons we may do it. When we're trying to do the best job possible, often the root motivation is so that we won't be *shunned by the group*. That threat might not exist in our reality, but that's what the part of our brain trying to protect us might be telling us.

Or we may be afraid to actually take a risk and put something out into the world, because we feel too vulnerable. So we deliberate and delay on creating that thing, overworking to perfect it, but never actually 'shipping' it.

In this case, perfectionism is another form of procrastination (an emotional response to stress). *If you need a refresher, head back to the chapter on procrastination.*

The need to people-please and be perfect happens across all facets of our lives, at the expense of our wellbeing and happiness. It's no wonder many of us feel so exhausted.

We may all feel the need to do some people-pleasing from time to time, and women are particularly prone to these behaviours.

For women especially, much of this stems from archaic cultural norms, prevalent from the dark ages to present day, where women were/are subjugated by, and expected to pander to, the needs of men.

Thankfully, these perceptions and behaviours are changing, despite patriarchal systems still being imposed on our freedoms. However, when you've been *indoctrinated* into a specific way of being, it can be extremely challenging to step out of that role and stay out of it.

These are heavy topics, but they are not the only things we have to contend with!

OTHER BURNOUT TRIGGERS

POOR NUTRITION

There are a lot of suspicious additions to our pre-prepared and processed foods that serve as bulking agents, flavourings, sweeteners, and so forth. Our delectable fast foods, snacks, and treats are loaded with trans fats, unhealthy sugars, MSG, and hollow calories.

There's plenty of research that shows how these things can disrupt our endocrine systems, the physiological processes in our bodies, and how our brains function. Some are even known to cause cancer.

Too much sugar, too many nitrates and nitrites, and too many of the "wrong" carbs and fats, are slowly poisoning our system.

A poor diet can put stress on our bodies, causing strain and fatigue. It can also lead to serious health conditions such as cardiovascular diseases, cancer, and diabetes, which are the primary causes of death in many countries.

It can also adversely influence our concentration, our wellbeing, performance and productivity. Eliminating harmful ingredients and improving your nutrition helps with focus and attention.

This is one reason why diet plays a central role in managing the attention-related symptoms of behavioural and neurodiverse conditions, such as ADHD and autism. The same applies for neurological disorders or diseases, such as Parkinson's, Alzheimer's and dementia.

POLLUTION

Air pollution is influencing not just our ability to breathe, but also our ability to concentrate.

Studies referenced by Johann Hari in his book *Hyperfocus* found that the particulates from traffic pollution are causing damage in our brains. Amongst other things, it's affecting our focus and attention in very negative ways.

Children and young adults are particularly at risk as their brains are still developing, but we are all in danger of losing our minds. And that is not an overstatement!

Research reported in July 2022 confirms that dirty air leads to general cognitive decline, and causes dementia in older people.

Microplastics and forever chemicals have also found their way into our bodies via our water, air and food. These break down and release poisons which disrupt our endocrine system, affecting our reproductive systems and overall development.

Personally, I've wondered often about the potential correlation between plastic and other pollutants, the rise of behavioural disorders, and the increase in crime, volatility and gun violence prevalent in our society.

Is it something in the water (and our food) that is making us so aggressive and less empathic? From a few things I've read, it would appear they may play a role in manipulating our behaviours on a chemical level.

So, consider what can you do to limit your exposure to bad quality air, toxic food ingredients, and other pollutants?

THE CLIMATE CRISIS

Aside from a pandemic, the environmental challenges we face are a genuine threat to our long-term survival.

Witnessing and experiencing the effects of things like polluted seas and rivers, extreme weather, runaway fires, deforestation, food and water scarcity, extinction threats to wildlife, displaced populations, etc. takes its emotional toll. It's causing what is known as **eco-anxiety**.

The scale of these problems is vast and can feel beyond our control to stop or change them.

Constantly feeling helplessness and hopelessness about these challenges can wear us down. It's easy to develop compassion fatigue. And then we feel the need to shut down or close ourselves off, so we can cope instead of burning out.

Taking small actions that are within your locus of control can help to manage your anxiety while you do your bit to save the environment. If we want to get involved in finding big ideas that can help solve these challenges, then we need to be more intentional in supporting our health and productivity.

This is how we can leverage our brain's power and problem-solving capabilities to the max.

For inspiration on things you can do to take effective climate action, check out 'The Carbon Almanac' for informed ideas from a host of contributors, including Seth Godin.

The climate emergency is a big world issue, but what about things closer to home?

FAMILY RESPONSIBILITIES

If you're in midlife, you form part of the sandwich generation where you may juggle caring for elderly loved ones, with looking after children, alongside managing a heavy workload.

You may be a single parent working two jobs to cover rent and childcare, spending your little free time helping your kids with their homework. Or perhaps you have a teenager struggling to get over some form of addiction, and you are trying to support them through this, alongside caring for your other kids, too. Maybe you're trying to oversee the care of a sick or incapable parent or partner.

According to the Family Caregiver Alliance, 66% of caregivers are women. In the situations I've described above, 50% of women are more likely than men to take on the primary caring responsibilities.

These types of challenges place extra burdens on our coping skills and our resilience. And if they are ongoing over a longer period without pause, they are a recipe for burnout.

> Prior to my burnout, I found myself in a situation where my in-laws both succumbed to illness and then died within a few years of each other. While this was unfolding, my husband was regularly travelling upcountry to be with them, so was away a lot and also trying to deal with his own worry, stress and subsequent grief.
>
> During this time, we had also been trying to have a baby unsuccessfully. The problem seemed to be me, and we were at the point of considering going through IVF. Aside from the uncertainties that come with this invasive procedure (and you usually require several rounds), it was going to cost the equivalent

of a down payment on a house, which added to our money worries.

On top of my work stress, each of these factors also played a role in my subsequent burnout. And, as mentioned in the Prologue, at the time, I didn't have the tools to adequately deal with the barrage of stresses and strains we were facing.

The reality is that we are all going to be subjected to extremely challenging situations in our lives. We can't avoid this.

So, the way to look at this is to consider how we can go about preparing ourselves to handle these situations should we encounter them. It won't make them go away, but it will help us to manage our response to them better.

We do so by gathering the tools that can support us and developing the skills that help to build our resilience. In this way, we can approach these challenges with a stronger mindset, and bounce back from them more quickly, too.

Working on being our better selves makes us better for others.

As mentioned earlier, when we experience burnout, it can dull our empathy and increase our negative moods. Not ideal in situations where our loved ones need even more of our care and kindness.

I'm not a therapist or mental health practitioner, so I don't have specific solutions for dealing with family crises and trauma, as every situation is different. However, in airline speak, "putting our own air mask on first" is an approach I've discovered can help in these situations.

We need to ensure we support our own wellbeing first, with dedicated self-care practices, so that we can be strong for those who need our support.

THE INTERPLAY OF BURNOUT INFLUENCES

Getting back to productivity, these last few chapters are proof of the dangers which stress, environmental factors, procrastination and burnout pose to our performance.

Even if the stress isn't originating from our work, we carry how we feel with us, so it influences our ability to work. And vice versa.

Despite the challenges we are likely to face, which will affect our work and our life, there is a way through.

Intentional productivity is about creating outcomes and outputs that have meaning, and following practices which are designed and developed to support our wellbeing, as part of getting our work done.

> To help us work better, I'm <u>not</u> advocating doing more at the cost of our wellbeing.
>
> Instead, I'm recommending doing less, but better, smarter and simpler.
>
> It means radically changing the way we approach our work and our life. With intention.
>
> ~ MICH BONDESIO

In Part 3 about How We Work, we'll consider how several work-related variables affect our ability to work well.

But first... to make changes, we need to be clear about which challenges we're facing.

The following section recap and reflection exercises will help you clarify which of these challenges impact you in your specific situation, and how.

TEN
REFLECTION EXERCISES NO.2

STRESS

To tackle excess stress, we first need to understand what internal and / or external stressors are causing the stress.

Physical and mental self-regulation are the quickest and simplest ways for us to complete the stress cycle so that we can manage our stress better.

Consider what causes excess stress for you, and how you deal with it / or don't?

- How do you typically respond, react, and feel when you feel stressed?
- When it comes to managing your stress, what is within your locus of control? And what is not?
- What might be good ways for you to shake off your stress?
- How can you manage your stress better?

REFLECTION EXERCISES NO.2

Changing your state by getting out of your head and into your body through movement, meditation, or laughter are good ways to complete the stress cycle.

PROCRASTINATION

Procrastination isn't about our inability to manage our time or control our willpower, it's our coping response for dealing with too much stress and challenging emotions.

Our brain battles against thoughts of doing something it finds uncomfortable or painful, in favour of doing something that makes us feel better.

How does procrastination show up for you?

- Identify your default procrastination activities. How can you create friction so that it's easier to stick with the task at hand?
- Identify your arduous tasks. How can you make them easier to do?

When you discover you are procrastinating, get to the root of why in the moment.

- What are you feeling? Name the emotion. Is it fear, uncertainty, boredom, anxiety, insecurity, or something else?
- Why are you feeling it? Get to grips with the real reason you're procrastinating.

Make it more difficult to default to avoidance tactics. And set yourself up to win by making the things you want to do as easy as possible to get started on.

BURNOUT

Stress and procrastination lead to burnout. All three are challenges which affect our productivity, performance and wellbeing.

Even if the stress isn't originating from our work, we carry how we feel with us, so it influences **our ability to work. And vice versa.**

Are you experiencing any of the following in relation to your work?

1. An unsustainable workload
2. A lack of autonomy or control over how we work
3. Feelings of self-doubt and a loss of self-efficacy
4. A lack of connection with our work community
5. Insufficient recognition or reward for our perceived value
6. A sense of depersonalisation, where we feel unrecognised as an individual
7. Unfair discrimination or judgement against us
8. A disconnect between external circumstances and internal values.

Are you at immediate risk of burning out?

Consider if you are displaying any of these signs or symptoms? If you have a few of these symptoms, you may be at risk of burnout.

- Depression
- Anxiety
- Insomnia
- Adrenal fatigue
- Gut issues
- Hormonal imbalances
- Food sensitivities
- Inflammation
- Low energy and being tired all the time
- Lack of motivation
- Listlessness and languishing
- Low morale with a strong negativity bias
- Over-reactive emotional behaviour: cynicism, hostility, anger or irritability
- Recurring dreams or nightmares
- Tearfulness

REFLECTION EXERCISES NO.2

- Fearfulness
- Brain fog
- Feeling unproductive
- Continuous procrastination
- Indecision
- Relationship conflict and breakdowns
- Feeling less sociable
- Avoidant behaviour, such as not answering emails or responding to texts
- Living and working in a state of clutter and disrepair

SOCIETY, ENVIRONMENT & CULTURAL INFLUENCES

Think about how your work habits, relationships, nutrition, physical environment, work culture, and the outlook of your larger community and their social norms affect you.

Are you influenced by patriarchal systems and/or discrimination? Are you affected by pollution or unhealthy nutritional choices? Are you overwhelmed with juggling a lot of family responsibilities?

Consider:

- How might they be influencing your wellbeing in a way that leads to chronic stress and burnout?
- What is not working / unhelpful / needs to change?
- What slight changes can you make to support yourself better?
- Make a note of these recommended changes, so you can add them to your Cadence Canvas framework as part of the exercises we do at the end of the book.

CULTURE & YOUR CADENCE CANVAS

The stressors you face daily and the challenges you encounter at work and home are also part of the culture in which you live and work. Once you've worked through these reflection exercises, it's time to decide which cultural elements you want to either improve and keep as part of the new intentional productivity framework you are designing.

Consider which of these elements you would also add to the CULTURE section of your framework?

Keep a note of your answers so that you can incorporate them into your Cadence Canvas Framework™ once you've completed all the exercises, and you will see how everything comes together.

Part 3 is about How We Work.

We'll start by considering the idea of seeking flexibility, before we examine how factors such as work styles, work environments, workflows, and our work tools impact on our ability to work.

Each chapter in this next section includes suggestions for what you can do to improve your set up and working practices.

NOTES

PART THREE
HOW WE WORK

6. Next Steps

4. Opportunities

5. Focus & Flow

1. Introduction

3. HOW WE WORK

2. Challenges

ELEVEN
SEEKING FLEXIBILITY

> … have the flexibility to evolve.
>
> ~ MARC BENIOFF

In our work environments (whether in person or online), to achieve our goals and outputs, we need to work well together, both as a team and as individuals doing business with others.

This requires flexibility.

Flexibility in how we work is also part of the intentional productivity approach. However, there is still much resistance to this idea, especially in certain industries where traditional working practices are the norm.

For example, I'll reference a 2018 report of SMEs in the North West of England, where I'm located at the time of writing this book.

Based on a collaborative study undertaken by the Centre for SME & Enterprise Development at the University of Central Lancashire, the findings showed that the ready adoption of Workplace Flexibility

Practices (also known as Flexible Working Arrangements) was <u>not</u> commonplace.

To quote from the report:

> "Despite the fact that flexible working practices are well documented as potentially influential in the improvement of productivity, the notion that workplace flexibility could be used to improve productivity was rejected by a significant proportion of businesses. Small businesses in particular were less inclined to report using such practices."

By my reading of the report, with less than 15% of companies surveyed offering their workers job autonomy, the main reasons appeared to be because of a lack of awareness or understanding on the matter, inflexible working practices, and/or leadership mindsets firmly entrenched in traditional ways of working.

The pandemic working experience has no doubt forced changes in this regard.

Based on the exciting research results being shared about the outcomes of companies implementing 4-day work weeks, it's clear that businesses, with some education, thought and planning, can introduce flexible working, without negative productivity impacts.

In the age of digital, with all these technologies and tools at our fingertips to help support our productivity at work, there is no reason we shouldn't.

However, when things opened up after the pandemic, many businesses across the world also seem to have returned to their original, inflexible working practices.

This step backwards forces us to question the notion of "good business leadership".

INFLEXIBILITY IS A LEADERSHIP ISSUE

Sound leadership skills can improve the productivity of a business. But the responsibility for achieving this goal, doesn't just lie in the hands of the boss or manager.

Everyone in the team plays a role in the success of a business. And how we enable people to play a more effective role is to first help them improve **their self-leadership skills**.

What does it take to do this?

- Providing access to learning resources.
- Teaching intentional approaches for sustainable working practices.
- The autonomy to implement our learning in ways that suit our needs.

A 2023 LinkedIn Workplace Learning Report suggested that L&D (Learning & Development) is the best way to "elevate people and their skills for business impact".

The report stresses the importance of building resilience and creating agility in companies by placing learning, tools, and skills in the hands of each team member and employee in a way that works for them.

An agile approach to learning and leadership development must be a flexible approach. This applies whether you manage a team, you are a team member, or you work on your own.

The knock-on effects of improving self-leadership skills transfers into our performance, our actions, and our communications at work.

This is how we help to enhance the culture of a workplace and improve its productivity.

HOW WE WORK

There are four specific aspects of how we work that can influence our leadership skills, productivity, and wellbeing.

- 1. Behavioural aspects - our work styles
- 2. Environmental aspects - our work space
- 3. Digital aspects - our work tools
- 4. Process aspects - our workflows

We cover these elements in the next four chapters, and you're likely to find some examples that apply to your situation.

As we work through them, consider your workspace, work tools, work styles and workflow.

Is how you work flexible or inflexible?

Think about the environmental, structural and logistical aspects of your work and whether there are any specific situations, habits, activities and behaviours in these areas that you identify with.

For example:

- How much of your typical day are you spending on each type of work you need to do in your role?
- What's your predominant communication style? And how do your environment, tools and processes impact on your ability to focus?
- Which aspects of your work style and workflow might not be supporting your productivity and wellbeing?
- Does the way you engage with these four aspects of your work support or hinder your focus and productivity? What can you do about them?

At the end of this How We Work section, you will have an opportunity to pause for deeper reflection, with a series of exercises and questions to help you get clear about where you are now, and where you might need to make change.

Let's start the process by considering how typical Work Styles affect our wellbeing and productivity.

In the next chapter, we are going to explore the actual cost of busyness and consider alternative ways of working from what has become the norm.

TWELVE
WORK STYLES

> Being 'busy' is not being productive, it is code for being 'functionally overwhelmed'.
>
> ~ RYDER CARROLL

In this chapter, we're going to look at how our style of working influences our wellbeing and productivity, and what we can do about it.

THE REAL COST OF BUSYNESS

When someone asks you how you are, how often do you respond to that question by saying, "fine, just very busy!" or something along those lines?

The word 'busy' links to being industrious.

Busy means being actively engaged in an activity. It's supposed to mean something good, but in our modern workplace, it's become a sign of overwork.

It also derides the importance of leisure time in the bigger picture of what's required to support us being industrious in the long term.

'Busyness' has incorrectly come to be seen as a sign of social status.

However, our brains don't deal with it well. Being busy too often for too long makes us over-stressed. It is both taxing on the body and tiring for our mind, so can lead to burnout when we are chronically busy.

Often the busyness we experience in a workday is because of our work tools, all those emails and messages flying around demanding that we react to them. They force us to multitask even though the science has proven that task switching has a terrible cost on our attention.

We need to change the way we think about busyness.

We can start doing that by examining our existing work styles and workflows.

- Do they allow room for deep work, creativity, and critical thinking?
- Do they enable time for rest?
- Do they exacerbate our busyness?

To manage our busyness, we can set limits on communication time and/or set specific times in the day when we do communication-related work. By creating those boundaries, we create space outside of those communication windows for the deep work to be done.

WORKPLACE COMMUNICATION STYLES

There are two common types of communication styles associated with our digital work - synchronous and asynchronous communication.

Both words are derived from *'Chronos'*, the Greek word for 'time'. In Greek mythology, Cronos / Kronos was the god of time, overseeing its destructive force.

THE CADENCE EFFECT

1. SYNCHRONOUS COMMUNICATION

We have got into the habit of being available, accessible and responsive to the communication demands of our work, continuously, in real time, all the time.

Communicating synchronously prioritises being connected over being productive.

So, when we engage in synchronous comms, usually through calls, emails, meetings, and messaging, we have a deluge of demands and information coming at us all the time.

In his book, A World Without Email, Cal Newport calls this continuous, collective conversation *the hyperactive hive mind*.

Working this way creates continuous interruptions. It forces us to multitask (which fragments our attention) and it puts us in fire-fighting mode.

This reactive style of working damages our concentration over the long term.

When we're permanently on distracted standby, our adrenalin is repeatedly being activated, causing elevated stress and anxiety, both of which are terrible for productivity.

A lot of us are spending as much as 80% of our work day on email, messaging and status meetings. Being plugged into these perpetual conversations makes it impossible to have long, uninterrupted periods of time during the workday to get the 'real work' done - the work you were actually hired to do.

For knowledge workers, this 'real work' might be writing, coding, designing, creating, making, or building something online. It usually involves thought, creativity, structure, planning, and focus.

We usually do better at this work when we have the space to do it in an uninterrupted manner. This is often why we find we may need to start work extra early or work late to find that undistracted space. I shared an example of this from my experience in a previous chapter.

Why do we extend our work day by starting early or working late? Well, usually it's quieter, and we have more time and space to think, so we can focus better and get more done.

Extending our work day has other costs, which I'll cover elsewhere, but being able to engage in a more focused style of work falls on the other side of the comms spectrum.

2. ASYNCHRONOUS COMMUNICATION

Working asynchronously means 'working out of time'. This communication style places productivity <u>before</u> connection.

When working asynchronously, you have more control over how and when you communicate with your team, colleagues, or clients.

What does asynchronous communication look like?

- It means turning off notifications, closing messaging apps, and only responding to other's requests or communications at a time that works for you.
- Or communicating at an agreed, designated time, where you and your teammates all come together to have a collective discussion.

Being able to designate when we work and when we're available to communicate proves to be better for our wellbeing and productivity. Working asynchronously also helps us to accommodate the other responsibilities in our lives better too.

After the big global "stay at home, work from home" experiment brought on by the pandemic, even more companies are incorporating this style of working into their culture.

MAKING TIME FOR BOTH

There will always be times when you need to be accessible. So the solution is a blended approach, blocking sections of time in your days for both types of work.

THE CADENCE EFFECT

Important Note: working this way revolves around you having a degree of control over your own calendar.

What does a hybrid-working style look like?

1. Managing your calendar to include time for asynchronous work.

Block off designated times when your clients or collaborators know that you're unavailable (unless it's an emergency), because you're doing focused work.

- Your focused work could be designing a new feature cover, programming a website, or preparing for that big client presentation. Whatever it is, it requires that you can work for certain time periods without distraction.

2. Setting specific times in your day and diary for real-time communication.

- This could be for weekly meetings, specific office hours for troubleshooting chats, or a designated daily slot to process your inbox or to do the logistical or administrative parts of your work.

3. Using shared documents.

Discussions based around a shared document enable people to brainstorm individually and allow for a more rounded, diverse and equal contribution 'in the document'.

Using a central document for feedback gives everyone the opportunity to be 'heard' rather than the loudest person in the room dominating any live conversation.

- Using shared documents for commenting, suggestions, recommendations, etc. in advance of meetings allows people to respond at a time that suits them.
- It creates the space for thinking and processing time prior to sharing thoughts.

- Meetings are then used to discuss and firm up those actions, rather than spending meeting time gathering the info.

4. Keeping meetings to a minimum and keeping them short.

Is a meeting really necessary? Do you need everyone in the room? How much time is needed?

According to Otter.ai's research, those surveyed preferred 15 to 30 minutes as favoured time slots.

5. Setting boundaries around your time.

Whether you work for yourself or in a team, it's important to set boundaries at the start of every project and new working relationship (whether it's with colleagues or clients).

If you are a freelancer or entrepreneur:

Can you put your working times and hours in the terms & conditions of your contract agreement (whether it's with your employer or your client)? Can you add a line at the bottom of your email about your working cadence?

If you work in a team:

Can you reach a consensus on how you can work and communicate more asynchronously together, so everyone can get more done without more stress?

> Personally, I have adopted each of these elements as part of my way of working. I also set very clear boundaries at the start of new working relationships to clarify how I work, when I work, and why I work this way.
>
> Obviously, I try to accommodate my clients' needs where possible, but I see my work projects as collaborations, where both parties need to come to the party. I don't work for these clients; I work with them. As I'm up front about this style of working, my clients rarely have a problem with it. And, if they do, from experience,

that's usually a warning sign to me they probably aren't a good fit, and it could lead to issues of overwork down the road.

Our experience during the pandemic has also led to the relaxing of certain social norms around how we work. As a result, people have become more understanding of the responsibilities outside of work that might impinge on our work days.

When we inform and communicate with our people **up front** about our preferred work styles, based on our other responsibilities, they are usually even more understanding and respectful of our boundaries. So, there is no harm in having the conversation.

How can you communicate your working styles in a way that is clear, appropriate and acceptable?

OVERWORKING REVISITED

This brings me to talk about the effect that working too much has on our productivity. I touched on this in the Challenges section, but it's also relevant to this conversation about our work styles.

Studies from 2017 found that, on average, most modern workers are only productive for 3 hours in total during a typical workday.

We typically spend the rest of the day interacting with coworkers, task switching on busy work, engaged in endless meetings, and so forth. While some of these things have their place in our workday, they can also distract our attention and affect our concentration.

What often happens is that we become so disrupted during the week by all those distractions that we end up working on the weekend to catch up and stay on track.

This is on top of any chores or side projects or social engagements we may have planned for the weekend.

When we do this, we end up working twelve-day weeks.

Let me explain.

12-DAY WEEKS

I first came across this term a few years ago in the book *It Doesn't Have to Be Crazy at Work* by the team at 37 Signals (makers of Basecamp and HEY).

Does this scenario sound familiar?

Say you work a full week, and then you have to put in time on the weekend too, so that's seven days of work. Then you're back on your usual schedule from the Monday after that weekend.

The Monday is not day one of week two. If you haven't taken a break, that Monday becomes day eight of week one. This means by the Friday of that second week, you've worked twelve days in a row, and may have to work more again on the next weekend.

This style of relentless work without sufficient rest depletes our resilience and wellbeing. It leads to less productive outcomes over the long term.

> As an entrepreneur, I admit I often do work on the weekends, as there is always something I'm interested in progressing in my business. I usually reserve weekdays for client-facing work - the stuff the involves working in my business - and weekends for learning and working on my business. On this entrepreneurial journey, I would find that there were times when weekends became like any other workday, and that is a recipe for burnout when it becomes the norm!

> Once I learned about 12-day weeks, I became a lot more intentional about how much time I devote to work on the weekend. I started ensuring that, where possible, I took at least one full day off to rest, or reserved large chunks of time on both days to still do social and supportive activities, to aid my rest and recovery and provide time away from screens.

If long working stints on weekends are inevitable, can you take time off during the week to recoup your energy? Perhaps you have to work weekends by default as part of your job. So can you ensure you are taking adequate time for rest at other times of the week?

Now, the occasional deadline is always going to be a thing, and adapting to these fluctuating work requirements is part of building the cadence of your days. But there is a compelling reason why it's detrimental if we regularly work 12-day weeks.

MORE WORK = LESS PRODUCTIVE

Research from Stanford University has revealed that the quality of our work declines considerably after 40-55 hours of working in a week.

So working a full week and then putting in extra overtime at night or on weekends isn't quality time from a productivity perspective. The studies found that working less resulted in a higher level of creativity, productivity and output.

Repeatedly overworking also has life-threatening consequences.

The World Health Organisation (WHO) shared research in 2021 that suggests that longer working hours (i.e. 55 hours or more) *dramatically increase our chances of heart disease and stroke.*

So less work leads to better productivity and better health and wellness, but also contributes to our longevity.

There are also differences between overwork, too much work, just the right amount of work, and insufficient work to keep us engaged. It's a bit like a Goldilocks scenario.

We want to avoid overwork. However, the flip side of overwork is under working, and that isn't good for our health either.

We require a degree of challenge in what we do, as stretching ourselves can bring meaning to our work and create opportunities for learning and growth.

I cover this in more detail in the chapter on Flow.

If we feel we are being underutilised in our role, or doing insufficient work to feel like we are making progress or making a difference, then that is also an issue that needs to be addressed.

There are other social ramifications of working more too. Our relationships may suffer, and working all the time can lead to isolation and loneliness, which are other contributors to life-threatening health issues.

This is <u>not</u> about not doing work, this is about pacing ourselves with supportive practices, so that we can sustain and thrive in our work over the long haul.

REST IS BEST

An important part of creating an Intentional Productivity practice is ensuring that your brain can rest.

According to Alex Soojung-Kim Pang, the author of *Rest: Why You Get More Done When You Work Less*, "rest is an essential component of working well and working smart".

As I've mentioned previously:

We need to make time for rest and recovery, because our brains are both our most important asset and our weakest link in the digital workplace.

If you need to work long hours during the week and / or on the weekend, ensure you're also taking lengthy periods of time out during your week and around that work on the weekend.

It is essential that you have quality time to recover and to interact with things that don't involve work.

4-DAY WEEKS

Another way to support working that allows for sufficient rest is to employ 4-day working cycles, instead of following the traditional 5-day work week.

Overall, trials so far have shown that reducing working hours can improve happiness, health, and productivity.

- Between 2015 and 2019, the country of Iceland employed the world's the largest and longest trial, reducing 40-hour work weeks to 35/36 hours without a cut in pay.
- Findings included a reduction in worker stress and burnout, and people could have a more balanced experience of work and life because of having more time for rest and relaxation.
- The success of this trial led to a significant change in the country's employment policies, with nearly 90% of the population now adopting different working practices.
- Other countries have followed suit with similar experiments, such as Spain, Ireland, New Zealand and the UAE.

At the time of writing, a six-month trial has just concluded in the UK to determine the feasibility of four-day work weeks. It's the largest trial of its kind so far, and over 60 companies took part, offering their employees one paid day off each week.

According to a report on CNN business, the six-month pilot committed over 3000 workers across these companies to "work 80% of their usual week in exchange for promising to maintain 100% of their productivity."

At the halfway point in October 2022, more than half of these companies reported no detrimental effects to productivity. And in some cases, major improvements in productivity were apparent.

The ultimate results of the trial, which concluded in December 2022, are encouraging. Most of the companies involved could maintain productivity levels and there were visible improvements in staff retention and wellbeing, with business revenue staying level. 90% of the participating businesses have opted to continue testing the four-day week, and 18 organisations have adopted it permanently.

With more people, employers and governments accepting the business benefits of a four-day work week, this bodes well for creating better, more intentional working practices that can support how we both work and live.

HABITS AFFECTING OUR WORK STYLE

When we have too much on our plate, it's natural to default into autopilot mode with habitual behaviours.

Whilst habits are shortcuts that help us save time, being perpetually overwhelmed by work is also fertile ground for breeding bad habits, particularly around how we use our digital communication tools.

On top of all those digital distractions, there are the physical habits that we develop which affect our working behaviours.

- We consume stimulants, which then cause anxiety and sleep disruption when we over-caffeinate.
- We sit for long periods of time hunched over a computer, which affects our posture and causes pain in our body and serious health issues over the long term.
- We eat lunch at our desks, while we scroll, so we don't eat mindfully, which can lead to overeating.
- We forgot to blink and look away from our screens, straining our eyes and increasing our risk of needing glasses. (This is also happening in children, who are using screens from a younger age).
- We don't move enough, which contributes to weight gain and serious health issues.
- We don't hydrate enough, which affects our concentration, our physiology, and mood.

When we're working in open-plan offices, we often have insufficient personal space and there are constant disruptions. So we unconsciously modify our behaviour to create space and set boundaries.

- We put our headphones on and hunch our body to create an imaginary perimeter.
- The flip side of this is that it can also make us seem unapproachable, which can have an adverse effect on communications in a shared work environment.

Alternatively, if you work on your own with little contact with others, it can be a lonely experience. A sense of isolation can affect your mental health and performance.

So, it's important to understand how these more physical and habitual aspects of our work style also affect our productivity. When we know what isn't supporting us, that helps us to work on developing habits that will support us better.

I cover simple things you can do to build better habits in both the Opportunities and Preparation for Focus & Flow sections of this book.

CONSIDER YOUR OWN SITUATION

At the end of this section, you'll have time to reflect on every aspect of how you work, including your work styles.

For now, contemplate which of the above influences, habits, activities and behaviours apply to your work environments.

- Is your work style more synchronous or asynchronous?
- Are you overworking?
- What is suffering because of your current work style?
- What parts of your work style are working well for you?
- Where can you improve? And what would that look like?

Next up, let's look at the role which our physical work environments play in supporting our wellbeing and performance.

This next chapter is about the tactile and sensory elements of your physical work set up and the impact they can have on focus and productivity.

I'll also suggest some small ways you can make enormous improvements.

THIRTEEN
WORK ENVIRONMENTS

> Most of us do our best work in a place of our own.
>
> ~ STEPHEN KING

In this chapter, first we're going to consider the elements that make up our environments, which can affect our productivity. Then, I'll recommend ways to make adjustments to your environment that can have positive effects on your wellbeing and your work.

Our surroundings help us create meaning. They help us make sense of the world.

Our typical modern workplaces and spaces affect our productivity, irrespective of whether we work from home or away from home.

Studies from the field of Ecological Psychology have found that places in which we choose to work matter because of the way we interact with the objects within that environment.

So, place making supports our performance, because our perceptions of our environment influence the actions we take within it.

WORK ENVIRONMENTS

LOCATION, LOCATION, LOCATION

The environmental, structural and logistical aspects of our location influence our ability to work well.

Irrespective of whether you are based in an office, or work remotely, or in a hybrid or distributed way, your physical work environments can affect your performance in many ways.

> Factors such as workspace layout, noise, temperature, aroma, lighting, and interruptions all play a role in supporting our focus, attention, creativity, wellbeing and productivity, or hindering it.

And if we work from home, there are other distractions that can also come into play, such as family members demanding attention, pets that need to be fed or walked, and chores that need to be done.

Let's look at the main environmental culprits that can affect our performance.

LAYOUT

It doesn't matter if you're working from your dining table, a company office or from a coworking space, the workspace layout influences how you work.

- Is the space open plan? Is it crowded or cluttered? Do you have enough personal space?
- Is your workspace inspiring and energising? Or does it make you feel stressed and anxious?
- Is it a permanent space where you can close the door?
- Or, is it a multi-purpose space where you have to pack your tools away?
- Are your tools set up correctly? (E.g. your screen and chair at the correct height.)

Open Plan vs Productive

Studies have identified a link between large open-plan offices, poor productivity, and reduced collaboration.

Harvard Business School found that introducing open-plan layouts caused face-to-face interactions to drop by 70%. More interactions were deemed to be counter-productive, as they create too many distractions and interruptions for those trying to do focused work.

As the leaders of these studies reported in the Harvard Business Review:

"The goal should be to get the right people interacting with the right richness at the right times."

To support this goal, employers with large offices can combine open plan layouts, with the addition of more quiet spaces and places for working in a less distracted fashion.

Clutter Causes Stress!

> Outer order contributes to inner calm.
>
> ~ GRETCHEN RUBIN

Chaos in our external world compounds our stress and anxiety. This includes clutter on our desks and messy workspaces. Clear space creates room to think and breathe.

- What are the actual contents of your desk? Is it a tidy workspace?
- Consider how many things are on your desk?
- Does it have a lot of gadgets and papers lying about?
- Is it clear and clean?
- What about your electronic desktop? Messy, disorganised online folders are just as stress inducing.

WORK ENVIRONMENTS

Clear away "the stuff" *(technical term)* related to your work, when it isn't being used or needed for a specific work activity. Have neat and organised filing systems in both your physical and digital workspaces.

NOISE

Sound can also affect productivity both positively and adversely, but it depends on the type of work you're trying to do, the type and volume of sound or noise you're exposed to, and how long you are exposed to it for.

- If you are in an office, do your colleagues talk loudly on the phone?
- Do you have to sit next to the annoying photocopier and shredder?
- If you work from home, are you on a busy street?
- Does your partner or house mate blast their music or talk loudly while you are trying to work?
- Or do you have to work to the sounds of the washing machine or vacuum cleaner, or the neighbour mowing their lawn?

Pumping up the volume pumps us up!

Loud noises can increase the release of epinephrine (adrenalin), which is a response to the stress the noise creates in our bodies.

Studies confirmed that repetitive tasks that require little cognitive energy are less likely to be affected by noise exposure. However, if you are trying to do complex tasks which are taxing to your cognitive load, then loud noises are detrimental to getting that work done.

Our productivity and creativity can thrive with certain sounds and ambient noise levels, usually in the region of between 50 and 70 decibels.

The higher end of this range is the equivalent of the white noise you might hear in a bustling coffee shop. It's also a continuous noise which the brain finds easier to tune out.

However, when that noise increases to 85 to 95 decibels (the equivalent of loud traffic noise), and / or is more intermittent or cyclical, it disrupts our brain's ability to focus.

Research has found that not only does this type of noise exposure affect our physical and mental health, but our "mental workload and visual and auditory attention is significantly reduced".

LIGHTING

- Is your workspace too bright, too dark or just right?
- Does the lighting give you a headache or force you to squint?
- Do you have your workstation set up so that the back light on your screens adjusts as the day progresses into the night?

It fascinated me to discover when researching this book that our eyes are actually a part of our brain, the only part that isn't shielded by our skull.

Being attuned to changes in light, our eyes also help to control our circadian rhythms.

We'll look at these rhythms in more detail in Part 4 - Leveraging Opportunities.

Eyes Wide Shut

The types of light we expose our eyes to, and the times at which we are exposed to them, affect how well we function, both when awake and when asleep.

They can strain easily when our lighting is too bright or too dark. And working in front of a screen is a nightmare for our eyes, as we can often forget to blink! Screens also expose us to radiation which can contribute to dry eyes.

Prolonging our day with artificial light, which is blue on the spectrum, can also disrupt our sleep patterns, and therefore our long-term wellbeing and productivity.

TEMPERATURE & AIR FLOW

The temperature in the room can affect your focus, just like Goldilocks. Too hot and you get sleepy, too cold and you get distracted.

In winter, we put on the heating and the air can get too dry, leading to dry mouth or congestion in our nose, which in turns affects our breathing.

When we can't breathe effectively, we aren't pulling in enough air to function optimally.

No Flow, No Go!

Working with the windows closed limits air circulation. Stale air contains more carbon dioxide, which makes us more sluggish.

The carpets, paint and finishes used in your workspace may also release chemicals that cause headaches and respiratory problems.

A lack of airflow and poor indoor air quality can cause symptoms which affect our ability to work accurately and efficiently. But, even more alarming, they can also cause a host of physical and mental health issues.

The Real Hazards of Bad Air

The situation is worse than you may realise.

If symptoms such as congestion, irritated eyes, dizziness, headaches, hypersensitivity, and/or fatigue persist and become chronic because of spending time in these environments, they can form part of a diagnosis for Sick Building Syndrome (SBS).

Studies by Ambius in 2018 found that 40% of US workers suffer from these illnesses because of poor air quality and insufficient air flow. Prolonged exposure to potentially toxic environments can even contribute to Alzheimers and Dementia.

So, I recommend you do an audit of your work environment to determine whether you might benefit from opening that window, using an air purifier or fan, upgrading your HVAC filtering, getting rid of old carpeting, and/or changing your heating settings.

SMELLS, ODOURS & AROMAS

We underestimate the power of our nose on our productivity.

- Fishy food smells emanating from the office microwave?
- Can you smell the acrid residue of the cigarette which your colleague just had on his break?
- Is last night's slightly burnt veggie lasagna still permeating the dining room where you work?
- Is the stench of the overflowing rubbish bin outside your window distracting you?

Our olfactory bulb has more projections on it than the brain has structures for dealing with vision and hearing.

The Nose Knows

Interestingly, there are several studies which link smell to how well we work.

Scent and odours affect our mood and therefore how we think and act. They also affect the mood of a room and how we feel within it.

Our mood affects our creativity too. Pleasant scents increase our levels of positivity, which have been found to improve our creative problem-solving skills.

SMALL WAYS TO MAKE BIG IMPROVEMENTS

So, as you can see, things like layout, lighting, sights, sounds and smells can create distractions, disruptions and discomforts for our brain and body.

Getting intentional about how you set up your workspace, so that your brain and body feel calm in that space, helps support your ability to be intentionally productive.

WORK ENVIRONMENTS

Here are three ways you can improve the environmental aspects of your workplace.

1. FLEXIBLE WORKING AREAS

Can you create flexible work spaces which support the different work tasks that you need to do?

Perhaps you have a dedicated quiet space for writing, idea generation, or other forms of focused work that is separate from where you do your email checking and admin tasks.

If you use a coworking space, or hot desk in a company setting, you could choose a desk in a more social space for when you're doing more shallow types of work where you don't mind being disturbed. And find a cosy, quiet corner for when you need to focus more deeply.

Regular clean ups, clean desk policies and having adequate storage for paperwork and miscellaneous items can help with reducing the stress caused by clutter.

2. SENSORY DESIGN

Touch, smell, taste, sight and sound help us connect with our environment and feel more rooted in it. And the more we work in a digital space, the more we need to create opportunities to reconnect with the natural world.

Can you design or redesign your space considering the 5 senses?

This could involve using natural and eco-friendly materials for your desk and chair, inspiring colours and textures in your workspace, and positioning your desk so that you have better access to more natural light.

Introducing plants and flowers to workspaces have been shown to improve people's mood. Whilst they don't replace the proven benefits of being outside in nature, their calming effect is a form of eco-therapy.

Studies have also found that scents like rosemary improve memory, and lavender promotes calmness and reduces anxiety. There are a variety of essential oils which can help support your productivity.

- **Problem Solving:** Rosemary, Vetiver, Coffee
- **Improving Performance:** Lemon, Jasmine, Citrus
- **Sustaining Attention:** Cinnamon, Peppermint, Ginger
- **Recharging:** Pine, Lemongrass, Lavender

A diffuser can help to circulate these scents. A humidifier mitigates the drying effect of electronics by moistening the air in your workspace. And an air purifier is a welcome addition, especially given the pandemic experience.

A secondary benefit of these appliances is the white noise they produce, which can provide ambient sound that helps with focus. Listening to certain types of noise frequencies (e.g. brown noise or pink noise) can also soothe an agitated mind, aid concentration, or improve sleep.

If, like me, you are sensitive to noise and high-pitched sounds, then you may benefit from using noise cancelling headphones to block out sound, or a set of earplugs especially designed to dampen certain frequencies. These earplugs enable you to still hear sounds and have a conversation, but without background noise creating unnecessary stress and anxiety.

I use a brand called Loop, which makes ear plugs for a host of different situations, and there are plenty of other brands out there too.

3. GET MOVING OUTDOORS

Do you need to be working inside all the time?

Being away from our desks is an opportunity to activate our creativity. Walking and being in nature are both highly beneficial for our brain's performance, and for improving our health and our mood.

Walking Boosts Our Brainpower

When we walk, our brainwaves synchronise with the pace of our footfall. This can create a calming effect on the mind, allowing it to engage in 'mental time travel'.

Walking also helps us to think. It is often when we have our best ideas, as our brain can percolate on challenges and problem solve, revealing innovative insights.

Studies have found that walking (and other physical exercise) improves concentration and memory and supports our mental health. It also boosts our creativity and slows our cognitive decline as we age.

As part of the larger movement towards 'social prescribing', doctors are increasingly recommending walking and cycling to ease the burden on healthcare sectors. And where we choose to walk can also play a role in supporting our wellbeing better.

Being in Nature Feeds Our Body

Shinrin-yoku - aka forest bathing - started as a healing practice in Japan and is now adopted as a practice around the world.

Forest bathing involves immersing yourself in nature, embracing the natural beauty around you whilst mindfully paying attention to your senses and the influence of nature on your body and mind.

While researchers recognise forested environments as having specific beneficial effects on our health, regularly spending time in any natural environment has been found to have a positive effect on our immune system and our cardiovascular system. Being outdoors in nature also reduces anxiety and helps with focus.

So make time in your day to head outdoors, for 5 minutes or 30. For a brainstorming session or a walking meeting. Or to let your thoughts from a recent deep work session percolate before the next one.

In this chapter, we've considered the effects that noise, light, temperature, air flow, smells and your office layout can have on your work performance.

THE CADENCE EFFECT

I also suggested some antidotes to poor work environments, which will help you improve not only your performance, but also your experience of your workplace.

The next chapter is about Our Work Tools.

We'll consider the positive and negative effects they have on how we work and things we can do to engage with them more optimally.

FOURTEEN
OUR WORK TOOLS

> We become what we behold. We shape our tools and then our tools shape us.
>
> ~ MARSHALL MCLUHAN

So, we've looked at our work styles and work environments and the impact they have on our ability to work well. The next important elements to consider are the tools we engage with daily to do our work.

For knowledge workers, our work tools typically comprise software programmes and applications that include:

- Email
- Calls
- Video/Audio meetings
- Shared folders
- Electronic documents
- Messaging
- Collaboration tools

There are also calendars, task monitoring and project management tools. And the specific specialist software we might use to create our work, whether that is to draw, make, design, write, or code, and so forth.

THE DIGITAL WORKPLACE

Collectively, these tools sit within online environments also known as **the digital workplace.** They are the digital architecture of your work environment.

With Web 3 and AI technologies now the norm, these environments have become increasingly complex and interconnected. We use AI-supported software to help in every facet of our business (and life) and we can interact in the spatial web, using tools such as headsets to engage in a variety of different types of metaverse (aka virtual reality spaces).

These emerging technologies are developing so rapidly, including the terminology used to describe them. So, there's a strong chance that descriptors like "the metaverse" and "web3" will quickly become outdated and replaced by something else.

Whatever we call them, these tools are meant to help us do our work well, but the way we use them can also hinder our focus and outputs. If not managed properly, these tools can cause digital noise, clutter, and distraction. They can also perpetuate that feeling of always being "on".

EMAIL & MESSAGING

With emails as a communication form, we're guided by someone else's requests and demands. We're also easily distracted by them, as our default response is to feel the need to immediately reply and comply.

When we keep our email or instant messaging open in the background, that draws us into participating in a perpetual collective conversation, aka the *hyperactive hive mind* I referenced in the chapter on Work Styles.

Now, I know that for many, email is the primary tool used to manage tasks. To make email an effective tool for task management, it requires discipline and a system. This is something that many of us are not adept at doing.

On average, we open emails within 6 seconds of their arrival, and many of us are on permanent standby, repeatedly refreshing whilst we wait for the next response (aka dopamine hit). Stats from 2016 put the average time we check for emails at 74 times per day!

Here are some more stats from a McKinsey Global Analysis report to shock you:

- On average, 28% of work time involves email.
- We check email on average 11 times per hour.
- 84% keep email open in the background while working.
- 64% use notifications to learn about new emails.
- 70% of emails are opened within the first six seconds of arrival.

Numerous studies have concluded that email makes us feel overloaded and overwhelmed.

According to Gloria Marks of the University of California, "the longer daily time spent on email, the lower was perceived productivity and the higher the measured stress."

The same goes for having your messaging or chat app - such as Discord or Slack - open while you work.

You end up getting distracted incessantly by what is meant to be a quick chat, when the cost of task switching means it takes much longer than planned for you to get back on track.

The time spent monitoring for emails and messages contributes to a loss in productivity. And interruptions from responding to notifications leads to a much larger cost than the short time taken to deal with the notification.

Research suggests that distractions derail our cognitive focus for up to 30 minutes each time. So, that 45 second distraction, when you quickly checked your email, is actually costing you 23 minutes and 45 seconds.

It's impossible to enter a state of flow and do what Cal Newport calls "deep work" if we are in a perpetual state of distraction.

The notifications, dings and pings associated with these conversations are also dopamine triggers. So we become addicted to the repetitive behaviour of clicking, checking, and refreshing. Again and again.

We find ourselves on permanent standby, whilst we wait for the next hit or response. This creates open loops which split our attention.

What compounds the situation is that we can access our emails on our phones. We become habituated to checking our emails outside of typical work hours and activities, too.

These are moments when we should be resting, relaxing or communicating with people and things we care about outside of work. Yet we're still on standby.

These compulsive experiences elevate our anxiety, our stress, and our sense of overwhelm.

TASK MANAGEMENT SOFTWARE

With the deluge of information coming at us, it is impossible to keep it all in our heads.

Working online, chances are you're using task management apps alongside a digital calendar to help manage your tasks, and the activities and information related to them.

What do I mean by task management?

- You could track ToDo's in Trello or ToDoist.
- Or build a 'second brain' database in Notion or Evernote.
- Or work with planning docs and spreadsheets in MS Office or Google Workspace.

OUR WORK TOOLS

There are countless productivity tools and frameworks that can help you tick those boxes. Aside from actual software, these methods encompass everything from Getting Things Done (GTD), Kanban, OKRs and the Eisenhower Matrix, to Eating the Frog or timing with Pomodoro, and plenty more.

> When working with clients, I prefer to be software and method agnostic, as there's *no one tool* or task management method that is 'the best' in the world.
>
> There is only what is right for you based on your needs and requirements at this moment in time. This might be one tool, or a selection of them, and these tools may need to change over time.

As I've mentioned before, there is no one right way to be productive, and all of these methods may work for you. However, you don't have to do or even try them all. You just need to find one, or a few, that feel like a good fit, which you can incorporate into your larger intentional productivity method.

If you work in a team, task management software can be an efficient way to stay on top of what everyone else is doing, and for everyone to be accountable for completing their tasks.

What is important with task management is that the software we use doesn't complicate our work day or steal too much of our time.

If you get distracted from work by spending a lot of time setting up and designing templates to capture the work, you're wasting precious time focusing (aka procrastinating) on the wrong thing.

If you're spending more time updating your task progress on the software than you are actually doing the work associated with those tasks, then that is also a problem!

So, what other tools are we using regularly for our work?

SMART PHONES

Achieving a flow state requires a period of unbroken concentration where we are fully absorbed in a task we're capable of doing.

Unfortunately, having our phones near us fractures our ability to focus and be in flow.

Ever pervasive, in the workplace, our phones aren't just used for calls.

Often they're a backup digital workspace when we're working on the fly, allowing us to send emails, schedule a meeting, book a business trip, publish a marketing campaign, deliver a slide deck presentation, or check our CRM dashboard.

In this regard, our smart phones can be extremely useful.

However, research has shown that having our smartphones in line of sight is detrimental to our productivity, as it splits our attention in two, negatively affecting our performance and concentration. When we need to do deep, focused work, this means we're only bringing half of our cognitive energy to the task at hand.

As part of our brain's procrastination tactics, we learn to self-distract using things like our phone.

Having our phone within arm's reach means it's easy to dip into social media when we feel bored or stressed by the task we're doing. And then seeking that distraction becomes a habit to do that whenever we feel uncomfortable.

These compulsive habits fuel our procrastination, so it becomes a negative cycle.

According to studies in 2015 and 2017, for many of us, this self-distracting behaviour we develop with our phones is happening on average every 10 to 20 minutes during work or focus time.

When our days become so fractured by these autopilot compulsions, it's no wonder we get frustrated at not getting things done.

I'll offer some suggestions at the end of this chapter for ways to alter this behaviour. Before we get there, what else is affecting our ability to work during a workday?

MEETINGS

A meeting is a synchronous form of communication, happening in real time with immediate feedback.

Meetings are a work tool. However, unstructured, unnecessary meetings are a drain on our time and energy.

Meetings have their place. However, having a meeting to decide what to have a meeting about is unhelpful, but commonplace in the workplace. This inefficiency has productivity and performance costs for all involved.

A 2021 meta-analysis by Otter.ai revealed that 70% of our meetings keep us from doing the work we are employed to do!

While video conferencing has been around for a long time, the pandemic threw us into the world of back-to-back online meetings. (*An average increase of 70% according to the Otter.ai survey*).

The enforced WFH (work from home) vibe meant meetings became the primary way to do work, with little space for catching your breath, never mind doing 'the proper work' in between.

Too many meetings impact on your ability to get this work done, affecting the bottom line.

The 'real work' is what might need to be created for another meeting, or because of the outcomes of this meeting. Plus, they often mean that you then work "out of hours" to get the work done, as your day is too full of meetings.

See how ridiculous this is! Yet, how many of us work this way, every day?

In early 2022, Harvard Business Review reported back on a 14-month survey of 76 companies who reduced meetings by increments of 20%, 40%, 60% and 80%.

The findings revealed some startling results:

> Fewer meetings have profoundly positive outcomes on autonomy, communication, cooperation, engagement, and productivity, and markedly reduce stress and incidences of micromanagement.

The Cost of Video Meetings

Video meetings with lots of people on a call are particularly fatiguing, as your brain is trying to make sense of multiple pictures of multiple people, rather than processing a single visual of the group in the room, as you would experience meeting them in person in a physical space.

In the online meeting format, it's also easy to miss the subtle cues that our other senses would pick up on, helping us form a "picture" of those people. So our brain is working overtime to make sense of things from the limited cues we have available.

Spending so much time in online meetings during the pandemic gave rise to terms like "Zoom fatigue" and contributed to our feelings of burnout.

However, when we started turning off our video to curb this fatigue, showing a photo of ourselves or a blank screen, people on the receiving end ended up feeling unseen, unheard, or ignored.

> In a digital room with no visual validation, we have no sign that what we are saying is being understood or having the desired effect.

Not "being" in the physical room with someone can leave lots of room for misinterpretation. If we don't bring our communication skills up to speed with how to interact in these online situations, it can cause stress and lead to mistakes and misunderstandings.

3D Virtual Meetings

Digital or online variations of meetings take on a greater level of complexity with the adoption of the spatial web with metaverse-type spaces as an alternative place to interact and collaborate.

Communicating in 3D, Extended Reality (XR), Mixed Reality (MR), Virtual Reality (VR), and / or Augmented Reality (AR) dimensions will become commonplace for three reasons:

- Emerging technologies are becoming more widely adopted.
- Our tools for accessing these spaces will improve.
- Hybrid working continues to grow in popularity and necessity.

In May 2022, Regus conducted a survey of 2000 office workers and 250 senior executives to find out their thoughts about the role of the metaverse in the future of business.

65% of business leaders considered the metaverse as part of the evolution of hybrid working, and over 40% of employees felt doing more work in metaverse environments would improve communication, teamwork and work opportunities.

The future of work is already here.

Since the Regus Report came out, Microsoft, Google and Meta, as well as hundreds of smaller software companies, have rolled out AI-assisted tools and XR meeting spaces as part of their existing workspace tool portfolios.

> Meetings in virtual reality spaces hold the promise of promoting social interaction, enhancing training opportunities, improving teamwork and fostering creativity.

However, there are cognitive and physical costs to spending time in these environments.

We need to be aware of the impact spending more time online will have on our wellbeing.

One example is wearing a VR headset, which can cause eyestrain, neck strain, and brain strain from focusing through a small viewing aperture, wearing a heavy headset, and trying to digest the plethora of incoming rich visuals you're taking in.

Some of these issues will be addressed as technology improves, but the fact remains, being in these spaces can negatively affect our wellbeing and performance. So, we should use them with care and intention.

RULE YOUR TOOLS

So how can you manage these elements of your digital workplace, to reduce overwhelm, limit distractions and support your wellbeing?

1. Know your tools.

Make a list of all the tools that you use to do your work daily. How do your tools connect? Do your tools integrate seamlessly or is there friction?

How complex is your system? Are there overlaps or redundancies in what they do? How can you scale down and keep things simple? Do you use them efficiently? Do they support you? Any problems they cause?

How can you improve how you use them? Are there any that are unnecessary / which duplicate the same service?

2. Create different routines for different types of work.

This could be writing or taking notes or brainstorming in a different place to where you are using your computer for other types of work, irrespective of whether you have a dedicated office space at home, in a company workplace, or in a coworking space.

Perhaps you like playing music while doing research or admin tasks, but prefer total silence when you need to be in thought mode.

Become more aware of how you work best. Do more of what supports your focus for your different forms of work, and do less of what irritates your attention.

3. Turn off your notifications and close apps.

The 25 tabs running in your browser, and the 7 software programmes waiting for you to do something on them, all cause open loops in your brain. All those loops take energy to keep circling in your brain.

Unless you're using them for the task you're working on, close them down so you can focus on the only thing you need to be doing at that moment.

The dings and pings of your incoming emails, chat messages and social media notifications are like blunt pins poking the balloon of your attention. Too many pokes and it bursts, but even before that, the incessant poking means you are being constantly nudged away from what matters.

Turn them off. Close them. You will lower your underlying stress levels and your brain and body will thank you.

4. Make your phone invisible.

Turn off unnecessary notifications. Better still, put it on silent. Even better, turn it off. Hard, I know, but once done, it's amazing what happens!

Hide your phone from yourself. Put it behind you, or in a drawer, or keep it out of line of sight. This makes it less easy to reach for when you have an urge to procrastinate during a focus period.

Becoming less reliant on your phone is one of the most challenging things you may have to do, but in these instances, that discomfort is usually only felt for the first 5-10 minutes. After that, your brain isn't paying attention to needing it.

The key here is to build a habit of _not_ automatically defaulting to reaching for the phone at the first sign of an external disruption, or your brain's yearning for distraction from a hard task.

5. Set clear boundaries.

Block specific time on your calendar for focused work, so that others cannot hijack that time for booking their meetings. Add an email footer below your signature to indicate your working pattern. Be clear in your communications as to when people can expect responses and deliverables from you.

Depending on the work you do, can you stipulate in the terms and conditions of your projects and how you prefer to work? For example, whether you will be contactable on holidays, weekends, or after hours.

Manage the expectations of coworkers, clients, and family members for when you are available and when you're not.

This isn't about being a hard arse. This is about clear communication. If you respect your boundaries, then other people will learn to, too.

6. Have a 'meetings protocol.'

Set some ground rules. Do your meetings have an obvious intention and planned outcome? Set agendas in advance, have a clear purpose in mind.

Are they really, really necessary? Could they be an email or a centralised document people can comment on instead?

What is the best format to have the meeting in? A video meeting, a call, a Slack chat, or in person? Or, how about a virtual campfire in a metaverse space with VR headsets?

Meetings take time away from deep work. So, consider which is more important and more effective for each project or task you're involved in. Ensure you can do what you need to do to achieve your goals and get things done.

How can you ensure that setting aside time and space for focused work becomes a norm in your work culture, even if you're a company of one?

OUR WORK TOOLS

Now let's look at Our Workflows, and how they can help or hinder our outputs.

This next chapter is more reflective than prescriptive.

We're going to consider how your systems and processes are helping you to perform at your best, or hindering your ability to focus.

FIFTEEN
WORKFLOWS

> The best preparation for good work tomorrow is to do good work today.
>
> ~ ELBERT HUBBARD

We are rounding off this section on How We Work by looking at the mechanics of workflows and how you can leverage them to support you better.

The term "workflow' refers to the set of actions used to define, execute and automate our business processes.

A workflow helps you to plan and organise how you begin, work on, and complete your tasks and projects.

Workflows can include activities, information, automation, documents, outputs, and deliverables.

They are meant to help you to work in a more focused, efficient and effective way.

So, according to the notion of intentional productivity, workflows should support your performance, but also your wellbeing.

WORKFLOWS

When we work on our own, or in small teams, we often fill many roles wearing many hats. As part of juggling these roles, it's easy to feel inundated with the amount of varied work tasks we need to complete. This is when having good workflows matters most.

Unsupportive workflows can hinder our ability to perform well at work, and this can have disastrous effects on our productivity and wellbeing. And as we saw in the section on Challenges, a 'hustle culture' style of working inevitably ends up creating unsupportive workflows.

THE MECHANICS OF WORKFLOWS

Before we consider ways to improve your workflow, let's understand the mechanics of workflows and how they connect to the concepts of systems and processes.

SYSTEMS & PROCESSES

- **Your System** is the overall way that you do things. It's the way you run your business and the framework for managing your team, clients, and projects.
- You may also use **an array of systems** (plural) to help you manage Your System.
- **Your Processes** work alongside those systems. Processes are all the things you do to make **Your System** work effectively and efficiently.

These systems and processes help you design, create, produce, sell and distribute your products and services. They enable you to convey your value to your clients or employer.

If you work in the digital realm, we often refer to this as "digital assets" or "content". By that I mean any output designed, created or manipulated by using software applications.

"Content" could be code, a completed website, a fiction eBook, an edited video, a podcast, a 3D graphic, architectural designs, etc.

Whatever it is, that content needs a workflow to help it get made and sent out into the world.

WORKFLOW LAYERS

Workflows typically have three overlapping layers in a digital workplace.

- There's some form of content storage, task database, and/or project management tool relating to this content.
- There's a task list of actions, activities and ToDos associated with producing this content.
- And we use a calendar and/or scheduling tool to designate, allocate and prioritise time for tracking these work activities and content creation tasks.

Depending on the complexity of our needs, we can use a single tool, or multiple applications, to manage these three layers.

DESIGNING A PERSONAL WORKFLOW

> The true method of knowledge is experiment.
>
> ~ WILLIAM BLAKE

Aside from any formal or specific workflows you may use to start, work on and complete tasks, there's also your personal workflow, aka Your System.

Whether you work for yourself or someone else, working with Intentional Productivity in mind requires you to devise a personal workflow.

A personal workflow considers not just your work tasks, but also the other things you need to do in your day to support your wellbeing and productivity AND the other people, things and responsibilities in your life, too.

Our digital calendars can be a powerful ally in supporting our Intentional Productivity and constructing our personal workflow.

Note: To do this effectively, you need to have some control over your calendar, and be able to schedule your tasks in a way that works for you and supports your focus.

Consider how you work best?

- Do you prefer to work on multiple projects in one day?
- Or is it more effective for you to take on a single project for a day or two before starting the next?
- How many tasks can you realistically block off time for (and do) in a day? *(It's usually less than we think)*

Consider the other things that take time in your day?

- Factor in the time needed for things like the school run or walking the dog.
- Can you schedule time for things like self-care practices, solitude, creative thinking, training, social moments, and rest periods within your work day?

Remember, if it's not in the diary, it usually doesn't get done!

How can you schedule your time to suit and incorporate your personal workflow?

Now, let's reflect on what we've covered in this section about How We Work.

After that, the next section is about Leveraging the Opportunities available to us to support more intentionally productive behaviours.

SIXTEEN
REFLECTION EXERCISES NO.3

> We can create opportunities for more intentional productivity when we develop and follow **simpler** workflows and processes.

The aim of this section is to help you identify what elements of your work are important, what matters and what's meaningful.

It will also help you realise which aspects of how you work might negatively affect your productivity and wellbeing. The following exercises will help you gain clarity on where you are right now and what you can do to improve how you work.

Whether you're the one setting your work priorities or someone else is setting them for you, it's important to get clear on what needs to be prioritised.

The essence of Intentional Productivity is to get THE BEST out of yourself and your coworkers, NOT the most.

So, as an individual, or as a team, as you work through these exercises, consider how you can embed wellbeing practices into your workflows as standard practice.

REFLECT - WORK STYLES

Our work styles play a large part in supporting our wellbeing and productivity. Work styles often revolve around the communication culture in our workplaces.

Consider how you work and the impact it has on you and the people you work with.

- Do you / your team currently communicate synchronously, asynchronously, or use a blend of the two?
- Any issues with the existing culture of communication in your workplace? What are they and why?
- Consider ways you can improve your culture around communication and setting boundaries?
- Agree on communication styles that are respectful of each other's space and focus.
- What can you change about your work style, to support you and/or your team better?
- Can you create boundaries without isolating yourself?

RECAP - WORK ENVIRONMENTS

Our working environments, and how we interact with them, influence our wellbeing and productivity. At work, there are 3 aspects at play - physical, digital and locational aspects.

Consider the lighting, layout, noise levels, temperature and air flow in your physical work space. Think about any friction you may experience in your digital workplace environment.

- Identify relevant influencers, habits, activities, behaviours and situational triggers for you in these three areas.
- Which of them supports your focus and productivity?
- What can you do about them if they don't?

LOCATION example:

My desk is located under the air cooling vent, and the cold distracts me and aggravates my sinus condition.

Action: Ask to move desks for health reasons / move your desk.

DIGITAL example:

My team chat online about work all the time, and expect everyone to be involved. I find it disruptive to my work.

Action: Turn off Slack for 2 hours per day.

PHYSICAL example:

I end up sitting for long periods trying to get things done, and my body is stiff when I get up.

Action: Set a timer to get up and move every hour.

REFLECT - WORK TOOLS

Consider which apps, tools and software you use to help you do your work and manage your time and tasks? Make a list.

- How do they connect?
- Do you use them efficiently?
- Do they support you?
- Do they cause any problems?
- How can you improve how you use your tools?
- Are there any unnecessary tools that duplicate the same service?

Action: Draw a mind map of what they help you do and identify any overlaps, redundancies, or repetitive tasks or tools.

Keeping things simple means reducing the amount of tools you need to use in a day.

REFLECT - WORKFLOWS

Workflows are the set of actions we follow when we define, automate, and execute our business processes. They include tasks, information, documents, outputs and deliverables that are passed between you, your clients and your suppliers.

1. What are the key types of work that you do as part of your job or role?

- Examples: design, programming, admin/HR, finances & accounts, proposal creation, quotes, client pitches, running workshops, marketing, finding clients, logistics, research, updates, etc
- Make a detailed list so you are more aware of what takes up your time.
- Also, consider which of these work types you enjoy most and least?

2. Break down the phases of your work/workflow.

- How do you track the process of how you work?
- Who does what?
- How do the phases of your workflow work?
- What's internal / client facing / requires input from people outside of you / the team?
- If you collaborate, with whom, and when? Who does what?
- Is there a bottleneck somewhere? Is it you?
- How can you improve your workflows?

3. Assess your work types and workflows, and your role in your company's workflows.

- Which of these elements do you consider to be deep or shallow work?
- Which of these require you to communicate in real time?

- Which types of work would benefit from you working asynchronously?
- How can you implement more of this style of work?
- Which types of work take the most time?
- Which ones are the most important?
- Which ones do you like / dislike?
- Is there anything you can change about how you do the various elements of your work?

As you do these exercises, consider ways you can change and optimise your systems and processes so that your workflows can support you better.

Action Steps

- Get clear on what needs to be prioritised in terms of workflows.
- Audit your work tools for suitability. Which of them support you best, which ones don't?
- Embed supportive wellbeing practises into your workflows and work styles.

How can you work smarter, more simply, and more sustainably?

HOW YOU WORK & YOUR CADENCE CANVAS

Based on your reflection exercises, review the key elements of your work styles, work environments, work tools, and workflows. Decide what you wish to implement or do more of from now on.

A summary of the outcomes from these exercises you're doing for this section will become part of your canvas.

Your work and personal workflows are the processes that support your overall system. These elements are how you want to work as part of implementing more intentionally productive practices.

REFLECTION EXERCISES NO.3

In the Cadence Canvas Framework™ these elements will sit within the PROCESS section of your framework, which we will compile once we've completed all the reflection exercises in the next part of the book.

In the next section, we're looking at ways to Leverage Opportunities.

We now need to consider things we can incorporate and implement to build the intentional productivity practices that help us transform how we live and work.

We will start with habits and behaviour change and how we can set ourselves up to win from the start.

NOTES

PART FOUR
LEVERAGING OPPORTUNITIES

1. Introduction
2. Challenges
3. How We Work
4. OPPORTUNITIES
5. Focus & Flow
6. Next Steps

SEVENTEEN
HABITS & BEHAVIOUR CHANGE

> Habits are automated solutions that solve the problems and stresses we face regularly.
>
> ~ JAMES CLEAR

In this section about Leveraging Opportunities, we're going to start at the beginning with habits, before looking at the role which mindsets, self-care practices, and cycles of productivity play in supporting our ability to perform at our best, both at work and in the other facets of our life.

To live and work in a more supportive way, we need to build better habits and behaviours to replace the ones that aren't serving us.

So, habits and behaviours sit at the heart of our intentional productivity practices.

Habits have become a popular topic in personal and professional development, fuelled by the work of people such as BJ Fogg *(Tiny Habits)*, James Clear *(Atomic Habits)*, Brendon Burchard *(High Performance Habits)*, and Nir Eyal *(Indistractable)*.

These authors have written extensively about habits and leveraging the components of habit creation to develop more supportive behaviours. I have referenced their work in this chapter, but also in other parts of the book.

If you've read any of these books, you may already be well-versed in the science of behaviour change and habit creation, but I think a refresher is always helpful.

So let's dive in to some science-based info to ensure we're up to speed.

MOTIVATORS FOR MAKING CHANGE

A behaviour is our response to a particular situation or stimulus. It determines why we do or don't take action or make change.

The research shows that there are three typical factors that prompt dramatic or lasting change.

1. Once off epiphanies or life-changing experiences
2. Changes in our environment (external motivations)
3. Changes in our habits (internal motivations)

We may not have control over when an epiphany arrives or how our environments affect us. But there is something within our locus of control.

We have the power to change how our life unfolds by changing our habits.

If you recall, we covered Locus of Control in the chapter about Stress & Stressors. If we become more aware of the drivers of our behaviours, we can take steps to manage our responses better.

WHAT DRIVES BEHAVIOUR?

BJ Fogg is an author and researcher who founded Stanford University's Behaviour Design Lab and created the Tiny Habits program.

In his book *'Tiny Habits - The Small Changes that Change Everything'*, BJ shares the FOGG Behaviour Model to describe how our behaviours develop.

The FOGG Behaviour Model:

B = MAP (Behaviour = Motivation + Ability + Prompt)

When the **motivation** to do something converges with a **prompt** to do that thing, and we have the **ability** to carry out the action needed to do that thing, the outcome that results is a behaviour.

As I mentioned in a previous chapter, all motivation is a desire to escape perceived discomfort and to ease perceived pain.

When we experience pain or discomfort, we are driven to change our state.

It's our habits and behaviours that help us achieve that change in state. If a behaviour was previously effective in alleviating discomfort, then we repeat it.

For example:

- If we reach for our mobile phone and/or dive into social media to avoid what we perceive as a stressful work activity, it can become a habit to do that every time we feel stressed about work.
- Then it becomes an autopilot behaviour or response. It turns into a habit.

Let's consider how and why this happens.

HABIT CREATION 101

> **Habits are behaviours we develop into mental shortcuts. They are a way for our brains to free up mental space and reduce our cognitive load.**

We apply them in new and future scenarios that share similar challenges to situations we've previously faced.

If the behaviour worked to solve that problem in the past, then chances are it will work again in this new, but similar situation.

So, to save time and cognitive energy, we default to that behaviour and it becomes an automated response in any situation that feels similar, *even* when the response *may not* be appropriate.

MAKING HABITS STICK

There are three elements that make it easier to create and cement habits.

1. Repetition

It's the frequency with which you perform an action, and not the time it takes, that builds the neural pathway which makes that habit become second nature.

The more you repeat an action or behaviour the more easily it becomes second nature to do when you aren't thinking.

2. Stable Context

If the context keeps changing, then so does the behaviour associated with it.

So, to build a supportive habit, you need a reliable environment in which to perform a repeated behaviour.

3. Positive Emotions

There's a saying that *'you gather more bees with honey than vinegar'*. The same is true for habit building (and the studies confirm it).

We are more likely to keep doing something - whether it involves eating sweets or going to the gym - if it makes us feel good.

We repeat things that give us satisfaction, joy, fullness, wellbeing, comfort, bliss, etc.

HABITS & BEHAVIOUR CHANGE

Essentially, we are seeking ways to increase the chances of a dopamine hit.

HABIT CREATION COMPONENTS

In order to change our habits, we need to understand the "technical elements" of habits in action.

It involves 4 steps:

Cue >> Craving >> Response >> Reward

1. **Cue** - The trigger that leads us to noticing a potential reward.
2. **Craving** - We have an emotional desire to achieve the reward.
3. **Response** - We perform the habit to get the reward.
4. **Reward** - It changes our state. (the habit's end goal).

A reminder that this change in state is fuelled by our need to avoid pain and discomfort and seek pleasure and comfort. So, the change we seek as our reward has to make us feel good in some way.

This is the case, even if the way we achieve that pleasure or comfort through avoidant or harmful behaviour that affects our long-term wellbeing or productivity.

CREATING GOOD HABITS VS CHANGING BAD HABITS

Let's consider ways we can leverage these four steps in building better habits.

As James Clear explores in his book *Atomic Habits,* there are ways we can leverage the four habit execution steps of *cue > craving > response > reward* to bring about behaviour change.

We can make it easier to create good habits that we feel more inclined to repeat. And we can create friction around unsupportive habits, so that we feel less inclined to do them.

Here are some examples...

1. CUE - Make Triggers Visible or Invisible

Make what motivates you to perform a habit more or less obvious.

Examples:

- If the goal is to stay hydrated during your workday, place a jug of water and a glass on your desk, so that it is a visible reminder to drink water.
- If you want to stop using your phone as much during work time, make the phone <u>less</u> visible. Turn off notifications and put it in your drawer or behind you.

2. CRAVING - Reframe Desired Outcomes - Attractive vs Unattractive

This is our emotional desire to achieve the reward that comes with carrying out a behaviour. How can we reframe the purpose of the habit so that we feel more or less inclined to carry out the action?

Examples:

- If I eat that extra chocolate bar, it's going to make my skin break out and make me feel hyper, so I can't focus. If I don't, I'll feel less grumpy later, and have a healthy glow for the party this weekend.
- If I do a great job with these presentations, instead of procrastinating every time by diving into social media, then that will create a good impression with my new manager. I can mention it at my next performance review, and that might lead to a raise!

3. RESPONSE - Make the Action Easy or Difficult

How can you make your response to your cue or craving more accessible or more challenging to do?

HABITS & BEHAVIOUR CHANGE

Examples:

- Lay out your exercise clothes and your yoga mat in a visible place the night before, to make using them first thing in the morning easier to do.
- Hide the sweet snacks and put healthy ones at eye level in your go-to snack spot.
- After every use, delete your social media apps from your phone or remove them from your laptop, so that every time you're tempted to use them, you have to reinstall them and log in. *(This sounds drastic, but if you have a problem with social media, it's one way of initiating a habit change in how you use these apps)*

4. REWARD - Is it Satisfying or Unsatisfying?

Habit change also requires changing our mindset about what serves us and what doesn't.

How can you reframe a short-lived pleasure into something which you can accept isn't helpful to you in the long run? What is more important than the short-term reward?

Examples:

- Every time you complete your daily exercise, remind yourself of how good it makes you feel the next day and how you are likely to sleep better tonight.
- Every time you want to reach for a bag of sweets, remind yourself of why it might not be a suitable response in this instance. What is a better way to respond? Avoid the guilty feeling by thinking in terms of positive outcomes.
- If we know that the rush we get from eating a bag of doughnuts is short-lived, but has far-reaching repercussions (*"once on the lips, twice on the hips", as they say*), what is a better activity to support us that will be more satisfying? It might be eating fruit or a lower calorie sweet snack. Perhaps it isn't

sugar we need at all. Maybe what we really desire in that moment is actually more hugs from our family? Dig deeper!

THE HABIT OF DISTRACTION

Our habits can support us or hinder us. But once they become ingrained, it becomes a challenge to change them.

Our biggest challenge to developing good, consistent habits and behaviours around the way we work is distraction.

As mentioned in previous chapters, our modern world has led to a distracted workforce. Our concentration is compromised, our focus is fractured and we've learned how to procrastinate like pros.

Distraction from all the uncertainties we face is a daily occurrence and we engage in a myriad of behaviours to avoid our discomfort.

Our satisfaction is temporary, so we often seek other ways to ease the discomfort, distracting ourselves even further. Anything that stops discomfort can become addictive.

The immediate reward we get for being distracted is a decrease in pain, but the long-term repercussions are that our productivity stalls and we get nothing done well, which arguably causes more pain.

Managing our time and our performance better is essentially a pain management exercise.

When we know the drivers of our behaviour, we can take steps to manage them better to reduce that pain. This is why developing our self-awareness skills is an important part of intentional productivity.

If we want to develop better habits to overcome distraction, we need to deal with the discomfort that comes with changing our habits. And that's where your grit mindset comes in, helping you persevere in making change.

I will talk more about mindsets in the next chapter.

HABITS & BEHAVIOUR CHANGE

Your personal system for intentional productivity takes time and practice to implement. It may need to be adjusted as your personal and work requirements change.

The important thing is to start small, so that the change is manageable and the level of discomfort is tolerable.

Changing our behaviours to support better performance requires focus and discipline, consistency in our actions, and also managing our environment.

- Cultivate a strong, self-aware mindset. This will contribute to your productive staying power and adaptability.
- Practice being more proactive and less reactive. Work on becoming more aware of the triggers and prompts that cause you to perform certain 'automatic' behaviours.
- Design and adjust your environments to support your habits and behaviours better.
- Make small (tiny) manageable habit changes that compound.

How can you leverage this knowledge about your habits to your advantage? What supportive habits are more rewarding to do? What unsupportive habits can you create friction around doing?

So, we've considered the science of habit creation and what we can do to make new habits stick. Creating new habits doesn't work in isolation though.

Making change also requires the right mindset to help you get there.

Up next, we'll be delving into Mindsets and the impact they have on our productivity.

From self-awareness to scarcity, grit to abundance, how our mind sees the world affects our drive, outlook, performance and success.

Understanding and leveraging supportive mindsets is essential for our wellbeing, creativity and productivity.

EIGHTEEN
MINDSETS FOR INTENTIONAL PRODUCTIVITY

> Your mindset matters. It affects everything - from the business and investment decisions you make, to the way you raise your children, to your stress levels and overall wellbeing.
>
> ~ PETER DIAMANDIS

Our habits and autopilot behaviours can dictate how productive we are at work. Our mindset also influences our outputs and performance. How we see the world can make us open up to opportunities and expansive thinking, or close us down and limit our thinking.

A mindset encompasses our set of attitudes, disposition, and philosophy on life. It's the frame of mind we cultivate because of our social influences and cultural values.

How we were raised and what we are exposed to in our environments can influence and create our mindset.

However, our mindset is not cast on stone.

MINDSETS FOR INTENTIONAL PRODUCTIVITY

When we work to develop our self-awareness - by doing things like building strong foundations and being more intentional in our daily actions - we can alter our mindset to support us even better.

We can also have more than one mindset or mindset approach for different aspects of our work and lives.

Having an open, determined mindset makes the difference between building the habit of intentional productivity because you appreciate the long-term outcomes. Or, giving up after a week or two, resigning yourself to being stuck on the treadmill of hustle culture.

> During my burnout, when I was in the depths of depression, I was very much stuck in a rigid way of thinking, preoccupied with scarcity, and crippled by the fear in my mind. It felt impossible for me to make any forward progress in my life. However, I finally accepted I needed to change my mindset, or I was going to be stuck in this quicksand of despair forever.
>
> At first, it felt like a mammoth undertaking to shift my mood and outlook from seeing my life as empty to seeing the glass half full. But, between my gratitude journaling practice and reinforcing my mottos of "What if I can" and "Tomorrow is another day", I found I could flip the script one day at a time in what turned out to be a manageable way.
>
> I started believing that "I was the kind of person who could follow through", who was capable of getting myself out of this place. And before I knew it, the glass wasn't only half full, it was full to the brim with possibility!

Remember, you have a choice in the matter, and your mindset affects how that choice will play out.

Let's consider aspects of building strong, positive mindsets that can help us on the path to developing our intentional productivity practices.

SELF-ACCEPTANCE

Excessive stress can lead to a negative self image, and both create barriers to activating our potential.

So we need to work on creating an open, resilient and accepting mindset to ensure we can follow through with our intentions.

How we respond to people says more about us than them. If we want healthy relationships with others, where we're able to communicate clearly, we need to start by having a healthy relationship with "I".

When we don't believe in ourselves, we are the obstacle to our improvement, progression, and connection.

When we're striving to make change, we're usually starting from a place of dissatisfaction.

During this transition, there will be times where the part we don't like has to tag along with the part we're trying to get to.

Self-acceptance involves feeling that we are enough, even when we are a work in progress.

To love others well and have them love us back, we first need to at least like (and eventually love) our SELVES, warts and all. That means we need to learn to be kind to ourselves. We need to train our inner dialogue to be a friendly, supportive voice of encouragement, instead of a harsh, screeching critic berating us for our failings.

Even when we're not quite where we want to be yet, being pragmatically optimistic about our capabilities leads to positivity within and positive interactions with others.

As Mel Robbins mentions in her book, *The High Five Habit*, we can't find the love we need from others if we don't first seek it within.

Now, most of us are hugely uncomfortable with saying things like "I love you" to ourselves in the mirror, but what is doable is giving yourself a high five in the mirror, and telling yourself that you've got this, even if you don't feel strong, beautiful or invincible today.

MINDSETS FOR INTENTIONAL PRODUCTIVITY

Imagine what life would be like if you accepted who you are and where you are... right at this moment... with no excuses?

- What if — despite any obstacles you're facing (internal or external) — you could still do what you needed and wanted to do with your life?
- Would you do it? Would you at least try?

A big difference between the 'you' you are now and the 'you' in that better life you want is your view of yourself.

When we live and give from a place of love and grace — which starts by accepting ourselves — it resonates out into the world and invites new possibilities back in.

If we're able to bring a calm confidence in our abilities and ourselves into our work, we can produce incredible things that connect more deeply with others. This connection is because we make these things with love.

When you're experiencing self doubt, ask yourself the question: "What if I can?".

Making changes you are in control of can only start with you. We have to take action to create the motivation to continue.

- So make a habit of asking: What if I can?
- If you can visualise yourself doing it or being it (despite where you are right now)… then it means you can!

Find small ways to follow through and do what "you can".

Build the habit of accepting that you can achieve great things by starting with the person you are right now.

By repeatedly and consistently taking small action steps over time, you then become more of the person you want to be.

Remember, the glass is always full. Full of possibility. It starts with where you are now, and accepting who you are now.

MINDSETS FOR SKILLS DEVELOPMENT

When we're making changes to the way we work, we have to learn new ways of doing things. It takes practice and it can feel challenging, especially at the start.

> As Robin Sharma says in his book *The 5am Club*:
>
> "All change is hard at first, messy in the middle, and gorgeous at the end."

Our ability, talent, and intelligence are not fixed. This means we're able to get better at doing difficult things when we're willing to put in the work.

When learning new things, it's helpful to accept that you may be a beginner in this new area, despite being accomplished in others.

Having a beginner's mindset opens your mind up to learning new things. When you think you already know all there is to know, that closes your mind down.

The best way to embed new behaviours when we are starting something new is to break our habit goals down into smaller steps. A beginner mindset can help with this.

THE BEGINNER MINDSET

Looking at our situation with fresh eyes can help us understand our context better and make change more easily.

The concept of "beginner's mind" originally comes from Zen Buddhism. It forms an important foundation in the practice of mindfulness. It simply means to adopt an approach where you see the world as if for the first time, like a child would, without bias, judgement or opinion.

Using beginner's mind as a guide, there are three overlapping mindsets we can employ as we develop our intentional productivity.

STEP 1: A TRAINING MINDSET

We activate this as we implement and practice new habits and routines.

- Imagine what you want to be like with these new behaviours.
- Visualise yourself working in a better way and being more focused and productive. What does that look like?
- This creates a positive imprint in your mind, as it builds neural pathways around what's possible.
- The more you train your mind to see yourself doing the hard thing, the easier it becomes for you to do and repeat these behaviours in your physical world.

STEP 2: A TRUSTING MINDSET

A trusting mindset involves having faith in yourself as you start physically performing what you've already practiced in your mind.

- Believe that you've got what it takes to do your best, based on the practice that you've put in.
- It's ok if you don't know how to do something. As part of accepting and trusting yourself, you know you've got what it takes to figure it out.
- You know you can do hard things!

STEP 3: A LEARNING MINDSET

Review your performance outcomes using a learning mindset.

This means being curious, instead of being critical, open and eager to learn from both your successes and your mistakes.

- When you don't get something quite right, that's ok. It's not a failure. Instead, see it as feedback.
- What can you learn from it, to course correct and improve over time? How can things be better next time?

- Ask yourself questions about how these new productivity-focused behaviours feel?
- Are they working, or do they need work?
- How can you make your productivity system better as you go, day by day?

Improving our performance requires that we get to know ourselves, so that we can lead ourselves better and engage in supportive behaviours more consistently.

There are two other mindsets that I want to share with you that can help or affect your intentional productivity practice.

SCARCITY VS ABUNDANCE MINDSET

> Wealth is wellbeing and prosperity in the form of money, caring, and service of yourself and others.
>
> ~ ROB MOORE

Our brains default to a scarcity mindset, because our minds are always assessing risk. It's just part of how our brains have developed to keep us safe. The downside is that a scarcity mindset can stir up limiting beliefs.

It's a common misconception that to be truly successful, you have to work more to earn more. As part of that approach and journey, there is something that has to be sacrificed. Most often, it's your wellbeing.

Making money, being successful and achieving a healthy rhythm in your work and life are not mutually exclusive.

The word 'wealth' comes from an Olde English phrase meaning "the condition of wellbeing". If we see wealth and success as more than just a material pursuit, it helps us work with more of an abundance mindset.

MINDSETS FOR INTENTIONAL PRODUCTIVITY

SCARCITY MINDSET

Seeing the world through a lens of scarcity means that when we gain, someone else loses.

A scarcity mindset puts us at a disadvantage because it makes us feel there isn't enough, and there will never be enough… whether "enough" is money, food, recognition, customers, and so on.

Examples of Scarcity Mindset:

- "There's too many people competing with me in this niche. There won't be enough customers for me to have a successful business and client base."
- "I could never price my work that high!"
- "If I don't take this project, another one isn't going to come along soon."
- "There isn't enough time to do my [dream activity], I've got too much on already."
- "I never get a break, I will never be able to start my [dream business]."

These probably sound familiar, as we've all found ourselves in situations where defaulting to a scarcity mindset was the natural thing to do in the circumstances. However, a scarcity mindset closes us down to opportunities.

It's forces a negative or pessimistic viewpoint on circumstances, and results in avoidant behaviour which doesn't always stand us in good stead.

ABUNDANCE MINDSET

An abundance mindset focuses on the profusion of opportunities available to us.

When we look at the world through the lens of abundance, we see that there are enough resources, enough customers, enough time and enough love for everyone, despite the challenges, competition and threats we may face in our work, our life and the world at large.

Examples of Abundance Mindset:

- "It's a competitive niche, but we all have different things to offer, and there are enough customers to go around."
- "If I price my work high, that gives me more room and my clients more opportunities, as I can then spend money on product development and offer special rates for repeat clients."
- "This project isn't the right fit for me. Although the money is good, the way they work doesn't align with my values, and I know that will cause me extra stress. So I'm going to create the room for a better fitting project to come my way."
- "If I keep working at a steady pace, and I keep trying new things, eventually one of my ideas is going to stick and I will have the success I'm dreaming of."

Being abundant in our thinking helps us to think more expansively. It opens the door to opportunities, collaboration, and innovation. It requires that we look at the world with an optimistic view.

It's easy to fall into a scarcity mindset when we face so many challenges in the world. However, despite these challenges, there is always hope.

As the Stoics say, "the obstacle is the way". There is always a way through, or another way to do things.

We are smart, creative thinkers and problem solvers, especially when we're able to focus our time and attention on what matters. And that means there are plentiful ways in which we can approach our lives and our work without it negatively affecting those around us. There's enough to go around.

The thing that may limit our growth is a fixed mindset.

FIXED MINDSET VS GROWTH MINDSET

Your view of yourself and your abilities can affect how you do everything.

The concepts of fixed and growth mindsets were coined by Carol Dweck, a psychologist and pioneering researcher in the field of motivation. In her seminal book *Mindset - Changing The Way You Think To Fulfil Your Potential*, she delves into how the way we think about ourselves affects how we fulfil our potential.

According to Carol Dweck, success <u>does not</u> come from intelligence, talent or education, even though these can help. Instead, success comes from our mindset around improvement and problem solving.

Let's look at how these types of mindset play out.

FIXED MINDSET

We believe that our intelligence is static, that we can't improve, and that we are incapable of change. This fixed mindset limits our success, as when things feel too hard, we tend to give up rather than persevere.

Examples:

- "I'll never learn how to speak French."
- "I'm useless with maths-type stuff!"
- "This situation is never going to change!"

GROWTH MINDSET

We understand we can develop our intelligence and that we are capable of change and improvement. With a growth mindset, we know that if we keep trying, we will improve. We put learning over approval and are more willing to persevere despite setbacks.

Examples:

- "This coding is hard, but if I keep at it, then I know I will eventually get it right."
- "This situation seems impossible, but I bet there's another way to approach this."
- "If I can climb a volcano in the dark, then I can definitely do this presentation!" (true story)

We can have both fixed and growth mindsets in different areas of our life or work.

Having a fixed or growth mindset in a particular area will affect how we respond to challenges, obstacles, effort, criticism and success in that area.

A growth mindset focuses on mastery through practice and persistence. It's an essential viewpoint to have to improve our productivity and performance.

When we understand we are inherently capable of change, we can develop and leverage our growth mindset.

It goes back to that simple question: What if I can? Then I know I can!

GRIT MINDSET

A Grit Mindset can help us build resilience, get through challenging times, and keep going so that we can succeed. Grit is a key performance indicator for success and it's _not_ linked to talent.

Psychologist and author Angela Duckworth conducted hundreds of studies to uncover what gives a person grit.

To develop your grit, you need a combination of passion and perseverance.

A growth mindset helps to build your grit mindset. This is because you know that your ability to learn is not fixed, and that with effort and perseverance, you can change your situation.

If we want to master distraction, we need to learn to deal with the discomfort that comes with changing our habits. That's where your grit mindset comes in.

Having a grit mindset regarding your productivity and outputs is about developing the stamina to pursue and adhere to your long-term goals.

It's also about building a solid work ethic. Through the lens of intentional productivity, that work ethic includes making time for rest and recovery.

Your personal system for intentional productivity takes time and practice to implement. And it may need to be adjusted and adapted as your personal and work requirements change.

Cultivating your grit mindset will contribute to your productive staying power, resilience and adaptability.

MOODS & MINDSET

> It is hard to do your best thinking when your mind isn't at peace.
>
> ~ BRAD STULBERG & STEVE MAGNESS

When we're in a negative mood, it inhibits our abilities to work on complex problems and be creative. Research using FMRI scans has revealed that when we're in a calm and positive state, we're more able to solve "challenging intellectual problems with creative insight".

Negative mental states can involve feeling tired, demotivated, angry, or anxious. They may also arise from having to interact with unsupportive people, or be in toxic places.

As mentioned in the section covering stress and burnout, if you're dealing with heightened recurring workplace stress, it's going to have a dampening mood on your mindset and your performance.

You may not have control over the external circumstances, but you can change your emotional state by focusing on improving your mood.

Become more aware of how your moods impact on your ability to work well.

For example, if I'm feeling irritable or emotional, it makes my busy mind go into agitated overdrive. When I'm in a bad mood, I find it challenging to come up with new ideas or write creatively because my focus is affected.

In situations like this, I have to change my emotional state. Exposing myself to something that makes me smile or laugh helps to break the tension I may feel, so that I can focus more clearly. As mentioned in the chapter on Stress, I can also change my emotional state by changing my physical state, and I usually do this by walking or dancing.

We will explore other ways to change our mood in the next chapter.

In the meantime, consider…

What can you do to limit or prevent negativity from influencing you and your day? If you are experiencing a case of the grumbles or feeling agitated, what can you do to adjust a negative mood?

Now that we're brimming with positive minds and 'can do' attitudes, let's look at other opportunities we can incorporate to transform our habits and behaviours more intentionally.

In the next chapter, the focus is on why we need to Build Strong Foundations to help us transform our lives for the better.

There are four cornerstones to building firm foundations which support our wellbeing and the practice of intentional productivity. Can you guess what they are?

NINETEEN
BUILDING STRONG FOUNDATIONS

> " The first wealth is health.
>
> ~ RALPH WALDO EMERSON

My burnout created immense turmoil in my mind and body.

I'd wake up at 1.30am and stare at the ceiling for 2 hours, then again at 4.30am when I would cry in despair or have a panic attack, frustrated by sleep eluding me and my problems crowding my mind. Then I'd feel totally whacked when I woke at 8am, and struggle to get focused before 9 or 10!

My anxiety and high stress levels meant I was eating erratically and craving sugar. I had inflammation in my body, with food intolerances and skin sensitivities going into overdrive. I also developed a stomach ulcer and gut health issues. When money became a problem, I would default to more affordable options that usually involved more processed foods and refined carbs, and less healthy choices. Not exactly a recipe for success!

During this fractious time before I started my road to recovery, I was in such a discombobulated state that my self-care and wellness practices were severely lacking, causing my stress-coping mechanisms to falter and my resilience to become severely depleted.

To handle the challenges we face daily, it's important that we find ways to maintain our stress management skills and keep building our resilience.

We've already looked at the role of stress and stressors, and what we can do about them, in the Challenges section. In this chapter, we're looking at wellbeing and productivity through the lens of resilience.

Mental, emotional, and physical resilience are rooted in good health and wellness practices.

The studies show that high-performing professionals, driven entrepreneurs, and cohesive teams thrive and endure over the long-term, because they build firm physical, mental, emotional and environmental foundations.

Strong foundations also form the cornerstones for creating cadence and building a supportive Intentional productivity practice. It's why FOUNDATIONS sit at the base of the Cadence Canvas Framework™.

THE 4 KEYSTONES

There are 4 areas where we can focus our attention to make small improvements that have far-reaching effects, not just on our health and wellbeing, but also on our productivity and performance.

1. Sleep
2. Breathing
3. Movement
4. Nutrition

These self-care fundamentals are all equally important as they're interlinked. Doing something in one area will affect the others. In fact, one small positive change in one keystone area can help our bodies bear the load of life better across all of them.

This means you <u>don't</u> have to dive into making change in all of them at once, which can be overwhelming and prevent you from progressing.

When overhauling your habits and making positive change, the point is to start somewhere. It can be anywhere within these keystone areas. You just need to make a start.

The bonus is that picking one area to improve in has knock-on effects, leading you to make positive changes more easily in the other areas, too.

Note: I've listed the keystones in the order I think is most helpful when getting started on making improvements. When you make your changes, you can choose to begin with any of them, although I highly recommend starting with sleep, and you'll see why.

1. SLEEP

Sleep is our biggest defence against the effects of hyper-connectivity, the dark arts of digital, and threats to our health and wellbeing.

We all know by now that a good night's sleep sets up us for the rest of our day.

The recommended daily sleep allowance to function at our optimum is between 7 and 9 hours, and many high-performing athletes aim for 10.

Yet, most of us are chronically sleep deprived!

What you might not know is all the other good things that sleep helps our bodies and minds do. Getting more zees is the thing we should focus on first to build up our resilience.

THE CADENCE EFFECT

Here's why.

- Sleep helps our body to heal from the daily stresses and strains we encounter. It performs a housekeeping function, cleaning out the plaques and waste that collect in our body and brain.
- It also helps us cement the memories and learning that have taken place during our day.

Sleep is also the number one body function that supports the maintenance of our immune system defences.

After the effects of the pandemic, we all know how important it is to build, strengthen and maintain our immunity. So sleep is the most important factor in ensuring our good health and wellbeing over the long haul.

I'm covering a few sleep basics here, but if you're interested in diving deep on sleep, then I recommend Dr Matthew Walker's book 'Why We Sleep' or The Matt Walker Podcast.

SLEEP 101

> A ruffled mind makes for a restless pillow.
>
> ~ CHARLOTTE BRONTË

Less than at least 7 hours of regular zees makes us crabby dimwits (literally)!

Anxiety, depression, or a busy mind can cause our sleep to become disrupted. When we're regularly not getting enough sleep, it compromises our immune system.

A lack of sleep also raises our stress hormones and limits our cognitive function.

These effects can take hold after even just one night of poor sleep, and the elevated stress it puts on our bodies in turn leads to more poor nights of sleep, which can become a vicious cycle.

Sleep deprivation can cause crazy moods, poor memory, bad decisions, weight gain, early wrinkles, the equivalent of drunk driver behaviour, and even scarier health issues too, such as heart disease, Alzheimer's and dementia.

It's not just how long we sleep, but also how well we sleep.

While a comfortable mattress, a cool room, and blackout curtains can play a role, good sleep starts with our habits <u>before</u> bedtime.

Late night screen time or stimulants at the wrong time wreak havoc with our sleep patterns. But when we create healthier rituals at night, we become so much better in our days.

Our sleep-wake cycles are driven by our circadian rhythms, which are affected by things like the amount of light exposure we get at certain times of the day, our body temperature, and the release of cortisol throughout the day.

How you wake up also determines how your day goes.

When we wake naturally, we move from the delta brainwave stage of sleep through the gentle waking states of theta and alpha before becoming fully awake in beta state.

> Checking your phone immediately upon waking forces the brain to skip the important theta and alpha stages, priming your brain for distraction.
>
> ~NEUROHACKER

Good sleep hygiene habits can include the following actions:

- Avoid stimulants like coffee or energy drinks after 2pm.
- Turn off bright lights 2-3 hours before bed.

- Stop using your laptop or blue-light devices at least 1-2 hours before bed.
- Make your bedroom a sanctuary, with no TV or phone use.
- Have a warm bath and/or do meditation before bed to relax your body.
- Get bright light (preferably natural light) on your skin and in your eyes in the first 1-2 hours of your day.
- Moderate exercise and meditation every day also support healthy sleep.

So, think about putting your pillow first for a change.

How can you prepare your body and mind for sleep, so that you can make the most of your time spent horizontal?

Note: I discuss circadian rhythms, sleep cycles, and chronotypes in more detail in the next chapter on Cycles of Productivity.

2. BREATHING

As breathing happens automatically, we forget about it. But paying attention to our breathing is one of the most reliable ways to change our mind and body for the better.

Our breath is our life force. It affects our state of being through every little cell in our body.

Good breathing supports our mood, sleep, focus, immunity and stress response, plus a host of other bodily functions.

When we don't breathe properly, the organs and cells that support us don't get what they need to help us function optimally.

- We feel our best when we're taking 5 to 6 deep, slow belly breaths a minute, but we tend to breathe faster, shorter, and shallower, especially when we're stressed.
- Breathing through our nose is better for our overall health, as long-term mouth breathing (especially at night) has been associated with conditions such as high blood pressure, gum

disease and poor oral health, digestive issues and chronic fatigue, as well as sleep apnoea which is a dangerous health condition.

When we feel stressed or anxious, we're usually running on fumes, but that's when we need oxygen the most.

Intentional breathing practices help us create a more relaxed or energised state from which to live and work.

CONSCIOUS BREATHING

Conscious breathing is where we control our 'in' and 'out' breaths for a set period. We can use focused breathing as part of a meditation practice. *(I cover meditation and productivity in an upcoming chapter).*

You can also leverage your breath as a simple resetting tool to help you change your state and get more focused. It helps you quickly release stress and get on with your day.

Here are four ways you can practise conscious breathing:

1. Simple Reset Breaths

If you're short on time, consciously inhaling and exhaling for a minute helps to clear your head of busy thoughts and calm your system.

- Slowly inhale and exhale through your nose 3-5 times, with your eyes closed or your gaze softened, to reduce external stimuli.

2. The Physiological Sigh

If you're feeling anxious or stressed, the physiological sigh is the quickest way to reset and activate your parasympathetic nervous system.

- It involves 2 inhales through the nose to open up the chest and belly, before a long exhale through the nose or mouth to release, clearing all the oxygen from your lungs. Do this 3 times slowly.

3. Four-Seven-Eight Breathing

If you're struggling with insomnia, 4-7-8 breathing is known to help slow the rapid breathing and fast heart rate associated with anxiety, to calm our system, reduce anxious thoughts, ease depressive moods and improve our ability to fall asleep.

- Exhale through your mouth with a whoosh, with your tongue held up behind your front teeth. Close your mouth and inhale through your nose for a count of 4. Hold for a count of 7. Exhale through your mouth with a whoosh sound for a count of 8. Repeat the process 4 times in total.

4. Box Breathing

If you have 3-5 minutes, you can do box breathing, also known as four count breathing.

- Inhale through the nose for 4 slow counts, pause for 4, exhale through the nose for 4, hold for 4. Continue at as slow a pace as your lung capacity allows, for 3-5 minutes.

There are several other breathing techniques rooted in ancient traditions that you can also use, but these are good starting points.

Breathing through our nose instead of our mouth is more beneficial for supporting our mind and body.

- The smaller size of our nostrils means we can control the speed of air flow and quantities we intake and exhale more easily, which helps to regulate our system.
- The hairs in our nose filter unwanted dust and irritants, improving the quality of the air we take in.
- The mucus in our nose moistens the air, making it easier for our lungs to process.

BUILDING STRONG FOUNDATIONS

It's healthier to breathe through your nose not just when you're awake, but also during sleep. The more you breathe nasally during your day, the more you train your body to do so at night.

Breathe deep, breathe slow, live long.

Try out these simple breathing practices to see which works best for you. Consider how you can build them into your day.

Note: We'll revisit breathing in the next section about Preparing for Focus and Flow, where we also consider meditation as a powerful productivity tool.

3. MOVEMENT

From an evolutionary perspective, our bodies are built for moving, not sitting for long periods. But putting our bums first has become our norm, and it's literally a killer.

Sedentary lifestyles, which include sitting at our desks for long periods of time, cause all kinds of health issues — from stiff necks, rounded posture, and sore backs, to weight gain, heart disease, and blood clots, irrespective of your age.

A lack of mobility has a knock-on effect as we age, but often we only start addressing the issue when the creaks and the cracks start to show and begin affecting on our ability to move, to work and to live.

Our physical framework is like our best mate.

Our body is our built-in partner, supporting us in life. But to rely on our body, we need to take care of it too, by making the most of our body's natural movement abilities.

Regular movement helps to keep our muscles primed and toned and it supports the health of our bones. The sooner we can make movement a foundation of how we live, the better off our bodies will be in the long run.

Our modern lifestyles, including how we work, are threatening our life span and our health span.

We know fitness is important for us and the latest findings are that we need to be incorporating a variety of different types and styles of exercise into our weeks, spanning cardio, strength training and high-intensity movements.

The great thing is that we have so many options to choose from that we can certainly move in a way that we can enjoy. Your favourite movements might be walking, running, yoga, pilates, cycling, swimming, rowing, gym work, weights, HIIT, martial arts, dancing, and so much more!

With exercise, for most of us, that means doing something before or after work. But we can (and should) stay limber during our workday too, and a good place to start is with what I call *mini movements*.

Mini movements are simple and easy to do — once or twice an hour, get up and move your butt!

- 2 minutes of stretches or Qi Gong movements to keep your limbs limber
- Some push ups against the desk or kitchen counter
- Star jumps or walking up and down the stairs to get your heart rate up
- A quick walk around the block to get your legs moving
- Crank up a tune for some kitchen disco while the kettle boils

Whatever works for you, mini movements are like a reset for the body, helping it to recalibrate before we go back to sitting.

Building strength, facilitating mobility and improving stability are key factors in creating vitality, increasing longevity, and enhancing our lifestyles.

It's the little movements and efforts over time that keep you and your body in tune. Not only will your butt thank you, but your heart and mind will, too.

How can you introduce simple mini movements into your workday and build the habit of doing it regularly?

How do you like to keep fit - how can you do more of it in a manageable way?

4. NUTRITION

> Chronic, low-level inflammation seems to be the root cause of most serious diseases that kill and disable people prematurely, and the mainstream diet promotes inflammation.
>
> ~ DR ANDREW WEIL

Nutrition is the power smoothie in our self-care pack because proper nourishment supports us mentally, physically, and emotionally.

What goes into our gut affects our brain function, our behaviour and every part of our body, inside and out. Our gut is also known as *our "second brain"*.

In fact, the gut produces more neurotransmitters that send messages to the brain than vice versa.

According to Dr Calum Moulton, a psychiatrist interviewed by The Guardian for a piece on gut health:

> A full one-third of the world has some sort of disorder of gut-brain interaction. That might sound surprising, but that includes things like IBS, as well as many patients with persistent heartburn, constipation or pain. The gut and the brain as so closely linked, you do need to take both into account.
>
> ~ DR CALUM MOULTON

Looking after our gut improves our mood and our overall health.

Whether you are vegan, Paleo or flexitarian, or if you eat 3 traditional meals or fast intermittently, these are all choices that we make based on our lifestyle, culture and beliefs.

Choice is good, but when our lives are busy and stressed, we make our nutritional choices on autopilot. When the going gets tough, this can turn us into sugar-crazed doughnut junkies or head-bitingly "hangry" zombies.

The first step in improving nutrition is literally to listen to your gut. Understand how what you eat and drink affects your body and mind.

A few examples of how our nutritional consumption can affect our wellbeing:

- **An excess of sugar** (in all forms) and **additives** such as nitrates/nitrites (found in processed meat) are both known to poison our system and cause cancer.

- **Gluten** causes 'brain fog', inflammation and gut health issues, and can trigger a dangerous autoimmune response for those with coeliac disease.

- **Dairy** can affect our skin and gut in the same way, too.

- **Alcohol** contains sugar and hollow calories, as well as histamines, yeast and sulphites, all of which can stimulate allergy responses such as rosacea, hay fever, or asthma. Alcohol has also been shown to damage the brain.

- **Transfats** in junk foods, crisps, baked goods and processed foods line our arteries with gunk and cause cardiovascular issues such as atherosclerosis and heart disease.

- **Additives** and **bulking agents** can mimic or disrupt the hormones in our body, cause gut irritation, or result in us producing more visceral fat as our body's built-in insulin management system goes doolally.

BUILDING STRONG FOUNDATIONS

- **Phytoestrogens** (found in soy products and elsewhere) mimic and influence the oestrogen levels in our body, affecting things like our menstrual cycle. They can also cause cancer or man boobs, or increase our hunger, so we eat more.

- We are ingesting **heavy metals**, **forever chemicals**, and **microplastics** via our bottled water, seafood and other foods. As they break down, they release chemicals and toxins that are poisoning our system and affecting our brain function, never mind the larger environment around us.

The onset of allergy-type responses in the body means our body's immune system is fighting something it thinks is an enemy.

Food intolerances and autoimmune diseases are on the rise because of the impact that pollution, pesticides, forever chemicals, and processed foods are having on our physical systems.

All that internal battling to maintain balance takes energy away from other body and brain functions. The knock-on effect of poor nutrition is that we can't focus properly and we are less productive.

So we need to do whatever is within our power to combat the effects of these things. What is within our control is making healthier food choices, lowering / cutting alcohol intake, and eating more mindfully.

We gain power by eating for strength, energy and immunity, and nurturing the garden of good bacteria in our gut.

Water, nutrient-dense foods, and meals with a plant-based focus, are all good friends for our gut. To help our bodies operate at their optimum, we need to fuel our mitochondria (the energy cells in our body) with the best forms of energy. This also helps to maintain our systems in a way that supports our ability to concentrate.

When we regularly make or experience erratic lifestyle changes, it can also throw our gut out of kilter, because it likes structure and routine.

So, for example, if you're travelling long hours to a conference, or preparing for a big presentation, or have a big feast at the weekend eating lots of carbs, this can cause stress on the body. You may note how your bowel movements change in response to that stress. Everything might stop, or get overactive.

Neither are ideal situations from a comfort perspective.

Remember what I said at the beginning of this chapter about how efforts in one of these keystone areas cascades into the others? In the same Guardian article mentioned earlier, gastroenterologist Dr Sarmed Sami confirmed the correlation between regular exercise and a healthy gut.

> There is good scientific evidence that exercise increases good bacteria, independent of what you eat. Exercise also improves the gut integrity through increasing antioxidant defence and reducing inflammation, which, in turn, enhances the immune barrier function of the gut.
>
> ~ DR SARMED SAMI

This is a great example of how these keystones work together to help your body to maintain its integrity, immunity, and resilience.

Start thinking with your fork before you think you need to. Your future body and your brain will thank you.

If we can recognise the weak points in our nutrition, we can work to strengthen them, one bite at a time.

What changes to your meal planning and consumption can you make to help support your brain and your body better? Are there specific supplements that might help?

So we've looked at four key elements of health that impact on our wellbeing and productivity. Changing our habits in the arena of sleep, breathing, movement, and/or nutrition can have far-reaching, compounding effects to help strengthen our resilience, performance and longevity.

Where do the issues lie and what needs to change?

Which minor adjustments to your eating, breathing, sleeping and moving habits are you going to start with today, so you can experience benefits tomorrow, and the next day, and the next?

What will help you stay on track with these changes - could it be a fitness app, a gym membership, a wearable, or a running buddy?

Further resources on nutrition, brain and body health, from Functional Medicine specialists:

- Young Forever. The Secrets to living your longest, healthiest life - Dr Mark Hyman, MD
- The Doctor's Farmacy Podcast - Dr Mark Hyman, MD
- Outlive: The Science & Art of Longevity - Dr Peter Attia, MD with Bill Gifford

The next opportunity to consider are the Cycles of Productivity we can leverage to improve our focus, performance and creative outputs.

We're going to look at a variety of different biological rhythms, other cycles, and natural elements which can affect our productivity. This includes the moon and our menstrual cycle!

TWENTY
CYCLES OF PRODUCTIVITY

> Great performers don't fight their body's natural rhythm. They take advantage of it.
>
> ~ BRAD STULBERG & STEVE MAGNESS

In the chapter on Work Styles, I spoke about how we are typically only able to do 2-3 hours of productive work in a day. And how 12-day weeks are also an unhealthy norm, especially since our productivity diminishes after we've put in 40-50 hours in a week.

> After my burnout, when I first returned to working, I found myself in a position where I could not physically do any kind of work for more than 3-4 hours in a day before I succumbed to complete exhaustion.
>
> It's why I ended up being self-employed as a freelancer, instead of becoming an employee and having to work by someone else's rules. I needed to have control over managing my wellbeing and energy, so I could stop working before I put my health at risk, and work when my energy was at its highest.

It took a while to build up my resilience and stamina again, and even now, I find I cannot work intensively (i.e. long hours in a pressured situation) for more than a few weeks at a time.

I have had to redesign my life and work around my compromised energy.

But, what I have found over these last several years of working less and more purposefully, is that this does not equate to fewer outputs. For me, it has led to better results, more considered and meaningful outputs, and improved creative focus.

CHANGING OUR PERSPECTIVE

The answer to solving our productivity crisis is obvious, at least to me.

It lies in creating space.

We need to ...

>Slow.

>Things.

>Down.

>Work less.

>At a pace that's in tune with our natural rhythms.

Why?

Working less and working intentionally result in a higher level of creativity, productivity, and output.

By working less, I <u>don't</u> mean doing the bare minimum to scrape by.

Instead, I mean doing what is manageable, and which still gives us the space to fit the other important things into our days and lives.

Picture yourself as a rubber band. You want your work to stretch you just enough that it's easy to bounce back and maintain your original shape at the end of the day. If you stretch yourself too far, too often, for too long, the band breaks or can't rebound to it's original shape as it's structural integrity has been compromised.

Let's slow things down.

Our culture primes us for working towards the future rather than living in the present. And often we're rushing to get there for the wrong reasons.

Like the Slow Food Movement, we also have a growing collective of people joining what has been called the Slow Productivity Movement, as part of wanting to be more present in the work they're doing.

When we have more room, more space, more time, we can make better sense of our world in the present, at this moment.

The concept of Slow Productivity is deeply connected to the idea of creating intentionally productive practices.

Slow productivity involves being more intentional.

- Making time for rest.
- Making space for processing ideas and creative thought.
- Working according to our natural cycles of productivity to make the most of our energy.
- Adapting our approach to the cycles of responsibilities in our lives so we can manage them better.

We also need quality time to interact with things that don't involve work.

To better support our wellbeing and productivity, it is essential to incorporate periods of rest, play, and recovery into our work cycle to create space and support mindfulness.

We are so driven by the threat of time scarcity, which is a cultural construct.

Instead, we can shift our mindset to think about what's possible to achieve within the time we have, and at the optimal time within that time frame.

This perspective removes the threat of scarcity that elevates our anxiety, focusing on efficacy instead. It's about considering what's manageable and doable within the constraints we have (irrespective of whether they are time related).

BIOLOGICAL RHYTHMS

Even if we follow a slow productivity ethos, when it comes to having to do the work, how can we be more intentionally productive? The answer lies in leveraging our natural cycles of productivity.

It is possible to use whatever small amount of time we have available for deep work in a more focused and productive way, by adjusting our workflow to align with our body's natural biological rhythms.

1. ULTRADIAN RHYTHMS

The optimum length of time in which we can do focused work is connected to our ultradian rhythms. These are natural physiological cycles within our bodies that repeat for measurable time frames **within a 24-hour period**.

Examples of ultradian rhythms include our appetite, blinking, blood circulation, heart rate and pulse.

These ultradian rhythms also affect our levels of focus and alertness throughout the day.

Our attention span is typically limited to focus cycles of 20 to 90 minutes at a time.

Focus cycles differ slightly for everyone, so your current work schedule might conflict with your natural ultradian rhythms, as well as your circadian rhythms and your chronotype.

- Consider how long you can focus for when you are in a flow state and/or doing deep work. Is it 30, 60 or 90 minutes, or longer?
- Does your work schedule permit you to work on specific tasks for the optimal duration?

2. CIRCADIAN RHYTHMS

Circadian rhythms are biological rhythms with **a cycle of 24 hours or more**. They affect our sleep and waking cycles and control the release of melatonin in response to cues in our environment, such as light and temperature.

These rhythms are also linked to our physical and mental wellbeing, influencing everything from daily body temperature fluctuations to our cognitive performance.

Our sleep-wake cycle happens in roughly 90 minute sequences and these rhythms like us to stick to a routine, otherwise they get disrupted. As they are adaptable, we can train them to help us.

When we wake and go to sleep at around the same time each day, we function more effectively over the long run.

We have light receptors in both our skin and our eyes that help us manage our circadian rhythms. Getting insufficient daylight, or light at the wrong times, will adversely affect our rhythms' functioning.

What affects our circadian rhythms?

- Not getting sufficient bright light / natural light outdoors within the first 1 - 2 hours of waking. This triggers serotonin synthesis, which creates melatonin later in the day (which aids sleep).
- Staying up late glued to blue screens (TV, phone, iPad, gaming console). This depletes our melatonin. Regularly viewing blue light between 11pm and 4am also causes depression.
- Consuming food and stimulants later in the evening. This affects our digestion and sabotages our sleep cycles.

CYCLES OF PRODUCTIVITY

- Chronic sleep deprivation due to stress, stimulants, alcohol and other disruptions.
- Poor light conditions during winter can cause low moods, and in extreme cases, it leads to Seasonal Affective Disorder (SAD).

Consider what may be affecting your natural cycles

What can you do to improve your access to daylight (even through cloud) close to sunrise and also at sundown?

How can you limit your exposure to blue or bright light in the evenings?

For more on managing your Circadian Rhythms, I recommend listening to these Huberman Lab podcast episodes:

- "The Science and Practice of Perfecting Your Sleep" with Dr Matt Walker
- "Sleep Tools for Optimizing Your Sleep"

3. OUR SLEEP ARCHITECTURE

There are different phases we go through when we sleep, and each one of them plays an important role in helping our bodies heal, learn, process, and recover. Understanding how they work can help us improve our sleep hygiene so that we get more of the right types of sleep.

These stages and cycles form part of what is called our sleep architecture.

- Stage 1 - N1 = Dozing off stage (1-5 mins)
- Stage 2 - N2 = Subdued sleep state (10-60 mins)
- Stage 3 - N3 = Slow Wave Sleep (SWS) / Delta Sleep (20-40 mins)
- Stage 4 - REM = Rapid Eye Movement Sleep (10-60 mins)

Our brain activity patterns change in each stage, and these cycles repeat several times throughout the night.

Stages 1 to 3 are non-REM phases and the fourth (REM) is where our brains are most active.

Stage 3 (Slow Wave Sleep) is our deep sleep state, and it plays an important restorative role. It aids recovery and growth, boosts the immune system and supports other physiological processes in the body. This sleep stage also supports our memory, thinking, and creativity.

In REM Sleep (Stage 4), our brain activity is the equivalent of our waking state, despite being in a deep sleep. We dream throughout the night, but REM sleep is where we have our most vivid and fantastic dreams. Even more than Slow Wave Sleep, scientists believe REM sleep to be a critical support mechanism for our memory, learning, and creativity.

We don't usually commence REM sleep until we've been asleep for at least 90 minutes, and often we only enter REM sleep much later during our full period of sleep. So, if we cut our sleep time short for whatever reason, we may not be getting sufficient REM.

It's essential for our longevity and productivity that we are supporting our sleep cycles as much as possible.

However, getting enough sleep is often the first thing to be shelved when life gets busy.

If we aren't spending sufficient time in the healing and recovery stages of sleep, it affects our overall health and our mood, thinking, behaviour, decision making, and general cognition.

Consider your sleep cycles.

- How many hours do you typically get?
- What gets you up in the night?
- How can you track your sleep quality?

- What improvements can you make to support your sleep architecture?
- How can you make it a priority to get a decent amount of the right sleep every night?

Sleep tips:

Whether you need to sleep more or less than 7 hours, aim for 90 minute increments, while also factoring in the time needed to fall asleep. You're likely to feel more refreshed if you wake as you are coming out of a cycle than when you're in the middle of one, even if you've had less sleep than you desire.

The habit of pressing the snooze button so you can sleep for 5 more minutes (and then another 5), puts you into a micro-sleep as you start another sleep cycle. When you finally get up, you're typically in the midst of a sleep cycle and may feel groggier.

Getting up when the alarm goes off, or when your natural wake cycle dictates, is the better way to go!

4. CHRONOTYPES

Are you a night owl or an early bird? Or a wolf, lion, bear or dolphin?

Our chronotype informs our natural inclination to sleep, wake and focus at specific times.

Chronotypes are related to circadian rhythms, in that they also define our individual levels of activity and alertness. However, they are determined by our genes and also depend on factors such as age and geographical location.

Unlike our circadian rhythms, which we can manipulate and train, our chronotypes are more resistant to change and management. But understanding your chronotype means you can adapt your work schedule and workflow to support your ability to focus and be productive.

The key is to work in sync with your body's natural chronotype.

If you're unsure of your chronotype, it may be because of the following factors:

- The dictates of your work and life responsibilities. For example, do you have to get up super early to take the kids to school, have a long commute to where you work, or work nights as part of your job?
- The stimulants you consume to help you manage fatigue and focus, so that you can more easily achieve the demands of your day. For example, do you consume a lot of coffee to stay alert at work, or need to eat chocolates at 4pm to get through that last few hours?

In their book *Peak Performance*, Brad Stulberg and Steve Magness recommend resetting your system so that you can determine if your natural proclivity is to be a lark or a night owl.

To quote from the Peak Performance book:

> "The gold-standard way to learn your chronotype is to go seven days without setting an alarm clock or compensating for fatigue at any point of the day. Not only will you most accurately home in on your chronotype, but you will also benefit from a reset period during which your body can return to its natural rhythm."

Another way to check your chronotype is to take the Automated Morningness-Eveningness Test (AutoMEQ) online at the Centre for Environmental Therapeutics. *(Link in the Bibliography)*.

COMMON CHRONOTYPES

The Bear

- 55% of the population
- Traits: extroverted, continuous energy flow
- Best Sleep: 11pm to 7am

- Best Focus: 10am to 2pm

The Wolf

- 15% of the population
- Traits: creative, introspective, introverted
- Best Sleep: 12am to 7.30am
- Best Focus: 5pm to 12am

The Lion

- 15% of the population
- Traits: leaders, early risers, charismatic
- Best Sleep: 10pm to 6am
- Best Focus: 8am to 12pm

The Dolphin

- 10% of the population
- Traits: smart, creative, may struggle with focus
- Best Sleep: 11.30pm to 6.30am
- Best Focus: 3pm to 9pm

Note: these are guides only. Some people's sleep and focus cycles may straddle two chronotypes.

So consider:

- Which of these chronotypes might fit your natural rhythms the most?
- When during the day or evening is it more optimum for you to do certain types of work?
- How can you work according to your optimum wake and sleep cycles more regularly?

OTHER CYCLES

There are other energy patterns and cycles which influence our behaviours, actions and emotions, too.

If we can find ways to work in tune with them, it improves how we work.

For the guys reading this, please don't be put off by talk of periods, which I'm about to get into.

If you have women in your life, be they your partner, daughter, sister, friend, or coworker, it is helpful to know what they may experience at different times of the month, so that you can support them better.

1. WOMEN'S HORMONAL CYCLES

Working in flow with the phases of your cycle makes for a better work experience.

Hormones govern a woman's menstrual cycle. This cycle can affect energy, mood, and capability at different times of the week or month.

Depending on where you are in your ovulation cycle (which is roughly 28 days), you may feel more confident or productive, or more reflective or fatigued. You can also feel terrible pain and discomfort, which are distracting and stressful.

According to a research report from BMJ *(a medical journal and global healthcare knowledge provider)*, a woman's menstrual symptoms contribute to a loss of productivity.

Their findings show this loss adds up to almost 9 days per year per person, with 'presenteeism' being the biggest contributor.

What this means is that during their period, women may be present at work, but less productive for a third of their working time, as they're not able to perform at their peak.

First, we need to understand the patterns that repeat at certain times of the month.

CYCLES OF PRODUCTIVITY

With that knowledge, we can then adjust our workflow more effectively to schedule certain types of work that fit in, with, or around, those patterns.

MENSTRUATION PHASE

- Day 1 to 8 of the cycle (approximately).
- We have less energy and we feel more emotional.
- A good time for less strenuous or less challenging tasks. Slow things down, get more rest, and create more space in your day for reflective work.

FOLLICULAR PHASE

- Starts around day 6 and can run for 14 days into your cycle.
- Starts during or towards the end of our period.
- We feel a boost in creative and physical energy and we are more open to trying new things. It's a good time for planning and starting new projects and doing high energy tasks.

OVULATION PHASE

- Around the 15 to 17 day mark, lasts for 3 to 4 days.
- Our verbal skills become heightened, and it's a good time for communication and collaboration.
- This is when we feel our most charismatic, energetic, and extroverted. Schedule social events, networking and big, important meetings during this phase.

LUTEAL PHASE

- From around day 18, lasts 12 to 14 days.
- This is a calmer phase, where we are most task oriented. We find it easier to focus and pay attention to detail.
- Prioritise execution and delivery, or schedule admin tasks. It's a good time for wrapping up projects and bringing things to completion.

For a deeper dive, read Maisie Hill's book Period Power - Harness Your Hormones and Get Your Cycle Working for You.

MENOPAUSE IN THE MIX

Again, when women reach their 40s, their hormonal cycle starts changing, and they enter peri-menopause and later menopause.

Surprise, surprise, this phase also comes with experiences and health challenges that can affect focus and productivity. Even worse, this phase can, in itself, lead to burnout.

Women may experience symptoms such as brain fog, memory and focus issues, fatigue, hot flushes, insomnia, mood swings, hormonal acne, dry and itchy skin, and more.

These hormone-related "side-effects" can be a lot to manage on top of a full plate of responsibilities.

The experience of peri-menopause and menopause can certainly be challenging, but it shouldn't be the thing that excludes us from being able to still have a rich and fulfilling work life on our terms.

We can work better when we're able to manage our workload and adjust how AND when we work to accommodate these physiological changes, which are part of a natural cycle in a woman's life.

If you are experiencing these challenges, it's important to arm yourself with knowledge and take control of your workdays. Do what you can to build the strong foundations mentioned in the previous chapter to support you during this time of transformation.

For further reading on this subject, Maisie Hill has also written a book about Peri-Menopause Power.

2. PHASES OF THE MOON

The moon affects the gravitation of the earth, and us on it, "us" being every living thing. Just like the sun helps things to grow, thrive and photosynthesise, the moon can influence certain things in the natural world too. For example, the moon's gravitational pull affects the ocean's high and low tides, and moon phases determine when wildlife such as fish or coral choose to spawn.

That pie in the sky can affect our sleep and our emotions, particularly at full and new moon times.

The lunar cycle is roughly 29 days and there are 8 phases in total:

> The new moon; waxing crescent; first quarter; waxing gibbous; full moon; waning gibbous; third quarter; and waning crescent.

Historically and traditionally, full moon is considered a time of lunacy, despite 50 years of research refuting a direct causation.

What a full moon does do is affect our sleep and melatonin production because of the extra light in the sky at night.

As I mentioned in the earlier section on sleep cycles, we have light receptors in our skin. So if your curtains don't adequately block light, you're likely to sleep less when the moon is full.

Scientists surmise that the "lunacy effect", which anecdotally gives rise to more car accidents, violent incidents, and A&E visits, is probably due to us feeling grumpier, groggier, or angrier, because of a lack of good sleep!

Less sleep can throw our hormones out of whack, and no man, woman or child is immune.

> Personally, I find I get a lot crabbier at full moon time, despite having light blocking curtains. I'm not sure if it's a correlative or causative effect, but if I can't find an identifiable reason for why I'm being particularly cranky, I'll check the lunar calendar and sure enough, it's usually full!

Nowadays, however, there are plenty of other bright light sources we use daily which affect our sleep as much, if not more, than the moon does.

THE MOON & PRODUCTIVITY

From a symbolism perspective, for centuries, people have referenced the lunar cycle phases.

They form part of specific traditions and ceremonies that honour the four seasons and our patterns of life throughout the months and years.

Different phases of the moon can also help us manage our tasks, goals and productivity, as we can connect each phase to specific energies suited to certain types of activities.

To keep things simple, I'll focus on four of the eight moon phases, and how we can leverage them to manage what we work on when.

NEW MOON

- **Stillness:** Focus on rest and reflection. Gather your energy and plan for the coming month by setting new goals and intentions and starting new projects.

FIRST QUARTER

- **Performance:** A good time for doing. Take deliberate action, make progress on your projects, and refine or pivot as needed.

FULL MOON

- **Culmination:** Launch projects, make announcements, gather the rewards of your actions, appreciate and celebrate the outcomes of your efforts.

THIRD QUARTER

- **Release:** A time of clearing, letting go and re-assessment. Tidy up your workspace, and wrap up loose ends on your projects.

Using the lunar cycle to plan your work is a great example of being intentional about your productivity.

Similarly, when seasons change, can you adapt your workflow to accommodate the shorter or longer days, in a way that helps you preserve your energy and support your sleep, wellness and focus?

If you have control of your calendar and have any autonomy over how and when you do the different types of work you do, then it's worth experimenting to see how working in this way can improve your business and life.

3. FAMILY & COMMUNITY RESPONSIBILITIES

Other cycles which may affect your productivity and attention have to do with personal responsibilities such as caretaking or homeschooling.

- Perhaps you need to take your elderly mum shopping once a week.
- You may have a dog that needs walking twice a day.
- Or maybe you regularly do volunteer shifts at your community centre, food bank, or church.

These take time and energy and require your attention too.

If you have to work around these needs and constraints, how can you do so in a considered way?

Can you find a way that helps you be as effective as you can be, both in these moments and in the work you have to fit around them, whilst still looking after your wellbeing too?

CREATING YOUR OWN CYCLE

As explained in this chapter, there are various cycles which impact on our health, focus and attention. Some are beyond our control, but we have the power to influence others. How can you leverage them, adapt them, or work around them, to create your own cycle of productivity?

Something to remember when creating your cycle is how you recharge best. Are you an extrovert, an introvert or an ambivert, or a bit of each of these at different times? Some people get energised by being more social, while others need quiet time.

Irrespective of your personality style, we all need alone time, from time to time, to reconnect with ourselves. This is where we can call on archetypes to guide us.

In the early twentieth century, psychoanalyst Carl Jung introduced personality archetypes as part of his theory of the collective unconscious.

However, the idea of archetypes has been around since the time of Plato, and the term originates from the Greek 'arkhetypos' which means 'first imprint'.

Then, in the early 2000s, Caroline Myss wrote a popular book called *Sacred Contracts* about 12 core archetypes which form and guide our purpose in this life.

BOOKING HERMIT TIME

Samantha Hartley, a coach and the host of the Profitable Joyful Podcast, recommends leveraging these energy pattern archetypes - and in particular the Hermit Archetype - to help structure our days.

As she explains, the Hermit is "the part of you that needs alone time for reconnection with self and rebalancing."

This archetype applies to both introverts and extroverts and relates to the activities we engage in to help recharge and ground us.

Hermit time is your "me" time, your thinking time, or time for reflection.

It involves intentionally taking time in your day or week to look inward, to reconnect with what matters to you, and to seek stillness and grounding.

When you feel aligned with your internal world, you're able to function better in your external environment. Reconnecting in this way improves your decision making, actions and interactions.

Creating "me" time looks different for all of us.

It could involve journaling and meditation, or walking the dog, or going for a run, or taking a long bath with a good book, or quiet time sitting in the garden or your local park.

Don't forget to consider this important element in your own cycle of productivity.

LESS IS MORE

An important reminder:

Intentional productivity is not about doing more, in terms of volume of work, or volume of time spent.

Spending more time doing more work is not the goal.

> Intentional productivity is about creating consistency in the way you work, following through by creating outputs that have greater meaning for you, irrespective of how much time you have.
>
> ~ MICH BONDESIO

The goal is to create foundations for consistent practices that fit in with, and around, the fluctuating cadence of each day.

So, being mindful about how you approach work also means stuffing LESS into your day.

If you can plan and carry out your tasks based on your personal energy cycles, capabilities and preferences, at different times of the day or week, then you're more likely to get more quality work done in the time that you have. Even if that's a small amount of time.

THE CADENCE EFFECT

Let's review all the Opportunities available to you in the reflection part of this section.

Then in the next section of this book, we'll look at ways to prepare your mind and body for Focus and Flow, with lots of practical things you can implement to help you.

But first, let's consider which of these Opportunities you'd like to incorporate into your plan for Intentional Productivity.

TWENTY-ONE
REFLECTION EXERCISES NO.4

1. HABITS & BEHAVIOUR CHANGE

A behaviour is our response to a particular situation or stimulus. It determines why we do <u>or</u> don't take action or make change. The desire to escape perceived discomfort and seek pleasure over pain motivates all behaviour.

A behaviour takes place when the **motivation** to do something converges with a **prompt** to do that thing, and we are **able** to carry out the action required to achieve that thing.

Habits are behaviours we develop into mental shortcuts. They become autopilot behaviours which can help or hinder us.

We carry out habits in the following cycle:

   Cue >> Craving >> Response >> Reward

We can make good habits stick through **repetition of a behaviour**, **creating a stable environment** to carry out the behaviour in, and through **associating positive emotions** with carrying out that habit.

- Identify what habits you want to change so that you can improve how you work?
- How can you make the cue for carrying out that habit more visible or invisible?
- How can you make your response to that cue feel more or less attractive?
- How can you make the action you take easier or more difficult?
- How can you make the reward feel more or less satisfying?

2. PRODUCTIVITY MINDSETS

Our mindset influences our outputs and performance at work. So your view of yourself affects how you do everything.

We can have different mindset approaches for different aspects of our lives.

Building positive, resilient mindsets can help us on the path to developing our intentional productivity practices.

SELF ACCEPTANCE

When we don't believe in ourselves, we are the obstacles to our improvement, progression, and connection.

- Visualise what your life would be like if you accepted who you are and where you are... right at this moment... with no excuses.
- Imagine how things would be different? How would you behave? What would you do? What would you say? How would you approach life and work?
- Now think about what can you do to implement some of that change in small, incremental ways.
- Take action, one step at a time.

The only difference between you and a better life is your view of yourself and what's possible.

Whenever you're experiencing self doubt, ask yourself the question:

What if I can?

Then do.

Remember, the glass is always full. Full of possibility!

MINDSETS FOR SKILLS DEVELOPMENT - TRAINING, TRUSTING, LEARNING.

When we're changing the way we work, we have to learn new ways of doing things. It takes practice and it can feel challenging, especially at the start.

The best way to embed new behaviours when we're starting something new is to break our habit goals down into smaller steps. Then employ supportive mindsets to help us achieve success every step of the way:

TRAINING MINDSET

- Imagine what you want to be like with these new behaviours.
- Visualise yourself working in a better way and being more focused and productive.
- What does that look like for you?

TRUSTING MINDSET

- Believe that you've got what it takes to do your best, based on the practice that you've put in.
- As part of trusting yourself, accept that you've got what it takes to figure it out, even if you don't know how to do something.
- Reinforce this by regularly saying to yourself, "I've got this!" In fact, there is research showing that speaking to ourselves in

the third person can motivate us. So perhaps you say, "You've got this, (insert your name here)!".

LEARNING MINDSET

- See failure as feedback. What can you learn from it, to course correct and improve over time?
- Ask yourself questions about how these new productivity-focused behaviours feel. Are they working, or do they need work? How can you make your productivity system better?

SCARCITY VS ABUNDANCE MINDSET

Understanding that there is enough to go around makes you open to opportunity and possibility.

A scarcity mindset makes us feel like there isn't enough, and there will never be enough.

An abundance mindset focuses on the profusion of opportunities available to us.

- Consider where you may have a scarcity mindset in your life.
- What triggers this response? How does it make you feel? How does it manifest in your body and in your actions and verbal responses?
- What things do you say or do in these situations that you can change?

FIXED VS GROWTH MINDSET

Your view of yourself and your abilities can affect how you do everything.

When we believe that our intelligence is static, that we can't improve and that we aren't capable of change, then we have a **fixed mindset**.

REFLECTION EXERCISES NO.4

When we understand we can develop our intelligence and that we are capable of change and improvement, then we have a **growth mindset**.

A growth mindset focuses on mastery through practice and persistence. It's an essential viewpoint to improve our productivity and performance.

- In what areas of your work and life might you have a fixed mindset?
- Consider examples of where or when you feel you want to give up?
- Where or when do you feel most sensitive to criticism? Which obstacles feel the most insurmountable?
- How much of the resistance you feel is caused by a fixed mindset?
- Consider how you would handle these situations if you could? It goes back to the question "What if I can?".

GRIT MINDSET

A Grit Mindset can help us build resilience, get through challenging times, and keep going so that we can succeed.

A *growth mindset* helps to build your *grit mindset*. Because you know that your ability to learn is not fixed, and that with effort you can change your situation.

Learn to get comfortable with discomfort. What activities can you do to help you build your grit and resilience?

- Can you turn the last minute of your shower into a cold one?
- Can you persevere in writing that report for another 30 minutes before you check your phone?
- Can you eat the fruit instead of the chocolate bar?

The only way to make change and create momentum is to do. So, take action, give it a go.

3. BUILDING STRONG FOUNDATIONS

Consider the 4 keystone self-care foundations of sleep, breathing, movement and nutrition.

What self-care activities are you already engaging in to support these foundations and which of these areas do you want to improve or add to?

- Pick two small actions you can start doing daily to support yourself better, (one in your personal life and one in your work life). Write them down.
- Practice doing these actions every day for a week, then assess their effectiveness. Do they need tweaking? If yes, adjust them and try again. If no, continue as is.
- How can you prepare your body and mind for sleep, so that you can make the most of your time spent horizontal?
- How can you introduce simple mini movements into your workday and build a habit of doing it regularly? How do you like to stay fit - how can you do more of it in a manageable and enjoyable way?
- What changes to your meal planning can you make to help support your brain and your body better?

Stating your intention helps your brain to identify with its importance and the need for you to do it.

It is the first step in helping you to automate positive actions so that they become habitual.

Be specific about WHAT, HOW, WHEN and WHERE you will perform these actions.

Tie them to an environment, a specific time of day and a specific trigger habit. Keep them small, manageable, and easy to include into your existing routine. Test for a week and make minor adjustments if needed, then keep going.

REFLECTION EXERCISES NO.4

Examples:

- Every day at work, when I get up from my desk to go to the bathroom or make coffee, I will stretch my arms and legs for 2 minutes.
- Before I go to bed at night, I will lay out my yoga mat so that when I get up, I will do 20 minutes of yoga / sit on the mat doing 10 minutes of meditative breathing, before getting ready for work.
- When I go to bed, I will place my phone on the other side of the room so that I get out of bed to turn it off. This helps me get up for the day and prevents me from pressing the snooze button.

How can you set yourself up to WIN at these activities?

Continuing to test and adjust is part of creating cadence in your days. What preventative actions can you take to reduce friction or create more resistance?

4. CYCLES OF PRODUCTIVITY

Reflect on your work requirements and the energy cycles which impact on your ability to work effectively.

- Consider your general energy levels and natural rhythms at different times of the day, week, and month. Make a note of times of the day when you feel more energised or more lethargic.
- What types of tasks are better suited for different times of days, or weeks?
- When are you typically the most productive and the least? Is it early morning, late at night, or just after lunch?
- How can you adjust your work schedule and workflow to accommodate the times when you are most likely to be more focused and productive?

- Are you doing your deep and important work during your most productive times?

If you track these variables and plan your tasks based on these cycles, you can develop a framework for better work and better wellness.

OPPORTUNITIES & YOUR CANVAS

Based on your answers to these reflective questions, consider which supportive habits, mindsets and foundational activities you'd like to include in the FOUNDATIONS and PERFORMANCE sections of the Cadence Canvas Framework™?

You will have the opportunity to pull this all together at the end of the next section.

For now, be aware of the changes you want to make, the existing behaviours you want to level up, and the new habits and activities you want to experiment with.

Which of these will you take on to improve your performance and activate more of your potential? Are you ready to try out making small changes?

In Part 5, we'll look at practical ways you can Prepare for Focus and Flow.

This includes ways to rewire your brain, manage your flow, and create supportive rituals.

NOTES

PART FIVE
MANAGING OUR FOCUS & FLOW

1. Introduction
2. Challenges
3. How We Work
4. Opportunities
5. FOCUS & FLOW
6. Next Steps

TWENTY-TWO
REWIRING OUR BRAIN FOR FOCUS

> Consistency is the key to achieving and maintaining momentum.
>
> ~ DARREN HARDY

To recap on things I've mentioned in previous chapters, developing intentional productivity practices helps us to thrive and endure over the long-term.

These practices are part of building sound foundations that support not just our productivity, process and performance, but also our health and wellbeing.

There are specific ways we can retrain our brains to support intentional, focused productivity. The practices, when done regularly, also help us achieve deep focus and flow states more often.

The key to rewiring our brain for focus and flow lies in improving our concentration and attention.

To keep our brains in top form, they need regular exercise as much as our bodies do.

THE CADENCE EFFECT

In several past chapters, I've spoken about the external influences which fracture our focus and attention. Too much time on our digital tools, including our phones, can decimate our concentration, but there are a few ways that we can rebuild our focus muscles.

Some of these suggestions may surprise you. Others are easy to implement. You may already do them, but might benefit from doing them more, and/or more intentionally. Some may take more time as part of a continued learning practice, as you work to develop mastery of a specific skill.

CONTINUED PRACTICES

These are activities and behaviours which you can build into a dedicated practice over time.

You can make them part of what you do regularly to build stronger foundations.

1. GO WALKABOUTS

It's not coincidental that many of the greatest minds throughout history also took long walks. Thinkers, writers and creators such as Aristotle, Henry David Thoreau, Charles Darwin, Albert Einstein and Virginia Woolf all used walking as a tool to help with their creative process. So, this isn't a new concept.

According to research out of Stanford University, walking is particularly good at boosting our creativity and creative problem-solving skills. The act of walking actually helps our brain to think about things differently than when we're sitting at a desk.

Getting active promotes a more active mind as blood flow increases to the brain and stimulates the growth of new neurons. The rhythm of our footfall also influences the pace of and shape of our thoughts. That's another example of cadence in action.

Walking also doesn't require a lot of conscious thought, which frees our brain to wander, enabling new ideas to percolate as we go.

REWIRING OUR BRAIN FOR FOCUS

If creating things, problem solving and critical thinking are part of the work that you do, then make walking part of your preparation and work process.

When is a good time to walk? Before work, during lunch, or at the end of the day? Twice a day? For 5 mins or 50 mins?

Give your walking time the same level of importance as you do to meetings, so schedule it.

Remember, if it's not in the diary, it doesn't happen!

2. READ MORE BOOKS & WRITE THINGS DOWN

Since discovering the joys of reading as a young child, I've always been an avid reader. However, as I explained in my intro story, when I experienced my burnout, it affected my ability to read and retain information.

> I've mentioned that, due to my burnout, I found I couldn't read more than two pages of a book before my distracted, fragmented brain rebelled. It took a long time for me to reconstruct my reading abilities and rebuild these neural pathways. The upside is that I'm now a better reader and learner, than I was before my experience.

Studies have found that reading doesn't just build our vocabulary, strengthen our brain and improve our memory. It also supports better sleep, reduces stress, alleviates depression, prevents cognitive decline and increases our empathy.

The act of reading longer pieces of written work (both fiction and non-fiction) prepares our mind for holding lots of information all at the same time.

The process is a combination of how our brain sees and identifies the words on the page, recognising patterns in the information, and then how our brain synthesises and stores that information.

So, developing our reading skills is important for developing our creative and critical thinking skills, where we need to consider many variables and hold complex thoughts and ideas in our heads simultaneously.

The more we read, the better we get at concentrating and processing information.

Yet, publishers have confirmed that reading 'book' books has declined in recent years. Many of us now default to audio-based formats which enable multi-tasking, but also because our attention spans are totally shot due to all the things we've covered in sections 2, 3, and 4 of this book.

> I'm no different, not just because I couldn't physically read during my burnout situation. Like many, I also love hearing clear, soothing and strong voices, and I listen to many non-fiction books in audiobook format. I find audio a good way for me to remember information, as I usually listen while I am walking.
> However, I do also read books in eBook and print format, as I like to highlight or scribble notes in the margins.

This brings me to a related point about the power of writing and the role it plays in supporting our focus and intentional productivity.

The act of writing is another way to strengthen our learning, retention, and recall capabilities.

We use a different part of our brain when writing things down versus typing things up.

When we're taking notes, typing is like transcribing. We don't really have to think as deeply about what it is we are putting down. However, with writing, as most of us can't write as fast as we type, instead we're forced to synthesise what we read, see or hear, and summarise the information in our brain before we write it down.

Writing things helps us to process information on a deeper level, which improves our likelihood of retaining that info.

> The value of writing by hand cannot be overstated. When we read (or listen to something) and then write down key takeaways by hand (not by typing) it engages motor circuits in ways that deeply embed information to memory. Writing by hand, however cursory, is the best way to recall information.
>
> ~ DR ANDREW HUBERMAN

Writing also slows things down to a more manageable pace.

It creates space for thought and mindfulness, as we are present with our task in the moment, even if we are writing about something in the past or future.

The power of writing is also one reason I give talks and workshops on paper-based & analog productivity, using the bullet journal method. This way of task tracking and data capture is also a key tool in my personal intentional productivity toolkit.

Aside from writing more, how can you read more 'book' books?

- To build (or rebuild) the habit of reading, start small. One or two pages at a time. It doesn't matter if the subject matter is fiction or non-fiction, it's the act of reading we're focusing on. It could be a magazine, or a long blog post, or a newspaper.
- Create quiet, distraction free blocks of time and space for reading.

Personally, I've discovered that when insomnia strikes, reading fiction when I can't sleep actually helps to calm me. So even though I may wake in the morning feeling tired, I feel less anxious as I've enjoyed the quiet experience of reading, (even if it happens to be in the middle of the night)!

Remember why you may love reading? Consider what it can do for you, to improve your life, your work and your relationships.

THE CADENCE EFFECT

3. DO BORING THINGS

Include small, mundane tasks in your workday, to help your brain get used to doing things that can be tedious. Aside from priming your brain to feel more comfortable with cumbersome tasks, it's also a chance to add mini movements into your workday.

- If you're working at home, this could be taking 5 minutes to vacuum the living room or fold clean laundry.
- If you're at the office, it could be tidying up the stationery cupboard. Or doing some admin, filing and archiving.
- If the task has to be done on your computer, shut down all the other bits that might vie for your attention while you're doing it (like email, chat, etc).
- Mundane online tasks could be things like entering data into a spreadsheet, updating your contacts list, or adding receipts to your accounts software.

Find something repetitive and non-taxing to do.

Why make a point of doing this? Training our brain to become accustomed to doing boring things means we become less likely to rebel against the discomfort of doing long stretches of focused work, where procrastination is always a danger.

It takes practice, but it's doable. The knock-on effect is that if your brain isn't itching for distraction, you're less likely to feel the need to reach for your phone or whatever it is you do when you want to avoid doing the "hard work".

Remember, our brains like to move towards comfort and pleasure, and away from discomfort and pain. How can you get your brain to become more comfortable being uncomfortable?

MEDITATION

This is a topic which requires a slightly deeper dive than the three options for rewiring your brain that I've just covered, but it also falls within the category of Continued Practices.

> [Meditation is] a progression that takes us on a sweet journey through the field of thinking into the field of being.
>
> ~ LIGHT WATKINS

This ancient practice, which has been around in various forms for thousands of years, involves stilling the mind and grounding the body.

Regular meditation, especially if you do it over many years, can lead to altered states of consciousness.

It can be a divinely spiritual experience, but as *new age* as that sounds, the practice of meditation is actually more "oh wow!" than woo-woo!

Meditation has the power to totally transform your life (and your work). Doing it regularly is like charging up your superpowers!

Countless studies have confirmed that meditation supports not just our mind, but our health and longevity. It improves our sleep, strengthens our immunity, and bolsters our heart health.

Regular meditation also reduces depression, stress, and anxiety, enabling us to face the challenges in our lives with more patience and resilience.

Scientists have found that long-term meditation slows our rate of biological aging, reduces inflammation and increases the length of our telomeres. It also improves our memory and cognitive skills, and can even provide pain relief.

But there's more....

Chris Bailey, in his book *How To Train Your Mind*, cites research that proves **meditation also makes us more mindful and helps us to focus for longer.** And that's great news for our productivity and being more intentional about how we work.

There are many ways to do meditation, with many different styles and brands of practice. However, they all fit into just a few categories.

You don't have to learn how to do all of them to benefit from the experience of meditating. And there is no 'one' method that is better than the others.

What feels right for you is the right way for you to meditate.

However, choosing a style of meditation is also about what you want that meditation to help you achieve.

> When I first started meditating, I desperately needed it to help calm my anxious mind so I could sleep. Once that was achieved, I could then use it to help with my focus and attention.
>
> Nowadays, I mainly meditate to help my creativity and productivity. But I do still occasionally have over-anxious thoughts or feel very stressed. So knowing which specific meditation tools to use in each situation is helpful.

MEDITATION TYPES

There are three categories (or core types) of meditation.

1. Focused Attention Meditation

- Involves clearing the mind of busy thoughts by focusing on the breath, on objects, or on bodily sensations.
- Increases concentration, attention, and awareness.
- Reduces anxiety and depression.
- Improves sleep and productivity.
- E.g. Vipassana meditation

2. Open Monitoring Meditation

- Involves observing your thoughts rather than attempting to clear them.
- Practice focusing on being comfortable in the present moment with whatever thoughts and feelings are arising.
- Improves attention, regulates emotions and supports better cognitive control, such as better decision making.
- E.g. mindfulness meditation, body scan, guided meditation

3. Self-Transcending Meditation

- Requires no mental effort. You let your thoughts come and go.
- Guided by a mantra which helps you go deeper, moving you from the surface chatter to the stillness within.
- Health benefits include reducing high blood pressure and managing PTSD symptoms.
- Activates the brain's imagination network for improved creativity.
- E.g. Vedic meditation, Transcendental Meditation® (TM)

MANAGING A WANDERING MIND

The goal of focused-attention meditation is to change our mind state, moving from a busy mind packed with competing thoughts and chatter to a quieter mind with fewer thoughts vying for our attention.

So meditation helps to create space, which is part of creating cadence.

Building a regular meditation practice into our days reduces our mind's wandering to shorter periods of time.

A degree of daydreaming is natural and can be helpful for creative thinking and problem solving. However, we know that being distracted (by social media, by life, by stress, etc.) can be supremely detrimental to getting things done.

A reminder of the stats I've quoted previously…

- Chris Bailey's research shows that even when we're trying to do deep, focused work, our mind still wanders for 47% of the time. So, we're only concentrating for 53% of the time when we're actively trying to focus.

The good news, however, is that his study shows that a regular meditation practice can increase our concentration from 53% to as much as 70% during periods of deliberate, focused work!

Meditation also trains our mind to get back on track quicker when we get distracted.

These distractions stimulate our mind and increase our desire for novelty. The dopamine release associated with a distraction wrecks our focus and productivity. But meditation reduces this type of stimulation in our mind.

Meditation increases our working memory, which improves our attentional capacity to do more complex tasks for longer, and to switch between tasks more seamlessly.

So, with more practice, we get accustomed to needing less dopamine and, therefore, seek fewer distractions.

We've already seen how meditation can support our sleep, mood and immune system. The fact that it also supports our productivity makes it a no-brainer to develop the practice.

BUILDING MEDITATION INTO YOUR ROUTINE

To develop a practice, all it takes is 5 to 10 minutes per day, and you can build from there.

It's easier to make the habit of meditation stick if you attach it to your existing morning or evening routine.

For example, in the mornings I make a cup of tea, and while I'm waiting for it to cool, I meditate for 10 minutes.

Irrespective of meditation's origins, with these practices, you don't need to wear strange clothes, or sit in an odd pose, or get hippy dippy about it!

You don't need an internet connection, a live teacher, or anything external to drop into meditation.

- Simply find a comfortable seat that works for you while you create some space in your day for grounding, for learning to let go, and for developing your self-awareness.
- Slowing your breath is a key part of the practice.
- You need a grounding point to come back to every time your mind wanders. This could be focusing on a specific breathing style (e.g. box breath); on an object (e.g. a candle or a crystal); on an image (e.g. a visualisation); or a mantra (e.g. a simple phrase or meaningless primordial sound).
- Closing your eyes or softening your gaze helps to reduce the stimuli that can trigger your mind.

Meditation Resources:

You can use one of the many meditation apps out there to help guide you. From personal experience, I can recommend *Headspace*, *Calm*, *Tripp* or *Insight Timer*, but there are many more to choose from.

To learn more about how meditation works and science-based effective meditation techniques, I recommend listening to the *Huberman Lab Podcast (Episode 96)*. (Interestingly, the Huberman Lab has also been involved in some fascinating research around optimum length of time and the best style of meditation for enhancing performance.)

Meditation is <u>not</u> about banishing thoughts from your mind. As we know, that's virtually impossible!

It's more about creating the space to observe the chatter without being overwhelmed by it. And in time and with practice, it helps you to develop the skill of only hearing the thoughts that matter.

THE CADENCE EFFECT

Note: There are links to further meditation resources provided in the Bibliography for this section.

TAKING MEDITATION TO THE NEXT LEVEL

If you're already in the habit of meditating and want to take things further and deeper, then give **self-transcending or mantra-based meditation** a try.

This is a form of deep meditation and a powerful practice to increase your state of awareness. All it takes is using a mantra (a repeated sound or word) to transcend your thoughts for **two 20-minute sessions daily**.

You can learn self-transcending meditation from a Vedic meditation teacher or an organisation, such as Transcendental Meditation® (TM). Once you have your mantra, you will be a self-sufficient meditator!

You repeat a mantra in your mind which helps to ground you. Aside from the mantra, you don't attempt to control anything, you just let your mind wander where it goes, and take notice of where that is.

So, if you need to scratch your nose, you can do so. If you need to add an item to your mental shopping list, so be it. Whatever happens during the session is fine, there is no expected outcome. Just bring yourself back to your mantra in between your mental wanderings.

Note: Links to Vedic meditation resources provided in the Bibliography for this section.

So, we've looked at how developing the practices of walking, reading, writing, doing boring things, and meditating can improve our focus.

But what about quick go-to strategies we can use when we feel a bout of distracted procrastination coming on?

IN-THE-MOMENT PRACTICES

These are activities you can set up and then draw on in situ, for when you struggle with distraction, stress, anxiety or procrastination in the moment.

1. HAVE A PROCRASTINATION ACTION PLAN

We covered this in detail in the chapter on Procrastination, but in short, have a reboot system to help you step out of *procrasto* mode.

Here's an example of how to create a reboot system:

Imagine this is you talking to your mind…

First, identify it when it happens - call it out!

"Wait, why am I hanging out in front of the fridge, again?"
I don't have time for this, I'm on deadline. Dang it, procrasto has a hold on me again!"

Second, understand why you're procrastinating.

"Why am I doing this? Hmm, I reckon it's 'cos I'm avoiding writing that piece of work for that big project."

"Why am I avoiding it? Because it's my first BIG client, and I have to learn something new, and it feels hard, and I'm scared I'll blow it!"

Third, override avoidance behaviours by creating friction and make better actions easier to do. Understand how it benefits you.

"Right, I know I'm feeling stressed, so of course I'm looking for distractions. Here's what I'm going to do whenever I feel this way."

- Put fruit on my desk so I can snack on something healthy without having to get up. And remove all unhealthy snacks from the fridge.

- Visualise doing a great job on that proposal and having a good outcome. I will feel awesome at completing the work well, as I will know I have done my best. And I will impress my client, which might lead to more work!
- Break down the sub-tasks for doing this so that I can make it easy to get started. Why am I doing that? So that I can finish it with focused attention, do a good job, and submit it in adequate time, instead of rushing it.
- Meditate for 5 minutes before I get started, so I can clear my mind and focus on doing the work.

"Why will I do this? Because it will make me feel good about myself and will help my business and my clients."

Next, simplify tasks into teeny, tiny, easy steps — next action.

I find this works best if I write (or type) the list of smaller steps I must take to start, work on and complete this task. Here's an example:

- Open the browser, then type in the research key word.
- Then open the pages I want to research for competitors.
- Then review and make notes.
- Then open Word / Google doc. Create a summary outline with headers, etc.

Then, do the first, simple thing on that task list — take action.

- I'm opening my browser - tick
- I'm typing in the research keyword - check
- Carry on… :)

This might seem incredibly rudimentary, but this process works. Before you know it, you'll be on your way, leaving procrastination in your dust!

There's another helpful practice you can use on the go, to help you support yourself in the moment.

2. PRACTICE CONSCIOUS BREATHING

I first mentioned conscious breathing in the chapter about Building Strong Foundations.

It's a form of meditative breathing where you control the depth and speed of your breath for a set period.

Conscious breathing is a quick and simple way to change your state.

It can energise you and reduce any anxiety or stress you may be feeling. It's also a mindfulness technique, as it helps to bring you into the present moment.

Intentional breathing calms and clears our mind and focuses our attention, and it has many physiological health benefits.

The golden number for good health = 5 or 6 slow, deep breaths a minute.

We're usually breathing much faster, shorter and shallower (15 - 25 breaths per minute), which means we aren't taking sufficient oxygen into our lungs to be processed and sent to all the cells in our body.

Deep breathing (also called belly breathing) is where we take air right down into the bottom of our diaphragm, expanding our bellies.

Taking a deep breath, and then expelling it all the way, helps to release toxins, reduce inflammation and increase oxygen to our cells.

Conscious breathing helps to purify our blood, support our immune system and stabilise our mood and our mental health. It energises our body, calms our mind, and helps us build stamina and resilience, all things we need in a busy, stressful workplace.

The easiest way to practise conscious breathing is with a technique called Box Breathing.

- It involves 4 steps - an 'in' breath, a pause, an 'out' breath, and another pause (all through the nose).

- A common way to do this is to inhale for a count of 4, hold for 4, exhale for 4 and hold for 4, before repeating the cycle of breath for 3 to 5 minutes.
- You can vary the length of the breaths and pauses, depending on your personal lung capacity. E.g. another way to do it is to inhale for 4, hold for 2, exhale for 6, hold for 2. Or work with a 5, 2, 7, 2 count.

In the chapter on Building Strong Foundations, I also spoke about the physiological sigh and the 4-7-8 method, which are also excellent ways to change your state quickly in the moment. *Revisit that chapter for more info on how to do them.*

To understand how these types of conscious breathing exercises can truly support your productivity and wellbeing, you need to physically experience them first hand through practice. That means incorporating them into your daily intentional productivity practice.

So, give conscious breathing a go. Try a minute at the start of your workday, 5 minutes just before a meeting, or whenever you're feeling stressed and anxious at work.

In the next chapter, we're focusing on ways to Manage Our Flow

Now that we've looked at how to rewire our distracted mind for better concentration, the next step is to consider flow states, time blocking and task tracking, and how they can be integrated into our intentional productivity blueprint.

TWENTY-THREE
MANAGING OUR FLOW

> Three to four hours of continuous, undisturbed deep work each day is all it takes to see a transformational change in our productivity and our lives.
>
> ~ CAL NEWPORT

We've covered several ways we can develop our concentration muscles and protect our attention. Now let's look at ways we can manage how we use that attention in our workdays, so we can better support flow states that activate more of our potential.

Whether you're a company of one, or many, creating boundaries and setting aside sufficient time and space for focused work and creative thinking is a game changer for your productivity.

Our natural cycles of focus affect our work styles and workflows, and we covered this in the section about How We Work.

In the Opportunities section, we covered cycles of productivity and referenced ultradian and circadian rhythms, which affect the times when we are more or less alert in our days.

THE CADENCE EFFECT

As our attention span is typically limited to focused blocks of 20 - 90 minutes at a time, to achieve flow states, the key here is to connect how we work with our natural cycles.

THE RHYTHM OF FLOW

Creating a workflow and environment where you can have an uninterrupted focus for specific blocks of time helps you to achieve flow states more easily.

> Flow is a highly focused mental state which helps us perform at our peak, but it is not only a powerful productivity tool.
>
> Creating opportunities for achieving flow states forms part of creating cadence in every aspect of our lives.

Flow is a state that we achieve when the combination of challenge and skill is optimal.

When we're in flow, it can feel like we lose time as we become fully immersed in what we're doing.

According to the late Mihaly Csikszentmihalyi - a psychologist known as the "Father of Flow" - **flow states are the secret to happiness and success**.

Studies out of Penn State University reported by the World Economic Forum indicate that leisure activities that put us into a state of **flow can also combat loneliness**, which is a health epidemic in itself.

Their research found that doing meaningful activities that require a degree of skill and concentration improves our mental health and reduce our feelings of loneliness or isolation.

Based on Mihaly Csikszentmihalyi's work, the three key factors that help us achieve flow states are:

1. A goal that will direct our energy and action.
2. The goal needs to be meaningful.

3. The associated tasks stretch us, as they are at the edge of our abilities.

Getting into this peak performance state — often referred to as 'the zone' — helps us push our minds and bodies further, so that we're able to achieve incredible physical feats and unlock our creative thinking to solve colossal problems.

THE SCIENCE OF FLOW

A flow experience feels timeless and effortless. There is a richness to the experience and often a sense of selflessness.

There are several characteristics that support flow states or indicate we've entered one.

We have complete concentration on the task at hand and the challenge of the task is balanced with the skills we need to complete it. This means we feel in control of our task and experience effortless ease working on it, even if it is challenging.

We have a clear goal driving us and the opportunity for immediate feedback. The outcome of the experience is linked more closely to an intrinsic sense of reward than focused on external approval.

Our actions and awareness merge and we lose self-consciousness, becoming fully present. Being in the moment transforms our sense of time, so it can feel like it either speeds up or slows down.

There are also metabolic changes that occur in our bodies when we enter flow.

- When we're undertaking something challenging, our bodies release cortisol, which puts our brain waves into a beta state. *This is our typical work state when we are not in flow.*
- As we enter flow, alpha brain waves dominate and nitric oxide is released to counteract the stress by increasing blood flow and lowering blood pressure. *This calms our system.*

- In flow, our brain waves change to theta/gamma waves, and dopamine and endorphins are released, which promote alertness and endurance, helping us to perform better. *This is where we produce results in "the zone".*
- As we leave the flow state, our brain waves transition into a delta state and the accompanying serotonin and oxytocin make us feel a sense of wellbeing. *This is where the happiness happens.*

The more we practise entering flow states, the more engaged and happy we will become in our life outside of work too.

FLOW PROFILES

According to Jamie Wheal of the Flow Genome Project, we each have different ways that we're able to get into "the zone" more easily.

Based on his company's research with high performance athletes, thinkers and doers, Jamie and his team have identified specific behaviours and instincts which give rise to flow. They've grouped these into 4 personality profiles, which they call *hard chargers*, *deep thinkers*, *crowd pleasers*, or *flow goers*.

While you may find it useful to identify your profile, my view is that we don't need to categorise ourselves to get into flow.

However, having this knowledge and taking directed action can help us achieve productive flow states more regularly.

So, the simple way to do this is to **identify our typical behaviours** for how we approach challenges and when we perform at our best. Then we can **leverage our strengths** in these areas and **work around our weak points**.

> Personally, I use music to help me get into a focused state that can lead to being in flow. As this is the first book I've written, I have to admit that the resistance I felt to getting words on the page was quite challenging at times.

So, as part of my writing routine, I got into the habit of putting on a specific playlist every time I sat down to write. This became a ritual. *(I talk about rituals in the next chapter).*

Funnily enough, my choice of music was an ambient album called *Flow State* by Above & Beyond. (The B-side includes inspiring words spoken in dulcet tones by Elena Brower). As a result of repeatedly taking this action, now, when I hear the opening track play, I find it super easy to get into a zone of concentration really quickly, no matter what type of work I'm doing.

It's become a habitual response to help me prepare for a flow state.

I also have other playlists I use, but for me it needs to be music that is calming or ambient, usually with no singing or lyrics. That's a personal choice though. I know people who focus best listening to death metal, so each to their own!

The important thing to note is that this is an example of how incorporating music into your intentional productivity toolkit can be another way of creating cadence in your days. It is a helpful way to establish the required baseline of optimum conditions for entering a flow state.

FLOW TIPS

Reaching and staying in flow depends on what Mihaly Csikszentmihalyi called the *Challenges/Skills Equation*.

- If the challenge of the task you are trying to undertake is too hard, you'll struggle to stay in flow. So how can you simplify the task? Try focusing on your technique more than on the outcome.

- Likewise, if the task is too easy, you won't become immersed in what you're doing. So how can you mix things up to add a bit more challenge?

Consider when you are most likely to enter a flow state and how that comes about? How can you do more of that?

Now I want to get more specific with a productivity method that helps you work in flow with your natural cycles.

TIME BLOCK PLANNING

The purpose of time block planning is <u>not</u> to restrict your time, it is to help support flow.

A highly effective way to work with your daily rhythms is to block off specific periods of time in your day or week to do specific types of work.

Using your calendar as your guide, time block planning (also known as *time blocking*) is a helpful way to manage what you focus on in a day, or a week.

It also visually prepares your brain for the work you need to do, as you can see an overview of what you're working on.

Scheduling in tune with your natural productivity cycles.

In its simplest form, this involves allocating specific time, say 20, 60, or 90 mins, or 2 or 3 hour slots on your calendar for specific tasks. The duration will depend on their complexity, the time they may require to complete or progress, and the time you have based on your other responsibilities.

- Think about how you can block time in your days for the different kinds of work that you do, based on your energy levels and responsibilities?

- Consider whether you are better off doing focused work in the morning and handling meetings and admin tasks in the afternoon? Or perhaps another permutation works better?

Scheduling your time blocks accordingly will help to organise your mind, so you produce your best work in a focused manner, at the time best suited to how your brain works.

Important Note:

Not everyone likes, or is able, to work to a set schedule every day. If you become too pedantic with your time blocking, (e.g. logging everything to the 'nth degree), it can feel restrictive. We tend to abandon things that are too rigid. And the whole purpose of focusing on cadence is to create flexibility.

Remember, the purpose of time blocking is to support flow, not restrict your time. It is meant to help your pace of productivity.

So, this may not be something you do every day.

MICH'S TIME-BLOCKING PROCESS

My calendar and its notifications form the basis for my time-blocking activities. I review my tasks at the start of my week and coordinate my time blocking in my calendar with the tasks I may have noted in my bullet journal.

This means adding required tasks into my electronic calendar, estimating the time I may need, and colour coding everything based on the type of task.

At the end of each day, I review what's coming up over the next few days and adjust the time blocks as required, based on what I've been able to complete "today".

I don't find this method restrictive; I find it a fluid practice that helps me to stay focused on what matters.

My calendar is a living document.

THE CADENCE EFFECT

To ensure I'm focused on the right things, I'm constantly reviewing what I've done, what I'm doing and what I need to do. Time-blocking helps me stay on track with that.

You can use any format and method that works for you. It's all about experimenting with what works best, and then adapting and adjusting as you go along, doing more of what helps you to maintain momentum with your tasks.

As we've covered in earlier sections, momentum is an essential part of creating cadence.

TIME BLOCKING TIPS

Batch small, busy work tasks together into longer, single slots so that they don't scatter your attention when you do them willy-nilly.

- Set yourself up to win on the focus front by **addressing your notifications**. Set them to go at the time you need to move from one task to the other. I have my notifications come up 10 minutes before the time of the next activity, so that I can prepare to make the mental shift between tasks. If you don't use notifications, you could use a timer instead.

- Include blocks of time for **preparing to work, taking mini breaks from work** or between meeting slots, as well as **longer rest periods**. For example, include self-care, exercise, social time with people you feel connected to, meditation, hobby time or extra-curricular activities, or daydreaming time. (If it's not in the diary, it doesn't happen).

- If you're a visual person like me, you may find **colour coding your different tasks** is also a helpful visual aid for your brain. For example, my meetings are navy, client work is yellow, podcast work is orange, writing work is purple, admin is light blue, and anything related to health, wellness and 'fun stuff' is green. This way I can see at a glance what type of tasks and activities my days and weeks involve.

- If you need to maintain deep focus for the duration of a longer time block period, for example, 2 hours, then try setting a 20 minute or Pomodoro-style timer to **gamify the experience**. When I do this, I find I end up getting more done in each of those shorter slots and therefore more in total over the 2-hour period. Another example, my wearable reminds me to get up and move for a few minutes every hour, which keeps me limber without distracting me from my focus.

WORKING IN SYNC WITH YOUR CYCLES

Distractions disrupt focus and prevent us from entering flow, and a lack of purpose hinders our ability to do focused work.

Being overworked and overstressed are the enemies of flow, productivity, and creating healthy rhythms in our lives.

So, consider how you can connect how you work with your natural cycles in a way that aligns with your beliefs and your values.

Here are some prompts to guide you:

- Identify what work is truly important, what matters and is meaningful, and what is fluff.
- Get clear on your priorities, whether you're the one setting them or someone else is setting them for you.
- How much time do you typically spend doing various work-related activities? Track your time for each type of work.
- What's a good focus period for you? (20, 30, 45, 60 or 90 mins, or even 2 hours?)
- What's your energy typically like at different times of day? When are you most productive and least?
- Are you doing your deep and important work during your most productive times?

- What can you do to support entering a flow state more easily? What needs to change?

A NOTE ON PRODUCTIVITY METHODS

In this book, I've focused on just a few productivity methods that you can leverage as part of your intentional productivity practice.

However, there are so many other activities and systems out there. And don't get me started on the host of SaaS tools and tech stacks you can use to help implement these systems. Things like Asana, Trello, Notion, Evernote, ToDoist, and then there's all the Enterprise software out there too. It can be overwhelming!

Remember, there is no "one" right way to be productive, and the same applies to the tools you use.

Each of these methods and tools may work for you. However, you don't have to do or even try them all. You just need to find one, or a few, that works, which you can incorporate into your own toolkit or Cadence Canvas.

Keep it simple.

What we've covered so far has prepared you to think more deeply about your approach to how you work. Answering these questions is the next step on your journey to transforming your life with intentionally productive habits.

In the next chapter, I'll cover the importance of Rituals as part of our workflow.

This includes how rituals can connect us to a sense of purpose in our work, and ways we can use rituals to prepare ourselves for our digital work day.

TWENTY-FOUR
BUILDING RITUALS INTO OUR WORKFLOW

> The secret of your success is found in your daily routine.
>
> ~ JOHN C. MAXWELL

This may seem like a strange question, but do you have rituals you engage in as part of your work?

Rituals form a part of your daily routine, whether or not you're aware of them.

Being conscious of your rituals and how they prepare your mind for work and other activities is another part of developing your intentional productivity practice.

Rituals are important for three reasons:

1. They help to cement mindful habits.
2. They help us to make considered choices about how we want to approach our day.
3. They help us build firm foundations, so we can manage our stress and our tasks better.

Before we consider ways to implement them, let's first look at what rituals actually are and why they can be a powerful tool to support our focus and flow.

THE POWER OF RITUALS

Rituals are a grounding practice, but also a system that connects us emotionally to some sense of purpose.

We often associate rituals with big moments in our lives, like celebration and grief.

They can also help us deal with things like uncertainty, fear, anxiety, or under-confidence.

Rituals are, at their essence, a combination of multiple habits that create a process or system of behaviours.

Aside from rituals for the momentous occasions and experiences in our lives, we also have rituals in our day-to-day.

- They could be the small actions we take when we get ready to walk our dogs every morning, (e.g. put on shoes, grab the bags and dog treats, pick up the lead, call the dog, if they're not already tail wagging expectantly at the door).
- These rituals could be the things we typically do on a weekend morning if we have the luxury of a 'lie in', (e.g. make coffee, read in bed, have a late breakfast, go for a walk).

With us seeking more purpose in our work and dealing with huge amounts of uncertainty and change in our work lives, having rituals at work is important to help us stay grounded whilst maintaining momentum.

So how can we use rituals to benefit our work?

Here are a few simple examples of how I use rituals, and what I recommend to my clients to try out. You don't have to do them all to notice a difference, but these suggestions all serve a purpose and can become helpful allies in supporting your focus and flow.

MORNING & EVENING PAGES

Benjamin Franklin was a keen data capturer in that he kept a daily journal of his successes and frustrations. Not only does journaling improve our self-awareness, but it also helps us to stay on track with our goals and the larger plan for our weeks, months, and life.

Before I start my workday, I have a morning ritual around journaling, which I replicate at night.

> Journaling for me is a daily practice, one which I've done ever since it was prescribed to me as part of my burnout recovery protocol in 2016/17. In the morning, part of my practice involves documenting what I wish to achieve in my day. At the end of my day, I review what went right or "wrong", so that I can flag what I need to work on improving in future days.

I use an A5 or B5 sized notebook and write on both sides of a double-page spread, but you can use any format that works for you. Let's dive deeper into my practice, as an example.

In the morning:

- Within the first 5 minutes of waking, I write on one side of a double page spread.
- It involves noting 3 things I'm grateful for, and the top 3 things I want to achieve that day, how I want to show up for that work, and how I want to feel in myself.
- I might also write about what's on my mind, and what I dreamt about.

THE CADENCE EFFECT

In the evening:

- Before bed, I write on the other side of the page about what happened during my day, how I felt, what went well or didn't, and how I can make things better.
- It's a recap that helps me acknowledge my learning from the day, to let go of what's on my mind, and to prepare me for tomorrow.

This process of reflection helps me to stay on track with my goals and tasks. It also helps me manage my stress, as I'm taking my worries out of my head and putting them on the page. It can also aid sleep, as when I write things down, I'm less likely to have anxious, time-dependent ToDos swirling in my mind overnight.

My journaling practices take between 5 and 15 minutes for each session, but you can choose how long your write for. It doesn't have to be a time-consuming exercise, or you can take an hour. It's up to you.

Do you already have a journaling habit? How can you implement some of these reflective practices into your morning and evening?

EARLY MORNING RITUALS

Many well-known creative thinkers, including composer Ludwig Von Beethoven, leader and polymath Benjamin Franklin, writer Toni Morrison, neurologist Oliver Sacks, and biochemist and writer Isaac Asimov, were advocates of early rising to be more productive.

These visionaries and innovators made a habit of getting up between 5 and 6 am and completing their deep creative work before lunch time.

Getting up at the crack of sparrow fart is a practice also promoted by Robin Sharma in his book The 5am Club, which I referenced in an earlier chapter. Five am starts are also something I got into the swing of doing when I was writing this book.

When I first made plans to bring my ideas together into a book, I found I just wasn't getting to it during my usual work day. Client work and busy work were taking all my attention, and my creative brain was too exhausted by the end of the day to dive in. I was feeling frustrated and knew I needed to create space for the book.

I only had small pockets of time to write first thing in the morning. So, I'd journal and meditate first, and then jump into working on a chapter. The stillness in those early hours helped me enter a focused state really quickly, and I was incredibly efficient in those 90mins, before I got on with my usual day filled with busy client work.

I don't do this all the time, but what I like about getting up super early is that it creates space to ground me. It's a little pocket of time just for me. It helps me prepare myself, before the craziness of my day takes over and sometimes derails best laid plans.

Time feels slower and more expansive at this time of the morning. It's like being in a liminal space.

Rather than diving into my phone and emails and social media and freaking out my brain first thing, I find I wake in a way that is more attuned to the natural rhythms of my body. It's a brilliant way to start the day!

Whether you use early morning time for self-care, exercise, work, or other responsibilities, you may find it helps you level up your focus on what really matters, in a more intentional way.

As mentioned in the chapter on Cycles of Productivity, you may not be an early morning person, and that's totally ok too! Find a wake up time that works according to your own natural cycles.

Important notes:

With sleep being a priority practice for intentional productivity, if you are getting up early, you need to be going to bed early, otherwise an early morning routine isn't sustainable over the long haul!

THE CADENCE EFFECT

With cadence front of mind, your morning routines (whenever you rise) should be flexible enough that you can adjust them based on what's happening in your day. Sometimes you may only have 10 minutes to journal or meditate, and other times, 2 hours to include exercise and a creative writing stint. Know how to adapt your tools, so they can still support you, in the time that you do have.

STARTING & ENDING WORK RITUALS

Creating transition practices for beginning and ending our work day helps with focus and flow, as they prepare our mind for what comes next.

In traditional, pre-pandemic work environments, a typical commute to the office helped us transition into and out of work mode.

On the way in, we might mull over what needs to be done in the day, getting ourselves ready for work. And the commute home helps us decompress and prepare ourselves for who we need to be in our home life.

So, if we are now no longer "office bound", how do we replicate that transition without a commute when our desk might be 3 metres from our kitchen and 4 from our bedroom?

- It might involve a walk outside, some stretches or meditation, listening to a podcast while making breakfast, or getting dinner prepared after work.

At the start of your workday, what small triggers can you use to activate work mode before you open your email and dive into the demands of the day?

- This could be as simple as taking 3 long, slow, deep, conscious breaths in and out while your computer boots up in the morning.
- Or the ritual could be sipping a coffee while you open your planner and review your day ahead.

If you work from home, it's important to create a boundary between home and work life.

The writer Maya Angelou was a big advocate for separating home from work environments. For years, she rented a hotel room where she wrote for part of every day, but you don't need to be this drastic to create the space to be in work mode.

Even if you don't have a workspace where you can close the door, you can create a space within your environment that is designated specifically for work.

If you missed it, I covered the importance of work environments in the section on How We Work.

If the only space you have is the dining room table, then how you create your boundary is by shutting down and putting away your laptop at the end of your work day.

The aim is to clear and reset the room for its next usage, which may be dinner with your partner, or helping the kids with their homework.

Clutter also causes unnecessary stress, and clearing the space is about creating a mental shift.

HOW I TRANSITION INTO & OUT OF WORK.

I use these two simple rituals irrespective of whether I'm working from my home office, my coworking space, or with a client.

I have a preparation ritual for starting work.

- I place my coffee, tea, or water on the right side of my desk.
- After I turn on my laptop, I open my bullet journal, which sits to the left of my laptop.
- While the computer is booting up, I review what's on the task list for the day.
- And off we go!

- This simple ritual helps to prepare my mind for work, signalling the start of the workday and getting me into 'work mode'.

I follow a shutting down process.

- I review my electronic calendar for the next day and cross reference that with my bullet journal to make sure my tasks are up to date.
- Then I close ALL my applications and my browser and I shut down my laptop.
- This shut down ritual signals to my brain that work is now over.

Both rituals support my focus and productivity because they help to compartmentalise work, so it doesn't take over every second of my day.

I enforce boundaries around my availability.

I have clients in the USA, so sometimes I'm contending with a time difference that requires me to be available later than 5pm.

When entering into new contracts with new clients, I ensure they're aware up front that I'm available for calls, meetings, etc. for a specific time window on week days. So that might be 9am to 12pm their time (which is between the late afternoon and early evening for me).

I also have a hard stop rule. I need to be offline by 8pm.

This is irrespective of what webinars, talks, courses or training is going on that I may wish to watch. This hard stop is essential to ensure I have sufficient time for my brain to calm down, so that I can sleep well and get enough rest. If I don't do this, my mind gets too overstimulated to sleep.

Sometimes I need to be waking at 5am to ensure I can **keep an adequate morning routine** (time for myself, exercise, journaling etc), before I start my project work and client work.

If I am waking so early, to maintain my energy during a long day that may go into the evening, I will take a long rest period in the middle of the day, that may involve a walk and or some meditation or reading.

At times, I also work weekends, but that is my prerogative to do so. I am not available to clients, and I make that very clear. I also ensure that even though I am working on the weekend, I also make time for active or passive rest activities, such as exercise, socialising and time away from the screen.

These intentional actions help me stay focused and productive, and reduce my risk of experiencing burnout.

Enforcing boundaries is necessary to help our mind and body rest and recharge before we climb back into the hot seat the next day.

We've become so accustomed to checking emails on our phones before our official work day starts or after it is done. Or we leave our laptop on, sitting on the dining table, just in case we need to dip in again.

These actions just keep dragging us back into work mode, elevating our stress levels and preventing us from switching off from work. They are terrible for our productivity and our health!

Setting boundaries may feel challenging to do when our work habits and our client cultures are so ingrained.

But it's simpler than you think to initiate this change. It starts with a conversation. It starts by putting it out there, stating the reasons to your clients or your management team why it's important to do this.

- What transitions can you implement at the start and end of your workday? It could be clearing your desk of clutter and ticking off your To Dos. Shutting down your open programmes and closing your laptop screen signifies to your brain that work is done.

- What boundaries can you set with family, coworkers, clients and other things competing for your attention?

Consider what opening and closing rituals you can practise to support your mind and shift your attention from work to home life?

RITUALS AROUND PHONE USE

As mentioned repeatedly, our phone use contributes to a loss of focus and a fracturing of our attention. So we need to develop better habits around how we use them.

Out of sight is out of mind.

Our addiction to our phones is often beyond our control. But what is within our control is to put it in a drawer or put it out of line of sight and turn off notifications when we are trying to do our deep work.

Ask yourself, is having this temptation within arm's reach really more important than what you're trying to achieve in this moment?

HELPFUL MEETING RITUALS

Lengthy and unnecessary meetings are the enemy of productive, focused work. But when we have them, how can we make them a more supportive and valuable experience?

Here are two examples of simple ways to improve your meeting experiences.

1. Bring everyone out of their heads and into the physical / virtual room.

- Do a 1 minute mindful breathing exercise at the start of your meetings, preferably with everyone in the physical or virtual room taking part.

If this isn't possible, can you do the breathing exercise by yourself before the meeting starts?

2. Build empathy and connection during team meetings.

- If you have regular team or client meetings, create the habit of sharing. Get everyone to briefly mention one good thing that happened this week and one thing they have found challenging.

If you work on your own, you can still incorporate this practice as part of your journaling ritual.

What are other ways can you employ rituals to support your meetings?

- There might be small behaviours that you already engage in without being aware of them.

- What are they, and do they support you? If not, what can you experiment with changing?

MINI MOVEMENT RITUALS

As mentioned in the chapter on Building Strong Foundations, there are breathing exercises you can do to calm your mind and balance the two sides of your nervous system.

Building the ritual of regular movement into your workday is another practical way to do this so you can improve your focus ability.

Mini movements during work time help to re-energise your body and mitigate the strain of digital working.

They don't have to be disruptive or get you hot and sweaty. Instead, they are small physical movements you can do at your desk or next to it.

- Keep your wrists limber by rotating your hands a few times, clockwise and anti-clockwise.
- Rotate your feet in the same way.

- Repeatedly clench your fists and then release your fingers in a star shape.
- Rotate your shoulders backwards to compensate for the hunching posture that is common when we work.
- If you're feeling lethargic or tired, rubbing your hands together vigorously or shaking out your hands brings energy and heat into your body, which can make you feel more alert.

Do these mini movements for a minute or two at a time, at least a few times a day.

RITUALS FOR WORK EVENTS & OUTCOMES

Think about how you embrace both success and change. Acknowledging our success supports and reinforces the basic human need we have for belonging.

It's important to celebrate our work-related wins, no matter how big or small.

1. HONOUR THE WINS

Creating rituals for how you celebrate your success signals to your brain that you are seen, acknowledged, or recognised — and therefore valued.

- Priya Parker, author of the *The Art of Gathering*, talks a lot about incorporating fun and celebration into work gatherings to help build team cohesion.

What celebratory rituals can you incorporate into your working practice to acknowledge both the small gains and the big wins?

That could be a team pint at the pub, a spa treatment, tickets to the theatre, sharing an accomplishment on social media, highlighting it in a team meeting, or calling your friends and family? Every win matters, so make a big deal of it, even if you work on your own!

2. CREATE SPACE FOR TRANSITIONS

When one intensive work project completes, and before you get ready to start another, how do you separate the two?

Rituals are also great for honouring change and creating transitions between projects.

- A closing ritual is helpful so that you can start a new project with a fresh outlook, without the remnants and residue of one distracting you from the other.

What activities help you shut things down in your mind after an event or project, so that you can move on to another without any lurking baggage or stress? What do you to prepare your mind for starting something new?

It could be journaling, physically packing away paperwork, shredding old notes, archiving a digital file, or taking a few days off from deep work.

New rituals are like habits. They take hold more easily when we attach them to things we already do.

- What small actions or early morning rituals can you add into your existing daily routines?
- How can you build on existing rituals you do to support your mind for work?
- And how do you shift your headspace out of work mode, when it's time to call it a day?

The final section (Part 6) is about Next Steps.

We'll revisit making a cadence canvas with guidance on crafting and implementing your own. In the final chapter, I'll share where things are headed and what we need to look out for.

NOTES

PART SIX
NEXT STEPS

6. **NEXT STEPS**

4. Opportunities

5. Focus & Flow

1. Introduction

3. How We Work

2. Challenges

TWENTY-FIVE
MAKING A CADENCE CANVAS

It's time to consider your vision of what creating cadence and being intentionally productive looks like for you.

Looking back to the Cadence Canvas Framework™ introduced in Chapter 3, all the topics covered in this book come together to help you achieve the elements and outcomes of this framework.

There are two phases to this process, which will unfold in Part 6 of the book.

The first phase is about adding your specific practices, habits, behaviours and outcomes to each of the four sections of the canvas. The second part is about your plan for how you go about implementing those things.

Use this framework as your guide, but write or type your answers in a format that works for you.

First, let's recap what the canvas is and how it relates to the framework.

WHY A CANVAS?

I chose this word for the Cadence Canvas Framework™ because a clean canvas forms the base from which to create and iterate. With it, we can draw or paint a picture of the life we want to lead and the ways we want to live and work within it.

On your canvas, you can add the elements that reinforce your resilience, support your wellbeing, and underpin your productivity.

If the word 'canvas' doesn't resonate, consider these alternatives:

- Your **'Blueprint for Intentional Productivity'** — showing the dimensions which map out your foundations for working better.

- Your **'Toolkit for Doing'** — your collection of 'go to' resources that you rely on to stay the course in each facet of your work and life.

- Or your **'Recipe for High Performance'** — a shortlist of vital ingredients that helps you to experience your ideal daily productive state.

Whatever name you give your canvas, the point is that this collection of activities, behaviours and intentional habits are **your compass points**.

Your compass points are the foundational activities you implement daily.

They are the rituals and routines that ground you.

The tools you reach for when you're struggling to stay focused and productive.

The cornerstones that support a more resilient life in which you can thrive.

THE CADENCE CANVAS FRAMEWORK™

PROCESS

Developing a personal workflow of systems and processes supports our focus, wellbeing, creativity and productivity.

PERFORMANCE

Improving our self-leadership abilities and being more intentional about our productivity activates more of our potential.

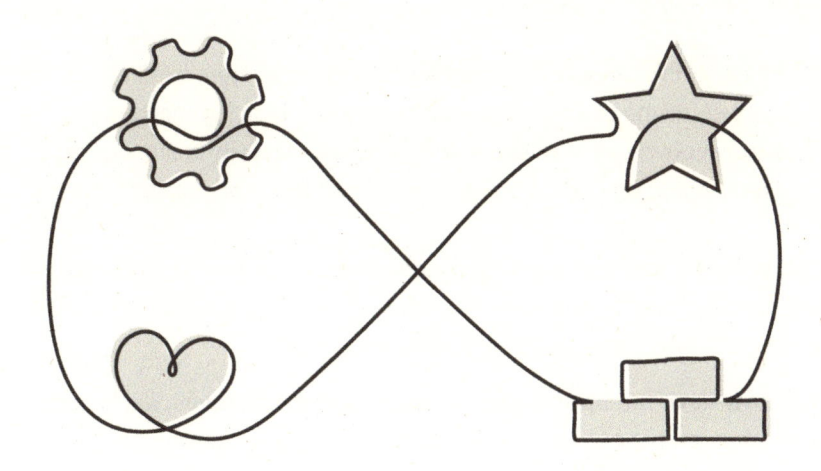

CULTURE

Placing purpose, wellbeing and meaning at the centre of how we work creates connection and aligns our values with our goals.

FOUNDATION

Building strong physical, mental, emotional, and environmental foundations helps us thrive over the long term.

The intention of the canvas is to help you activate your potential by:

- Building strong foundations
- Developing effective processes
- Cultivating a happier work and life culture
- Elevating your performance

These components are what help you to envision and achieve meaning, purpose and happiness, sustained wellbeing, and success in your life and work.

When we implement these elements and make them part of our daily activities, they enable us to create momentum, work with purpose and live with more intention. This activates more of our potential and helps us to craft a more meaningful life.

> I deliberately designed the framework around a figure 8 infinity symbol, as the practice of creating cadence, building momentum, and becoming more intentional with our productivity is an ongoing process and practice. It's like a dance that loops back and forth.

You will find that you continually revisit each of these sections as part of adapting your cadence, as you adjust your personal practices to suit your work and life needs at different times.

You now have the opportunity to craft your own Canvas, and I also share tips on how to take action consistently and adapt your canvas as you go.

Then, in the final chapter of the book, I'll share closing thoughts on what the future holds.

Now, it's time to pull together your answers and notes from each section, so you can put the final touches to your own Cadence Canvas.

TWENTY-SIX
CRAFTING YOUR CANVAS

In this section, first we're going to create your canvas, and then I'll share tips on how to implement it with ease.

The final chapter includes a quick recap, plus I'll also share my views on the future of work.

GETTING STARTED

You need a central place to gather and store all the ideas, notes, observations, practices, and tools that will support this vision.

This central place will act as your guide for implementing new habits and behaviours and staying on track with them.

It could be a notebook or an electronic folder.

Before we add notes to our canvas, we need to be clear on our starting points and our aspirations.

These exercises will help you decide what you want to keep and what you want to change about your habits, behaviours and goals.

1. WHAT'S YOUR BASELINE?

We can't make change if we don't understand where we are.

The first thing I ask new clients to do is to assess what they do in their day. We do this to establish a baseline to work from.

A baseline helps us understand whether these habits, actions and activities are having positive or negative effects on our behaviour, mood, creativity and productivity.

So consider:

- What are you doing in the first 1-2 hours of waking in your day?
- What does a typical workday's tasks involve?
- How much time do you spend on each type of task in a week?
- Which tasks are stressful, and which tasks are enjoyable?
- What are you doing in the last 2 hours before bed?

2. WHAT'S YOUR IDEAL DAY?

Next, consider what typically happens in your day-to-day.

What does a good day look like?

- What are the things that help to make your day feel great?
- What activities fuel your flow, inspire you, and bring you joy?
- What typically needs to happen for you to finish your work day thinking, *"today was an awesome day!"*.

These variables may be simple things such as making sure you drink enough water during the day and eat at regular times, so you don't get hangry. Or that you move around regularly, so you don't feel stiff.

They could be more communicative or relational, such as getting clear feedback on the work that you deliver, or being acknowledged for your contribution with a compliment.

CRAFTING YOUR CANVAS

A good day for you could be technical or process-driven, such as feeling more accomplished and productive if you get 2 hours of coding done *before* you respond to emails.

Or they could involve creating healthy boundaries, such as being able to set limits on the amount of Zoom calls and meetings you have during a day.

When we're aware of what makes our day run smoothly, what reduces our stress and helps us work better, then we can do more of those things to ensure that we have more of those great days at work.

Your ideal day reflects your activated potential.

In the context of the Cadence Canvas™, the ingredients for an ideal day and the outcomes you're able to achieve in that ideal day will sit under the PERFORMANCE section of the canvas.

Consider:

- What are the specific elements that make up an excellent performance at work, or a best day in your life?
- What can you do more of, to bring more meaning to your work and more joy to your life?
- "Who" is it you want to be at work and in life? How do you want to show up?

3. WHAT ARE YOUR ESSENTIAL ELEMENTS?

Now, consider the other exercises we've covered in this book.

If you've completed the questions and exercises from the various reflection sections, you can use those answers to help define your essential elements.

If you need a bit of extra help or inspiration, download the **FREE Cadence Canvas Cheat Sheet** which lists examples you can use to craft your canvas, and includes a blank canvas template. *Sign up to the Cadence Newsletter to get the Cheat Sheet - creatingcadence.co/subscribe.*

THE CADENCE EFFECT

These elements will become part of your recipe, toolkit, blueprint or canvas.

STEP 1:

Based on your observations, <u>list the top 10-15 habits</u>, behaviours, processes and/or workflow elements which can help you to be more focused, creative and productive.

These activities need to be things you identify with and can easily implement, activate, or communicate.

They can include a mix of things you can engage in before work, during work, and / or after work.

We want to keep it simple and manageable, starting small and building from there.

If you're stuck, the downloadable Canvas Cheat Sheet mentioned above provides examples.

STEP 2:

Group your selected habits and behaviours to fit into the remaining three Canvas categories:

- FOUNDATIONS
- PROCESS
- CULTURE

It's ok if you have more activities in one tier than the others. And some may straddle more than one category, pick the one that is most relevant.

If there are gaps, revisit what might be missing. You may discover there are other things you want to add to the 'Performance' section too.

Try to keep your selection simple and summarised. You won't stick with anything that involves a copious and convoluted list of instructions!

Reference the examples on the Canvas Cheat Sheet if you need help.

CRAFTING YOUR CANVAS

STEP 3:

Create a visual representation of your canvas, blueprint, toolkit or recipe that you can view every day as a reminder.

- This could be as bullet points jotted on a large post it, or a paper index card you put above your laptop.
- Or it could be a poster you design on Canva, a hand-drawn illustration, a digital diagram, or a spreadsheet of the most important things that help to support your ideal work experience.
- You can also turn this representation into a screensaver on your phone, laptop or desktop to serve as a daily reminder and to help you stay accountable for the changes you want to make.

Make your canvas an easy reference point, to inform and inspire you to bring more of these elements into how you work daily.

Be super specific in how you list your ideal work day and toolkit elements.

When things feel messy or unclear, we default to inaction, but being specific creates clarity for our brain.

So, don't state vaguely "I will do rituals during my day".

You need to specify the exact rituals and routines that are important to you.

For example:

- Journal for 15 minutes in bed before I start my day.
- Do mini movements when I get up from my desk to pour a glass of water.
- Breathe deeply for 2 minutes before every meeting, etc.
- A minimum of 30 minutes walking, yoga or weights every day.
- Take a 30 minute break from screens at lunchtime.
- A maximum of 2 Zoom meetings per day.

- No screen time between 8pm and 6am.

Note: You can find more examples on the cheat sheet.

STEP 4: (For Teams)

If you work in a team, do this exercise together, or compare notes.

Comparing your toolkit with your coworkers' versions enables you to spot patterns that may benefit everyone in the team.

This comparison can help you decide collectively about which activities, behaviours, habits or processes in your workday may be most important to implement to support you better as a team. This would be alongside any personal activities you want to engage in as part of this exercise.

You may feel awkward sharing the things you do outside of work, to support what do you within it. However, remember that we carry how we feel with us, so everything we do outside of work counts towards our performance at work.

It's all relevant, and sharing about it with team mates may create more relatable connections and boost empathy.

When we collaborate on identifying and implementing changes together, it helps to build those foundations for team cohesion, improved communication and high performance outputs.

Collaborating on improving work practices also leads to a healthier, happier work culture, which means your team commits to staying, instead of leaving!

Now for the next step … Implementing Your Canvas.

In the penultimate chapter, I share tips on how to take action, so you can implement your intentional productivity plan with ease.

TWENTY-SEVEN
IMPLEMENTING YOUR CANVAS

Great job on putting together your canvas!

The next stage involves taking action, one small step at a time.

When implementing your canvas, the aim is to create momentum by carrying out manageable actions consistently.

Step by step, these small changes create marginal gains, which compound over time to become far more than their individual steps.

IMPLEMENTATION TIPS

Remember, you're going for longevity, not speed.

Your canvas is a living, breathing thing just like you, so your steps or elements don't have to be carved in stone.

Experimentation sits at the heart of creating cadence and building intentional productivity. It's ok to pivot, add or remove certain habits, behaviours or activities, if they are not serving you.

This is a process of consistent practice and constant refinement.

However, before deciding whether to remove or change something, I recommend experimenting for more than a week, preferably 4-6 weeks.

Collect adequate data to make an informed decision about how best to change things.

The process and practice of being intentionally productive requires commitment, which means you need to keep showing up and trying again. That's that way you hone your practice.

How To Implement - An Example

- Try something out for at least 2, and preferably 4-6 weeks.
- Make a note of how certain behaviours and activities pan out during your week and your month.
- Then review and assess.
- If certain things aren't working, decide on how you can adapt them slightly to get a better result.
- Then try the new routines and rituals out for at least a few weeks.
- Review and assess, adapt, and continue.
- Repeat :)

A gentle reminder that this is not supposed to be a rigid process.

It is meant to be fluid and flexible, to fit into the changing needs and cadence of your days, weeks and years. And it can be fun!

These aren't rules, they are compass points to guide you.

They are what you come back to when external factors take you off track.

Over time, they help you build a consistent practice that becomes a part of your life, which then stays with you for life.

They form the structural framework for building a work-life that supports you better, because it helps you build better cadence into your days.

IMPLEMENTING YOUR CANVAS

This is a way of living and working that helps you create more meaning in your days and activates your potential in all facets of your life.

These transformational habits are the cadence effect in action.

NOW LET'S RECAP AND WRAP UP.

In the final chapter, I offer my observations on where I see things going.

I'm recapping what we've covered in this book, as well as sharing thoughts on where the future of work seems to be heading, and how that may affect our wellbeing and productivity.

TWENTY-EIGHT
MOVING FORWARDS

> Life is always moving, and we need to move with it.
>
> ~ MICH BONDESIO

Wow, this book endeavour was a labour of love, which has turned out to be a way bigger deal than I ever planned! Thank you for making the time to engage with it.

I hope it helps you to improve your life and your working practices in profound ways, in the same way that these methods and modalities have helped me.

Before I let you go, I'm going to briefly recap what we've covered. However, nothing we do happens in isolation.

So, aside from reviewing the key themes, in this chapter I also share my opinion on the larger perspective of where I see things are going with the future of work.

These are important developments which contributed to me deciding to write this book.

KEY THEMES

The concept of productivity in our modern work environment has changed. Meaning and purpose now form part of what we call productive output.

Changing your approach to work and productivity helps you to improve your focus and get more meaningful work done in a way that also supports your wellbeing.

Yet, we are still constrained by traditional work models, cultural norms, and social influences, all of which affect our productivity.

Outside of our immediate work, our global context, and societal and cultural norms, also affect our performance and wellbeing. Our workspace, work tools, work styles and workflow impact on our attention and our outputs. Stress and procrastination put pressure on our wellbeing and focus.

However, there are practical ways that we can counteract the impact of the stresses and strains which affect our lifestyles and work styles. It has been my intention in this book to share some of these helpful practices.

We can retrain our brains to support intentionally productive practices by:

- Creating better habits
- Leveraging our natural rhythms and cycles
- Developing supportive rituals and routines
- Placing self-care and wellbeing first in everything we do
- Improving our mindset about work

To master intentionally productive practices, we need to understand exactly how our behaviours and our tools are helping or hindering our wellbeing and performance.

Then incorporate more supportive practices into how we work and build stronger foundations that bolster our resilience and keep us strong.

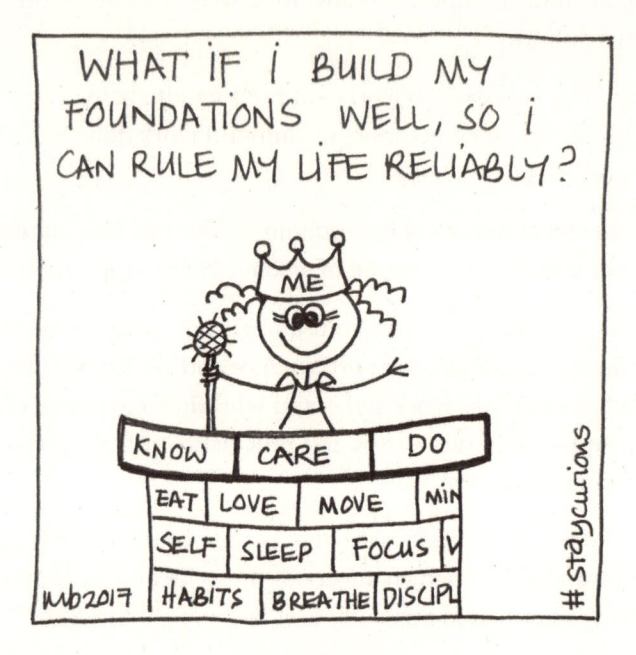

> WHAT IF I BUILD MY FOUNDATIONS WELL, SO I CAN RULE MY LIFE RELIABLY?
>
> ME
>
> KNOW | CARE | DO
> EAT | LOVE | MOVE | MIN
> SELF | SLEEP | FOCUS
> mb2017 | HABITS | BREATHE | DISCIPL
>
> #staycurious

© Mich Bondesio

Doing this aids our focus and productivity. It also helps us to build stronger foundations and healthier cultures at work, creating the space for doing more purposeful work and building a more meaningful life.

> **Intentional productivity is <u>not</u> about a rigid set of rules. And it's <u>not</u> about getting more out of ourselves or others.**
>
> **Instead, it's about finding the best within ourselves. It's a fluid framework to guide us in how we do everything.**
>
> ~ MICH BONDESIO

When we become more mindful and intentional about how we work, we can activate more of our business potential and create more meaning in our lives.

When we slow things down, that helps us to improve and sustain a healthier pace of productivity, a smoother rhythm in work and life, and continued momentum over the long term.

This is the cadence effect in action.

As I said right at the beginning … **you <u>don't</u> have to do everything** recommended in this book to experience the benefits of the cadence effect.

Start small and simple, pick a few manageable changes you can implement, and build slowly from there.

Remember, intentional productivity is about developing a lifelong love affair with activating your potential.

Fill this journey with learning, curiosity and fun. Be open to getting to know yourself better.

THE BIGGER PICTURE

The importance of purpose-driven working practices is coming to the fore, now more than ever.

This movement around "doing business better" has been growing for some time, supported by the popularity of movements such as B-Corp and those (like me) advocating for sustainable working practices that take account of the bigger picture.

It's about so much more than just work and business. It's about community, connection, thriving, and creating meaning in our lives.

One of my favourite thinkers and speakers on this topic is Simon Sinek, who sums it up well in this quote.

> The idea of purpose has nothing to do with business. It is a deep-seated human need. The need to belong is deeply ingrained in us. The more that we feel we belong to our tribe, that our company and work have meaning beyond the money we make and the products we sell, it

is incredibly fulfilling and joyful. And it just so happens that it's good for business.

~ SIMON SINEK

To me, putting wellbeing at the centre of how we work is a no brainer.

This is not just because of my lived experience with epic burnout.

It's also because when we are strong, healthy and resilient, we can be our "better selves". This makes us better for those around us, and better at what we do out in the world.

This is such a key differentiator from the way most people work and do business.

It's not just a competitive advantage, though. It's also an opportunity for us to activate so much more meaning and potential in our lives.

THE PANDEMIC LED TO MORE PURPOSE SEEKING, BUT ALSO PANDEMONIUM.

Seeking meaning in our work and life has also inadvertently led to the Great Resignation, an unexpected outcome of the Covid-19 pandemic.

Vast numbers have left their careers and jobs to work for themselves, or somewhere else which promises to be better. Unfortunately, the transition hasn't always been smooth. Often, unhelpful and unhealthy work habits - ingrained because of the culture people were previously working in - are transferred over to the way they now work for themselves.

When these people branch out on their own, they don't always have the same level of support around them they had before. They can also become overstressed and end up overworking, which we know leads to burnout.

MOVING FORWARDS

When this scenario plays out, it also means they don't find meaning in what they are doing, despite leaving their old jobs to do just that. This is just one example of how overwork can affect us.

Overwork is caused by having a lack of clarity, a lack of leadership, and a lack of clear boundaries.

Whether you work on your own, or with a team, being intentional with your productivity is an opportunity to design a better way of working.

It's a more manageable and sustainable way of working.

Whatever your circumstances and work situation, you have the power to make change.

© Mich Bondesio

You can create healthier habits that support better performance and outputs. You can find more meaning, both in your work and in how you carry out that work. You have the chance to set boundaries with yourself, your coworkers, and your clients, deciding what's acceptable and what's not, based on your values and purpose.

Remember, you need to respect your own boundaries first, if you want others to respect them too.

This book and the Cadence Canvas Framework™ are my attempt to help with these issues.

To help you to build better ways of working that create the freedom and space for you to include more meaningful experiences in your life.

This book is a call for us to transform how we work, to throw down the mantle of overwork and redesign traditional work systems that don't serve us.

There is always another way, and it's within our power to find it.

LIFE & WORK IN THE METAVERSE

> We stand on the precipice of fundamental transformation.
>
> ~ LEX FRIDMAN

Our work pressures are going to increase as we head further into virtual work landscapes with new AI coworkers powered by machine learning and a host of associated technologies.

Things are moving incredibly fast in this sphere, and the learning curve is currently steep.

It's the reason I purposefully haven't written much about this technological transition, as what I share will be out of date before I publish this book! But who knows, perhaps these advancements, and their impact on us, will be the topic of my next one. :)

On the plus side, these new tech tools will aid with efficiency, productivity and other elements of work that perhaps we haven't even thought about yet. In particular, Cal Newport believes they will improve our efficiency by providing more *shallow task automation*.

Some of these technologies are already proving to be helpful for our work and for our wellbeing, for our medical advancement and our environmental challenges. In terms of future applications, anything seems possible at this point.

The only limit is our imagination.

On the less helpful side, it's obvious that we will lose many jobs as AI takes over some work functions.

Those who can't adapt will struggle.

Issues such as ethics, legality, regulation, and responsible usage policies for AI, blockchain, etc., are slowly being hashed out. Yet most lay people feel terrified by the potential capabilities of these tools, as so much is still unknown.

These rapid and radical changes are perceived by our body and brain as a threat to our survival.

So, alongside the economic and political flux occurring in our world context, these tech changes are also causing stress, anxiety and pressure, which are affecting our performance and our health.

However, this is the nature of technological progress. We need to embrace and get involved in the change.

New roles will also be created as part of this transition. As will new ways of working.

I see it as an opportunity that we can leverage, with some caveats…

A mindful approach to using these tools and technologies is going to be critically important to help support our minds and bodies in this "fantastical future" that's already a part of our present.

We need to set boundaries around how we use our tools, as well as manage our stress and build our resilience. So we can keep up with

the pace of this life that is in perpetual motion (and moving exponentially faster).

© Mich Bondesio

Much of what I recommend in The Cadence Effect applies in these new spaces, too.

None of these tech advances will diminish the power of building strong foundations, and developing more intentional, sustainable practices to support our health, wellbeing, creativity and productivity.

With that in mind, I know that the contents of this book will stand you in good stead into the future, too.

THE NEXT STEP

Thank you for putting yourself first by buying and reading this book.

The next step is to take a step, and you can do this in two ways.

MOVING FORWARDS

1. TAKE ACTION

Today is the day!

It's time to activate your potential, transform your life and support your wellbeing and productivity better by implementing the practices suggested in this book.

Share your endeavours and progress on social media by tagging

#thecadenceeffect
#intentionalproductivity

© Mich Bondesio

2. SPREAD THE WORD

Please help me keep the conversation going, by sharing your experience of The Cadence Effect, so that together we can build the momentum to create profound and positive changes in the world of work.

I'll be over the moon if you could please leave a helpful review wherever you've purchased your copy, and tell all your friends about The Cadence Effect.

The more of us in the Cadence Club, the better outcomes we can create for ourselves, the world, and our future in it. :)

I wish you all the best on your journey! Thanks and keep moving forwards, with courage, curiosity and cadence.

Mich x

thecadenceeffect.com

creatingcadence.co

ACKNOWLEDGEMENTS

Despite requiring many long and lonesome hours in front of a laptop, writing a book isn't a solo mission.

There are a LOT of special people who helped, inspired, and guided me on this path. Both during the book creation process, and also well before the idea of doing this crazy thing was even a tiny spark in the back of my mind.

THE VIP'S

Without the support of these amazing people, I wouldn't have taken all the tiny steps that brought me to this exciting and momentous place.

> First, **BIG thanks and BIG hugs to MY FAMILY**. For being there for me, and for trusting in me, despite not knowing where this weird and wonderful adventure was taking me. Although you are far from me, I carry you with me always.
>
> **Catarina and Brendan King, Chris, Alex, Kally,** and the Society1 crew, for your friendship, camaraderie and brilliant advice. You are wonderful collaborators who always help me see the bigger picture, and your special workspace is where I found "my people" up North. society1.co.uk
>
> **Ed Matthews-Gentle FRSA** and **Jonathan Ball**, who both took a chance on working with me when no one else would. You are both gems! creativelancashire.org

MY BADASS BETA READERS

Shout out to this awesome collection of creative entrepreneurs who all do fantastic things in their own right!

Thank you for your time and careful attention. I appreciate your hand-holding, cheerleading skills, and incredible feedback.

Your contributions have helped make the book everything I wanted it to be. It was such fun having you along for some of this wild ride!

Trudi Roth - itsthetrustory.com
Kelly Berry - learnstartgrow.com
Susanna Hooper - everbetty.com
Jan Richards - jan-richards.com
Tom Bentley - tombentley.com
Catarina King - society1.co.uk

MAGIC MENTORS & COLLABORATORS

Thanks to the mentors and collaborators who advised me on this book-creation journey.

Danielle Hughes for strategic copywriting support with the development of my marketing materials, and for helping me find my voice. morethanwordscopy.com

Joanna Penn for her excellent podcast and writing resources, her encouragement and her infectious enthusiasm about life and tech. I'm so grateful for your help with finalising my book title! thecreativepenn.com

Rachel Simpson for creating my vision of this book cover, redesigning the framework, and creating the book illustrations. You are a joy to work with and I appreciate your patience. wearebird.co.uk

Jerod Morris, Brian Clark, Trudi Roth and the fabulous **Unemployable Initiative Community** (particularly the Monday Accountability Club) for their learning, support, feedback, mentorship and friendships. I am so fortunate to know you all. unemployable.com / movement.consulting

Pat Williams for helping me figure out how to Fix This Next, for being a huge Creating Cadence podcast fan, and for unforgettable adventures in Arizona! cybercletch.com

J. Thorn for being an accountability buddy, offering expert advice and good laughs. I appreciate being able to learn from you and your excellent writer community. theauthorlife.com

IN THE WINGS

Thanks also to these wonderful people in my network who have supported me over the years, collaborated with me, attended my early workshops, and helped me get to this point.

The teams at **Lancashire Forum Creative** (Laurie, Lena and Juliane), the **Centre for SME Development**, (The two Sues, Alison, and Becky), **iROWE**, (Val and Adrian) and the **University of Central Lancashire LSBE**. I'm so grateful for the many opportunities for learning and support. uclan.ac.uk

The team at **Boost**, for training, business mentorship, and featuring my progress over the years on your blog. boostbusinesslancashire.co.uk

The Lancashire crew of collaborators, guinea pigs, experimenters, participants, and peanut gallery contributors - **Amanda; Amy; Ben & Rachel; Emma; Garth; Gordie & Laurie; Jacqueline; Jill, Sally & Ellie; Kieran, Barrie & Simon; Matt, Jack & Steph; Mel B; Mel J; Paul; Sarah & Stephen; Simon P;**

Sirka; and **Steffan**, plus so many more lovely people than I can mention here - thank you.

Veronica Fossa (veronicafossa.com) and **Magdalena Rungaldier** (ma-people.com) for being my sounding board squad and EU cheerleading contingent.

The inspiring creative thinkers I met at **The Do Lectures** (thedolectures.com) back in 2016 at the start of this journey. This includes **Barrie Thomson** (feastsandfables.co.uk); **James Taplin**; **Juliet Simmons**; **Michael Burne**; **Mark Shayler** (thisisape.co.uk); and **Penny Lee** (thebranddirectoress.com).

Peter Jones, my (now-retired) career coach. You showed me that there is always another way, when I was struggling to find mine.

THE MISFITS, REBELS & CRAZY ONES

That's you my lovely reader!

Like me (and Steve Jobs), you see things differently.

And by engaging with this book, you're ready to change your own status quo.

Thanks for supporting me, now it's your turn.

Off you go!

Onwards, with courage, curiosity and cadence. :)

thecadenceeffect.com

creatingcadence.co

FULL AUTHOR BIOGRAPHY

ABOUT MICH BONDESIO

Michelle Bondesio is a writer, speaker, coach and entrepreneur.

Mich *(pronounced Mish with an 'ish')* is the founder of Creating Cadence, the host of The Creating Cadence Podcast, and the author of The Cadence Effect.

The focus of her work is on transforming our habits and practices to activate more of our potential, both at work and in life. Mich's aim is to change the global conversation around traditional views of productivity, so that we can create better cadence in our days, more momentum in our work, and more joy in our lives.

Originally from South Africa, Mich currently lives between the UK and France, and works with clients around the world. Through her podcast, talks, workshops, courses and coaching programmes, she helps high-achieving strivers step off the treadmill of overwork, so they can thrive in mid-life and beyond.

After gaining a degree in English and Psychology, and a post-grad in Journalism, Mich cut her teeth in the film industry. She then worked as a project manager and communications consultant for tourism and events companies, design houses and digital marketing agencies.

Her second career, as an entrepreneur, came about in her 40's, after a brush with epic burnout forced her to redesign how she lives and works.

Mich's passions include learning and travel. She is an adventurer at heart, who has made memories and experienced local cultures in over 23 countries to date. Her travel highlights include:

- **In her 20's:** Working 2 ski seasons in Europe, and mountain biking the West Highland Way hiking trail in Scotland with a bunch of lads, (she was the only girl).

- **In her 30's:** Hiking the Annapurna Sanctuary in Nepal, and climbing a live Indonesian volcano (in the dark) while backpacking SE Asia for 6 months.

Despite her now creaky knees, Mich's adventures continue!

For more information about Mich's projects, and to work with her, visit **creatingcadence.co**

Sign up to Mich's bi-monthly Cadence newsletter (and grab the Canvas Cheat Sheet) at **creatingcadence.co/subscribe**

Instagram: instagram.com/michbondesio

Twitter: twitter.com/michbondesio

YouTube: youtube.com/@MichBondesio

LinkTree: linktr.ee/michbondesio

BIBLIOGRAPHY

PROLOGUE

Bird By Bird - Anne Lamott
https://www.penguinrandomhouse.com/books/97395/bird-by-bird-by-anne-lamott/

Cognitive Behavioural Therapy Overview - NHS, UK
https://www.nhs.uk/mental-health/talking-therapies-medicine-treatments/talking-therapies-and-counselling/cognitive-behavioural-therapy-cbt/overview/

The Do Lectures - https://thedolectures.com/

Creating Cadence Website - https://creatingcadence.co/

UCLan LSBE Entrepreneurs in Residence
https://www.uclan.ac.uk/schools/business/entrepreneurs-in-residence

CADENCE VS BALANCE

The Fourth Industrial Revolution (Definition) - World Economic Forum
https://www.weforum.org/focus/fourth-industrial-revolution

Cal Newport - Non-fiction Author and Computer Science Academic
https://www.calnewport.com/

The Minimalists - Joshua Fields Millburn and Ryan Nicodemus
https://www.theminimalists.com/

The World Needs Netflix Minis - Dan Pink
https://www.theatlantic.com/technology/archive/2018/06/the-future-of-television-is-being-able-to-pick-shows-by-length/562547/

WHAT IS INTENTIONAL PRODUCTIVITY?

Meta-analysis of Happy Employees - Gallup & London School of Economics
https://blogs.lse.ac.uk/businessreview/2019/07/15/happy-employees-and-their-impact-on-firm-performance/

BIBLIOGRAPHY

Productivity Definition - The US Bureau of Labor Statistics
https://www.bls.gov/k12/productivity-101/content/what-is-productivity/home.htm

What is 'The Great Resignation'? - World Economic Forum
https://www.weforum.org/agenda/2021/11/what-is-the-great-resignation-and-what-can-we-learn-from-it/

Microsoft Work Trend Index 2022
https://www.microsoft.com/en-us/worklab/work-trend-index/

The Signs of Quiet Quitting - Washington Post
https://www.washingtonpost.com/business/2022/08/21/quiet-quitting-what-to-know/

LIFE IN THE DIGITAL AGE

Dare to Lead - Brené Brown - https://brenebrown.com/book/dare-to-lead/

Dopamine Nation - Finding Balance in the Age of Indulgence - Dr Anna Lembke
https://www.annalembke.com/dopamine-nation

Stolen Focus - Why You Can't Pay Attention and How to Think Deeply Again - Johan Hari
https://johannhari.com/

Hyperfocus - How to Manage Your Attention in a World of Distraction - Chris Bailey
https://chrisbailey.com/books/

Eustress vs Distress: Positive & Negative Types of Stress - Hailey Shafir (Choosing Therapy)
https://www.choosingtherapy.com/eustress-vs-distress/

The Chaos Machine: The Inside Story of How Social Media Rewired Our Minds and the World - Max Fisher (Quercus)
https://www.quercusbooks.co.uk/titles/max-fisher/the-chaos-machine/9781529416367/

The Guardian Review of The Chaos Machine: The Inside Story of How Social Media Rewired Our Minds and Our World - Max Fisher
https://www.theguardian.com/books/2022/sep/22/the-chaos-machine-by-max-fisher-review-how-social-media-rewired-our-world

Max Fisher Interview - How The Algorithmic Overlords are Rewiring Our Brains - Rich Roll Podcast
https://www.richroll.com/podcast/max-fisher-703/

BIBLIOGRAPHY

Excessive Smartphone Use is Associated with Health Problems in Adolescents and Young Adults - Frontiers Psychiatry
https://www.frontiersin.org/articles/10.3389/fpsyt.2021.669042/full

Definition of Nomophobia - National Library of Medicine
https://www.ncbi.nlm.nih.gov/pmc/articles/PMC6510111/

STRESS & STRESSORS

Make Stress Good for You - Human Performance Resources
https://www.hprc-online.org/mental-fitness/sleep-stress/make-stress-good-you

Are you too stressed to be productive? Or not stressed enough? - Harvard Business Review
https://hbr.org/2016/04/are-you-too-stressed-to-be-productive-or-not-stressed-enough

When does stress help or harm? the effects of controllability and subjective stress response on stroop performance - National Library of Medicine (R Henderson, H Snyder, T Gupta, M Banich)
https://www.ncbi.nlm.nih.gov/pmc/articles/PMC3369195/

Chronic stress puts your health at risk - The Mayo Clinic
https://www.mayoclinic.org/healthy-lifestyle/stress-management/in-depth/stress/art-20046037

What Is The Vagus Nerve and How to Stimulate it for Increased Stress Resilience - Sara Adaes (Neurohacker)
https://neurohacker.com/the-vagus-nerve-what-it-is-and-how-to-stimulate-it-for-increased-stress-resilience

What The Vagus Nerve Is And How To Stimulate It For Better Mental Health - Sarah Jeanne Browne (Forbes)
https://www.forbes.com/sites/womensmedia/2021/04/15/what-the-vagus-nerve-is-and-how-to-stimulate-it-for-better-mental-health/

Wim Hof Method - https://www.wimhofmethod.com/

The Stress Prescription - 7 Days to More Joy & Ease - Dr Elissa Epel, PhD
https://www.elissaepel.com/the-stress-prescription

Burnout - The Secret to Solving the Stress Cycle - Emily & Emilia Nagoski
https://www.burnoutbook.net/

BIBLIOGRAPHY

PROCRASTINATION

Procrastination, Health & Wellbeing - Science Direct (T Pychyl & F Sirois)
https://www.sciencedirect.com/science/article/pii/B9780128028629000086

Procrastination is not only a thief of time, but also a thief of happiness. - Emerald Insight (A Silva, P Neves, A Caetano)
https://www.emerald.com/insight/content/doi/10.1108/IJM-05-2022-0223/full/html

Effects of Procrastination, the good and the bad - J Marks & V Saripalli - Psych Central
https://psychcentral.com/health/good-and-bad-things-about-procrastination

Personality & Individual Differences - Procrastination, Stress & Mental Health - Science Direct (R Stead, M Shanahan, R Neufeld)
https://www.sciencedirect.com/science/article/abs/pii/S0191886910001625?via%3Dihub

Procrastination among university students - Frontiers in Psychology (A Rozental, D Forsstrom, A Hyssoon, K Klinsieck)
https://www.frontiersin.org/articles/10.3389/fpsyg.2022.783570/full

Learned Optimism - How to Change Your Mind & Your Life - Martin Seligman
https://www.amazon.co.uk/Learned-Optimism-Change-Your-Mind/

The new era of positive psychology - Martin Seligman - Ted Talk
https://www.ted.com/talks/martin_seligman_the_new_era_of_positive_psychology

Deep Work - Rules for Focused Success in a Distracted World. - https://www.calnewport.com/books/deep-work/

Hyperfocus & How To Train Your Mind - Books by Chris Bailey - https://chrisbailey.com/books/

Leverage Dopamine to Overcome Procrastination & Optimize Effort - The Huberman Lab
https://hubermanlab.com/leverage-dopamine-to-overcome-procrastination-and-optimize-effort/

BURNOUT PART 1 - WORK

How Burnout Physically Changes Your Brain - Jessica Stillman (Inc)
https://www.inc.com/jessica-stillman/burnout-brain-chemistry-mental-health.html

Burnout and the Brain - Association for Psychological Science
https://www.psychologicalscience.org/observer/burnout-and-the-brain

BIBLIOGRAPHY

Yerbo Burnout Index 2022 - State of Burnout in Tech Report - https://report.yerbo.co/

Convertkit State of the Creator Economy Report 2022 - https://convertkit.com/reports/creator-economy-2022

Burnout is caused by more than just job stress - Science Daily
https://www.sciencedaily.com/releases/2014/09/140916092703.htm

Burnout an occupational phenomenon - World Health Organisation
https://www.who.int/news/item/28-05-2019-burn-out-an-occupational-phenomenon-international-classification-of-diseases

Open Access Government Report 2022
https://www.openaccessgovernment.org/the-working-population-are-at-risk-of-job-burnout-mental-health-remote-working/136705/

Definition of hustle and the origins of the word and the concept of hustle culture - Isabella Rosario (NPR)
https://www.npr.org/sections/codeswitch/2020/04/03/826015780/when-the-hustle-isnt-enough

Tech Worker Burnout Article - Jenny Darmody (Silicon Republic)
https://www.siliconrepublic.com/careers/tech-worker-burnout

Productivity Dysmorphia - https://www.ohellothere.com/post/productivity-dysmorphia

Why I can't see my own success - Anna Codrea-Rado
https://annacodrearado.substack.com/p/why-cant-i-see-my-own-success

Mental health & entrepreneurship - 2015 Study - Michael Freeman (UCA Berkeley)
https://michaelafreemanmd.com/Research_files/Are%20Entrepreneurs%20Touched%20with%20Fire%20(pre-pub%20n)%204-17-15.pdf

Mental illness statistics - National Institute of Mental Health
https://www.nimh.nih.gov/health/statistics/mental-illness

Why entrepreneurs need to talk about their mental health - Dan Murray Serter (Forbes)
https://www.forbes.com/sites/danmurrayserter/2020/10/04/why-entrepreneurs-need-to-talk-about-their-mental-health/

Dare to Lead - Brené Brown - https://brenebrown.com/book/dare-to-lead/

Thrive - Arianna Huffington - https://www.ariannahuffington.com/thrive/

BIBLIOGRAPHY

BURNOUT PART 2 - LIFE

Burnout: The Secret to Solving the Stress Cycle - Emily & Emilia Nagoski - https://www.burnoutbook.net/

Abolition - The Rise of the Anti-Slavery Movement - National Portrait Gallery
https://www.npg.org.uk/learning/digital/history/abolition-of-slavery/abolition-the-rise-of-the-anti-slavery-movement

The Abolitionist Movement - History.com
https://www.history.com/topics/black-history/abolitionist-movement

The Women's Movement - UN Women
https://interactive.unwomen.org/multimedia/timeline/womenunite/en/index.html#/

The Suffragette Movement - Parliament UK
https://www.parliament.uk/about/living-heritage/transformingsociety/electionsvoting/womenvote/overview/startsuffragette-/

Sexism & Ageism Alert: Was She Fired Because of Her Gray Hair? - Next Tribe
https://nexttribe.com/sexism-and-ageism-lisa-laflamme-firing/

Dare to Lead - Brené Brown - https://brenebrown.com/book/dare-to-lead/

The Gifts of Imperfection - Dr Brené Brown - https://brenebrown.com/book/the-gifts-of-imperfection/

Hyperfocus - Johann Hari - https://alifeofproductivity.com/hyperfocus/

Air pollution causing dementia - New Scientist
https://www.newscientist.com/article/2330483-air-pollution-likely-to-be-causing-dementia-say-uk-science-advisers/

The Carbon Almanac - It's Not Too Late. - https://thecarbonalmanac.org/

Women & Caregiving - Family Caregiver Alliance US
https://www.caregiver.org/resource/women-and-caregiving-facts-and-figures/

SEEKING FLEXIBILITY

Four-day week: 'major breakthrough' as most UK firms in trial extend changes - The Guardian
https://www.theguardian.com/money/2023/feb/21/four-day-week-uk-trial-success-pattern

Report: Productivity in Lancashire: Sparking New Ideas - Centre for SME Development, University of Central Lancashire, 2018 (S. Smith, P.B. Whyman, A.I. Petrescu, A. Wright and V.Moon)
https://www.uclan.ac.uk/business/support-for-smes/centre-for-sme-development

2023 LinkedIn Workplace Learning Report
https://learning.linkedin.com/resources/workplace-learning-report

The Bullet Journal Method - Ryder Carrol - https://bulletjournal.com/pages/book

On Writing - Stephen King - https://stephenking.com/works/nonfiction/on-writing-a-memoir-of-the-craft.html

WORK STYLES

A World Without Email - Cal Newport - https://www.calnewport.com/books/a-world-without-email/

The Truth About Open Offices - Harvard Business Review
https://hbr.org/2019/11/the-truth-about-open-offices

Workplace stressors & health outcomes - health policy for the workplace
https://behavioralpolicy.org/articles/workplace-stressors-health-outcomes-health-policy-for-the-workplace/

Dear Manager, You Are Holding Too Many Meetings.
https://hbr.org/2022/03/dear-manager-youre-holding-too-many-meetings

The Productivity of Working Hours - John Pencavel, Stanford University
https://docs.iza.org/dp8129.pdf

Long working hours increasing deaths from heart disease and stroke - World Health Organization
https://www.who.int/news/item/17-05-2021-long-working-hours-increasing-deaths-from-heart-disease-and-stroke-who-ilo

How Resting More Can Boost Your Productivity - Alex Soojung-Kim Pang
https://greatergood.berkeley.edu/article/item/how_resting_more_can_boost_your_productivity

To Get More Creative, Become Less Productive - Harvard Business Review
https://hbr.org/2015/11/to-get-more-creative-become-less-productive

It Doesn't Have To Be Crazy At Work - Jason Fried & David Heinemeier Hansson
https://37signals.com/books/#calm

BIBLIOGRAPHY

How the world's biggest four-day workweek trial run changed people's lives - CNN Business
https://edition.cnn.com/2022/08/01/business/4-day-work-week-uk-trial/index.html

4-Day Workweek Brings No Loss of Productivity - NY Times
https://www.nytimes.com/2022/09/22/business/four-day-work-week-uk.html

Which countries have already adopted a 4-day working week? - Madison Bridge
https://madison-bridge.com/which-countries-have-adopted-a-four-day-working-week/

Results from the World's Biggest Trial of the Four Day Work Week - World Economic Forum
https://www.weforum.org/agenda/2023/03/four-day-work-week-uk-trial/

WORK ENVIRONMENTS

An Ecological Approach to Personality: Psychological traits as drivers and consequences of active perception" - Compass Journal, April 2021. (L.P. Satchell, R.O. Kaaronen, R.D. Latzman)
https://compass.onlinelibrary.wiley.com/doi/full/10.1111/spc3.12595

Background Noise & Productivity - Krisp.ai - https://krisp.ai/blog/background-noise-and-productivity/

The Effects of Noise Exposure on Cognitive Performance and Brain Activity Patterns (August 2019) - National Library of Medicine NCBI
https://www.ncbi.nlm.nih.gov/pmc/articles/PMC6901841/

Ventilation in the Workplace: Productivity & Health - Hitachi Aircon Magazine
https://www.hitachiaircon.com/id/en/magazine/ventilation-in-the-workplace-productivity-and-health

Inspiring Workplace Wellbeing Report 2018 (TSK Group & Carter Corson) and WorkplaceRESET Report 2020 (TSK)
https://www.tskgroup.co.uk/

OUR WORK TOOLS

The Social Economy - Unlocking Value and Productivity Through Social Technologies
https://www.mckinsey.com/industries/technology-media-and-telecommunications/our-insights/the-social-economy

Email Duration, Batching and Self-interruption: Patterns of Email use on Productivity & Stress - Gloria Mark, University of California (G. Mark, S. Iqbal, M. Czerwinski, P. Johns, A. Sano)
https://affect.media.mit.edu/pdfs/16.Mark-CHI_Email.pdf

BIBLIOGRAPHY

Deep Work - Rules for Focused Success in a Distracted World. - https://www.calnewport.com/books/deep-work/

The Cost of Interrupted Work - More Speed & Stress - Gloria Mark, University of California (G.Mark, D. Gudith, U. Klocke)
https://www.ics.uci.edu/~gmark/chi08-mark.pdf

Ambius Air Quality Survey (2018) - https://www.ambius.com/offices/air-quality-survey/

Can Smell Really Affect Workplace Productivity (2016) - Initial Workplace Hygiene
https://www.initial.co.uk/blog/can-smell-really-affect-workplace-productivity/

Can The Right Smell Make You More Productive? (2022) - BBC - https://www.bbc.co.uk/news/business-61708789

12 Scents That Will Make You More Productive
https://www.fragrancex.com/blog/scents-that-help-you-work/

How Physical Exercise Makes Your Brain Work Better (2016) - The Guardian
https://www.theguardian.com/education/2016/jun/18/how-physical-exercise-makes-your-brain-work-better

The Link Between Walking and the Mind
https://www.newyorker.com/tech/annals-of-technology/walking-helps-us-think

Effects of Shinrin-Yoku (Forest Bathing) and Nature Therapy on Mental Health: a Systematic Review and Meta-analysis
https://link.springer.com/article/10.1007/s11469-020-00363-4

Building A Second Brain - Tiago Forte - https://www.buildingasecondbrain.com/

Which Productivity Method is Right for You? - ToDoist
https://todoist.com/productivity-methods

How Your Cell Phone Distracts You Even When You Are Not Using It - Time Magazine
https://time.com/3616383/cell-phone-distraction/

Smartphone addiction, daily interruptions and self-reported productivity - Eilish Duke & Christian Montag
https://www.ncbi.nlm.nih.gov/pmc/articles/PMC5800562/

How Metaverse Technology Can Boost Hybrid Working - Regus

BIBLIOGRAPHY

https://www.regus.com/en-gb/hybrid-working/how-metaverse-technology-can-boost-hybrid-working

HABITS & BEHAVIOUR CHANGE

Tiny Habits - The Small Changes That Change Everything - BJ Fogg, Phd
https://tinyhabits.com/

Atomic Habits - Tiny Changes, Remarkable Results - James Clear
https://jamesclear.com/atomic-habits

Indistractable - How to Control Your Attention and Choose Your Life - Nir Eyal
https://www.nirandfar.com/indistractable/

High Performance Habits - How Extraordinary People Become That Way - Brendon Burchard
https://brendon.com/blog/high-performancehabits/

MINDSETS FOR INTENTIONAL PRODUCTIVITY

The High 5 Habit: Gain Confidence and Erase Self-Doubt - Mel Robbins - https://www.melrobbins.com/books#the-high-5-habit

Money - Know More, Make More, Give More - Rob Moore - https://robmoore.com/books/#op3-element-q23WVjQy

Robin Sharma - The 5am Club - https://www.robinsharma.com/book/the-5am-club

Mindset - Changing the way you think to fulfil your potential - Dr Carol Dweck
https://www.amazon.co.uk/Mindset-How-Fulfil-Your-Potential/dp/1780332009

Grit: The Power of Passion & Perseverance - Angela Duckworth - https://angeladuckworth.com/grit-book/

BUILDING STRONG FOUNDATIONS

Sleep & Immune Function - L Besedovsky, T Lange & J Born - National Library of Medicine - https://www.ncbi.nlm.nih.gov/pmc/articles/PMC3256323/

How Sleep Affects Immunity - Eric Suni (Sleep Foundation)
https://www.sleepfoundation.org/physical-health/how-sleep-affects-immunity

Checking your phone first thing primes your brain for distraction - Neurohacker

BIBLIOGRAPHY

https://www.instagram.com/p/CkTqqehscUi/?igshid=MDJmNzVkMjY

Why We Sleep - Unlocking the Power of Sleep and Dreams - Dr Matthew Walker
https://www.sleepdiplomat.com/author

The Matt Walker Podcast - https://www.sleepdiplomat.com/podcast

Is night-time mouth breathing affecting your health? - Joyce Lee-Iannotti, MD
https://www.bannerhealth.com/healthcareblog/teach-me/is-nighttime-mouth-breathing-affecting-your-health

Breathing techniques to reduce stress and anxiety - Dr Andrew Huberman - Huberman Lab Podcast
https://www.youtube.com/watch?v=ntfcfJ28eiU

Box breathing techniques and benefits - Dr Elizabeth Scott - VeryWellMind.com
https://www.verywellmind.com/the-benefits-and-steps-of-box-breathing-4159900

Four Seven Eight Breathing - CNN Health
https://edition.cnn.com/2022/09/16/health/4-7-8-breathing-technique-relaxing-wellness/index.html

Preventing Cognitive Decline - Interview with Dr Andrew Weil (Lewis Howes Podcast)
https://lewishowes.com/podcast/the-habits-foods-to-increase-brain-function-eliminate-inflammation-live-healthy-longer-with-dr-andrew-weil/

How to Have a Healthy Gut - 8 Things Nutrition Experts Want You To Know - The Guardian
https://www.theguardian.com/lifeandstyle/2023/mar/20/no-you-dont-have-to-poo-every-day-eight-things-nutrition-experts-want-you-to-know

Young Forever: The Secrets to living your longest, healthiest life - Dr. Mark Hyman, MD
https://store.drhyman.com/collections/books/products/young-forever

The UltraMind Solution - Fix Your Broken Brain by Healing Your Body First - Dr Mark Hyman
https://store.drhyman.com/collections/books

The Doctor's Farmacy Podcast - Dr Mark Hyman - https://drhyman.com/blog/category/podcasts/

Outlive: The Science & Art of Longevity - Dr. Peter Attia, MD with Bill Gifford - https://peterattiamd.com/outlive/

BIBLIOGRAPHY

CYCLES OF PRODUCTIVITY

The Rise of the Slow Productivity Movement - Amy Blankson (Forbes)
https://www.forbes.com/sites/amyblankson/2022/10/24/the-rise-of-the-slow-productivity-movement/

Ultradian Rhythms Definition - Biology Online - https://www.biologyonline.com/dictionary/ultradian-rhythm

Circadian Rhythms Definition - Biology Online - https://www.biologyonline.com/dictionary/circadian-rhythm

Stages of Sleep - Eric Suni (Sleep Foundation) - https://www.sleepfoundation.org/stages-of-sleep

Chronotype vs Circadian Rhythm - Danielle Pacheco (Sleep Foundation)
https://www.sleepfoundation.org/how-sleep-works/chronotypes

Sleep Chronotypes - Casper - https://casper.com/blog/chronotype/

What is your Chronotype - Amerisleep - https://amerisleep.com/blog/what-is-your-chronotype/

Peak Performance: Elevate Your Game, Avoid Burnout, and Thrive with the New Science of Success - Brad Stulberg & Steve Magness
https://www.bradstulberg.com/books
http://www.stevemagness.com/books/

Automated Morningness-Eveningness Questionnaire (AutoMEQ) - Center for Environmental Therapies
https://chronotype-self-test.info/

Sleep Toolkit - Tools for Optimizing Sleep-Wake Timing - Huberman Lab Podcast (YouTube)
https://www.youtube.com/watch?v=h2aWYjSA1Jc

The Science and Practice of Perfecting Your Sleep - Dr Matt Walker - Huberman Lab Podcast (YouTube) - https://youtu.be/gbQFSMayJxk

What The Vagus Nerve Is And How To Stimulate It For Better Mental Health - Sarah Jeanne Browne (Forbes) - https://www.forbes.com/sites/womensmedia/2021/04/15/what-the-vagus-nerve-is-and-how-to-stimulate-it-for-better-mental-health/

Menstrual symptoms linked to lost productivity through presenteeism - BMJ - https://www.bmj.com/company/newsroom/menstrual-symptoms-linked-to-nearly-9-days-of-lost-productivity-through-presenteeism-every-year/

BIBLIOGRAPHY

How Women Can Use Monthly Periods As A Productivity Tool - Alexandra Mysoor (Forbes)
https://www.forbes.com/sites/alexandramysoor/2018/05/10/how-women-can-use-monthly-periods-as-a-productivity-tool/

Period Power - Harness Your Hormones and Get Your Cycle Working for You - Maisie Hill
https://www.maisiehill.com/

Peri Menopause Power - Navigating Your Hormones on the Journey to Menopause - Maisie Hill
https://www.maisiehill.com/

The Moon and Sleep - Scientific Studies
https://www.sciencedirect.com/science/article/pii/S0960982213007549
https://pubmed.ncbi.nlm.nih.gov/10363673/

How The Moon Phases Can Increase Your Productivity And Planning. (Futurism)
https://vocal.media/futurism/how-the-moon-phases-can-increase-your-productivity-and-planning

Using The Moon Cycles in Business & Life - Jenessa MacKenzie (Thrive Global)
https://thriveglobal.com/stories/using-the-moon-cycles-in-business-and-life/

How to use the power of the moon to achieve your goals - Sonya Chen
https://medium.com/@sonya.shen7/how-to-use-the-power-of-the-moon-to-achieve-your-goals-fe1259003bd6

How and why to hack your life with moon phases - Amanda Warton Jenkins
https://medium.com/well-woman/how-and-why-to-hack-your-life-with-moon-phases-78b4b4e84f2e

A historical perspective on archetypes - Archetypist - https://archetypist.com/what/more-on-archetypes/

The Hermit Archetype - Know Your Archetypes - https://knowyourarchetypes.com/hermit-archetype/

The Hermit Archetype - Samantha Hartley (Profitable Joyful Podcast)
https://samanthahartley.com/the-hermit-archetype-for-consultants/

REWIRING YOUR BRAIN FOR FOCUS

The Compound Effect - Darren Hardy - https://store.darrenhardy.com/products/the-compound-effect

Why Walking Helps Us Think - Ferris Jabr (The New Yorker) - https://www.newyorker.com/tech/annals-of-technology/walking-helps-us-think

BIBLIOGRAPHY

9 Famous Thinkers from History Who Were Habitual Walkers - Blake Miner, Flaneur Life - https://www.flaneurlife.com/famous-thinkers-walkers/

Stanford Study Finds Walking Improves Creativity - May Wong (Stanford News) - https://news.stanford.edu/2014/04/24/walking-vs-sitting-042414/

The Science of Why You Do Your Best Thinking While Walking - Jessica Stillman (Inc.com) https://www.inc.com/jessica-stillman/the-science-of-why-you-do-your-best-thinking-while-walking.html

Hyperfocus & How To Train Your Mind - Books by Chris Bailey - https://chrisbailey.com/books/

The Benefits of Reading - R Stanborough (Healthline) - https://www.healthline.com/health/benefits-of-reading-books

Reading Skill and Structural Brain Development S House, C Lebel, T Katzir, F Manis, E Kan, G Rodriguez, E Sowell (NCBI) https://www.ncbi.nlm.nih.gov/pmc/articles/PMC4128180/

Reading Comprehension and Reading Experience Aid Vocabulary Development - K Cain, J Oakhill (PubMed) https://pubmed.ncbi.nlm.nih.gov/21772058/

The Bullet Journal Method: Track The Past, Order the Present, Design The Future - Ryder Carroll - https://bulletjournal.com/pages/book

The Best Way to Remember Valuable Information - Dr Andrew Huberman, The Huberman Lab https://www.instagram.com/p/CqL7qHYv0Bx/?igshid=MDJmNzVkMjY%3D

Meditation Resources

- Headspace - https://www.headspace.com/
- Calm App - https://www.calm.com/
- TRIPP - https://www.tripp.com/
- Insight Timer - https://insighttimer.com/

Huberman Lab Podcast - https://hubermanlab.com/how-meditation-works-and-science-based-effective-meditations/

Meditation Goes Plural - Beth McGroarty - https://www.globalwellnesssummit.com/2019-global-wellness-trends/meditation-goes-plural/

BIBLIOGRAPHY

How to Choose the Best Meditation Practice for You — https://further.net/best-meditation-practice/

Vedic Meditation Resources

- What is Vedic Meditation - London Meditation Centre https://www.londonmeditationcentre.com/vedic-meditation/
- Light Watkins - How Vedic Meditation Works https://www.youtube.com/watch?v=wImaO6mTXNk
- Shakti Sisters Vedic Meditation Practitioners https://www.theshaktisisters.com/
- How to Choose the Best Meditation Practice for You - https://further.net/best-meditation-practice/

MANAGING YOUR FLOW

Flow - The Secret to Happiness - Mihaly Csikszentmihalyi - https://www.ted.com/talks/mihaly_csikszentmihalyi_flow_the_secret_to_happiness and https://positivepsychology.com/mihaly-csikszentmihalyi-father-of-flow/

Flow as a simple solution to loneliness - Victoria Masterson, World Economic Forum - https://www.weforum.org/agenda/2022/04/leisure-activities-for-loneliness/

Your Attention Didn't Collapse, It Was Stolen - Johann Hari (Guardian) - https://www.theguardian.com/science/2022/jan/02/attention-span-focus-screens-apps-smartphones-social-media

The Flow Genome Project - https://www.flowgenomeproject.com/

Flow State - Above & Beyond (Anjuna Beats) - https://www.aboveandbeyond.nu/flowstate/tracklist/

Which Productivity Method is Right For You? - ToDoist - https://todoist.com/productivity-methods

BUILDING RITUALS INTO YOUR WORKFLOW

Productivity Habits of Famous People - ToDoist - https://blog.doist.com/7-productivity-habits-famous-people/

Robin Sharma - The 5am Club - https://www.robinsharma.com/book/the-5am-club

The Art of Gathering: How We Meet & Why It Matters - Priya Parker - https://www.priyaparker.com/thebook

BIBLIOGRAPHY

MOVING FORWARDS

B Corporation - https://www.bcorporation.net/en-us/movement

Purpose and Business - Simon Sinek Interview Snippet - https://www.instagram.com/reel/CpnNhlvMIx2/

Thoughts on ChatGPT & Other AI - Deep Questions Podcast Ep.244 - Cal Newport - https://www.thedeeplife.com/podcasts/episodes/ep-244-thoughts-on-chatgpt/